**Publisher and
Creative Director:**
B. Martin Pedersen

**Design Director:**
Hee Ra Kim

**Designers:**
B. Martin Pedersen
Hee Ra Kim
Hiewon Sohn

**Editor:**
Brittney Feit

**Associate Editor**
Stephanie Ginzburg

**Japanese Advisors:**
USA: Toshiaki & Kumiko Ide
Japan: Taku Satoh
Sakura Nomiyama

**Chief Executive Officer:**
B. Martin Pedersen

**Financial Officer:**
Arna T. Pedersen

**Legal Counsel:**
John M. Roth

**Cover Art:**
"Omahyra, Crown of Thorns,"
New York City, 2004
Photo by Albert Watson

**Published by:**
Graphis Inc.
389 Fifth Avenue, Suite 1105
New York, NY 10016
Phone: 212-532-9387
www.graphis.com
help@graphis.com

**Distributed by:**
National Book Networks, Inc.
15200 NBN Way
Blue Ridge Summit, PA 17214
Phone: 800-462-6420
customercare@nbnbooks.com

**ISBN 13:** 978-1-931241-80-9
**ISBN 10:** 1-931241-80-5

I am glad to relate that we are getting enthusiasm and interest from a number of Clubs to present Graphis Exhibits in their locations. We will announce in the future on our website where these shows will take place. Additional information can be found in the digital copy of this Journal.

In my past, I used to attend award shows, especially the AIGA and Art Directors Club Exhibits, that were an extremely important influence in my early days as a developing designer.

I would usually arrive early before the crowd, so that I could visually digest some of the brilliant work that was on display, and get myself charged. I would then witness some of the legends that were there for that evening, such as Herb Lubalin, Massimo Vignelli,and Milton Glaser, etc.

Today, there are few of these exhibits around with this kind of talent. I know that the millennials are probably getting inspiration, however, mostly postage stamp-sized from their iPhone.

At our first Atlanta display of 100 Posters, Ads, Photos, and Student work, the young people were pulling each other around to show each other work that excited them. It was a highly successful social evening, but more important, people left feeling inspired.

In the fine arts, one goes to museums; but in the commercial arts, one should see what their competitors are creating. The Annuals, of course, also provide influence. However, seeing the work displayed full-sized in front of you is magical.

My mission is to make Graphis Exhibitions available to AIGA Club locations around the country with the Award-winning work from our Annuals. We will display all of the disciplines, as well as exciting new talent from the Education community that competes at the professional levels.

With this issue, I'm proud to present remarkable international talents, all of whom have been consistent Graphis Platinum and Gold award winners in each of our Annuals.

First we have work in design that has shaped the landscape in each of their respective countries. Fons Hickmann (DE), an imaginative graphic designer; Jennifer Morla (U.S), an outstanding designer, with over 300 awards of excellence for her firm Morla Design; and also the work of Chiii Design Ltd., an influential firm from Macao.

In Advertising, we present Graphis award-winning ad agency, Young & Laramore, based in the U.S. Young & Laramore has garnered national recognition for their creative branding.

In Photography, the legendary Albert Watson (UK), whose range of work is vast and continues to inspire. Gregory Reid (U.S.) takes influence from Pop Art and Surrealism for his still life photography. Also, Frank P. Wartenberg (DE), with his impressive collection in portraits and fashion.

Illustrator Jeff Foster's wild spirit roams free in his retro and vintage digital art. Based in the U.S., his work qualifies as a representation of how modern art can rely on classic styles of illustration and still provide a sense of never-ending curiosity.

In Products, we feature modern innovations in transportation, including the Audi R8 (DE), the Sole of the UX by Tej Chauhan (UK), and the Lime Electric Scooter (U.S).

We also present sustainable architecture, with ZGF Architects and Skidmore, Owings & Merrill LLP (SOM) for the Architecture 2030 Challenge, along with the Writer's Shed from Matt Gibson Architecture + Design (AU), whose work demonstrates how design can transform the world.

B. Martin Pedersen
*Publisher & Creative Director*

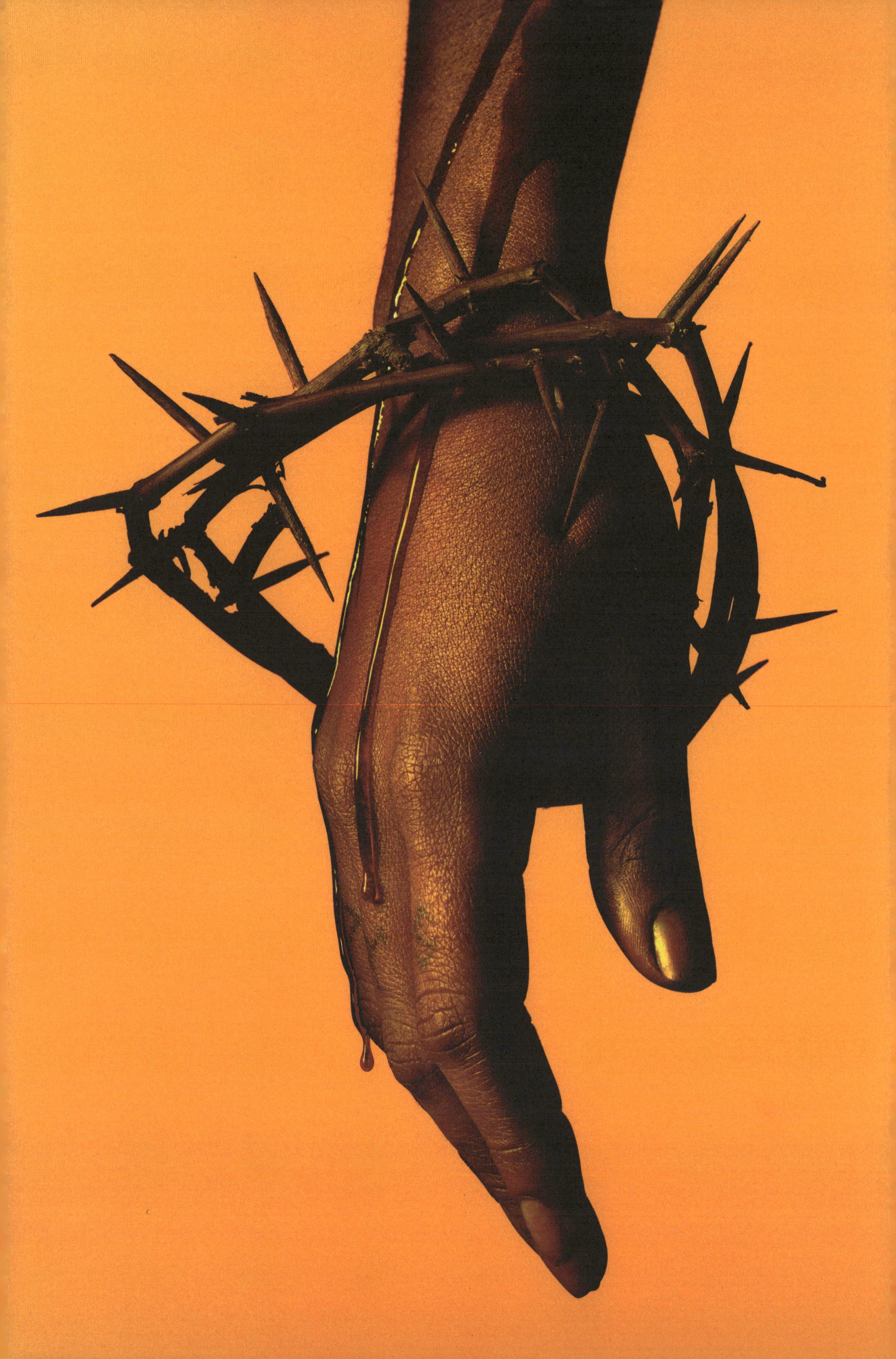

# Contents



*(Opposite page) Omahyra, Hand with Thorns, New York City, 2004; Photographer: Albert Watson*

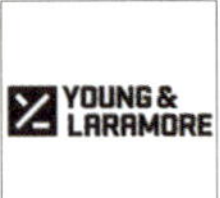



Without good creativity, the message has no power. Without strategy, it has no direction. Young & Laramore is a nationally recognized, proudly independent advertising agency based in Indianapolis. Each day, 65 employees come to work in an 1899 schoolhouse designed for Kurt Vonnegut's great-grandfather, creating work that's been featured in leading ad industry publications as well as the Wall Street Journal, The New York Times, and on The Today Show. Listed among Best Places to Work by both AdAge and Outside magazine, Y&L continues to build and reinvigorate regional and national consumer brands by helping them take a stand.

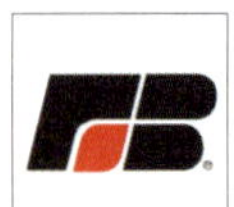

**Introduction by Kari St. Clair, Indiana Farm Bureau Insurance**

Indiana Farm Bureau Insurance has protected fellow Hoosiers since 1934. Organized by Indiana Farm Bureau, Inc., our family of companies has grown to include insurance products for auto, life, home, business, and farm. Banking and other financial services and products are also available. With a home office in downtown Indianapolis and local offices in all 92 counties, Indiana Farm Bureau Insurance serves Hoosiers with more than 400 agents and nearly 1,200 employees, who live and work throughout the state. Our company is a leader in auto and homeowner's insurance and is the largest writer of farm insurance in the Hoosier state.



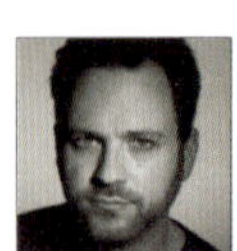

Albert Watson was born in Edinburgh, Scotland in 1942, and immigrated to the United States in 1970. He has made his mark as one of the world's most successful and prolific photographers since he began his career in 1970, blending art, fashion, and commercial photography into some of the most iconic images ever seen. From portraits of Alfred Hitchcock and Steve Jobs, beauty shots of Kate Moss, to Las Vegas landscapes and still life photographs of King Tutankhamen artifacts, Albert's diversity and body of work are unparalleled. His striking photographs and stunning handmade prints are featured in galleries and museums around the globe. The photo industry bible, Photo District News, named Albert one of the 20 Most Influential Photographers of All Time. Albert has won numerous honors, including an Order of the British Empire (OBE) from Queen Elizabeth II in June 2015 for his lifetime contribution to the art of photography. Other honors include a Grammy Award, three Andys, and a Hasselblad Masters Award.

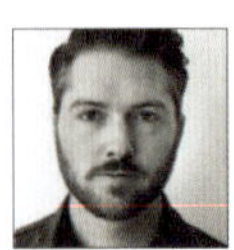

**Introduction by Michael Comeau**

Michael Comeau is a Brooklyn-based portrait photographer, focused on fine art projects and private commissions. His simple, evocative portraits are influenced by classic editorial photography from the 1980s and 1990s, as well as the New York streets he has called home all his life. Michael is also the creator of OnPortraits.com, an educational platform for aspiring portrait photographers.

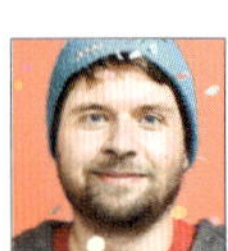



Gregory graduated with a BFA in photography from the School of Visual Arts. He currently lives and works in Brooklyn, NY with his studio located in Clinton Hill. Taking influences from Pop Art and Surrealism, he loves working with graphic and bold color compositions to bring in the next generation of still life photography. Gregory is a recent recipient of the Graphis Platinum Award. His work has been featured in editorial publications such as W Magazine, TIME, Newsweek, and The Atlantic; with commercial clients ranging from Coach, Saks Fifth Avenue, Stoli, and Sephora, among others.

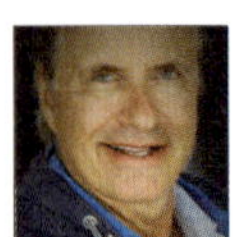

**Introduction by Dan Saelinger**

Dan Saelinger is a director, photographer, and visual collaborator. Raised in the era of MTV and 8 bit video games, he is drawn to all things graphic and colorful. He was named one of The Art Directors Club's Young Guns in 2009. His work has been recognized by American Photography, Communication Arts, Graphis, Photo District News, The Society of Publication Designers, and The American Society of Magazine Editors.



As a schoolboy, Frank Wartenberg was very interested in photography. His family didn't encourage him to choose photography as a profession, which is why he studied law at university. He never gave up his passion for photography. When he was a student, he worked as a press photographer at concerts for The Rolling Stones, Pink Floyd, Eartha Kitt, Madness, Astrud Gilberto, and many more. He decided to give photography a try and opened up his own studio in Hamburg, Germany. At that time, he did still life photography as well as people photography. He realized very quickly that people photography was the field that tempted him most, with a focus on portrait, fashion, and beauty. He worked for magazines like BRIGITTE, ELLE, STERN, DER SPIEGEL, MAX, COSMOPOLITAN, Men's Health, as well as for fashion and beauty brands like Peek & Cloppenburg, S. OLIVER, BRAX , NEW YORKER, GOLDWELL, WELLA, NIVEA, and L'OREAL. In the US, Frank Wartenberg worked in NYC for COTY, BLOOMINGDALES, LOGITECH, and ESPN. Today, Frank lives with his wife, daughter, and Golden Retriever in his hometown, Hamburg.

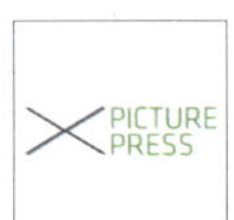

**Introduction by Stephan Braun, Picture Press**

Picture Press is one of Germany's major independent image agencies since 1995. Picture Press represents rights-managed images and illustrations of top quality. The customers are professional image researchers at magazines or newspapers, advertising and design agencies. The customers require special content and excellent service. The company's main strengths are: beauty & fashion, celebrities, animals, food & living. The Picture Press team are image experts, we've known the business for many years. Their team of photographers is highly professional and experienced. They produce a constant flow of exclusive material for Picture Press.

*(Opposite page) "Heart Health," 2019 AARP Magazine; Photographer: Gregory Reid*

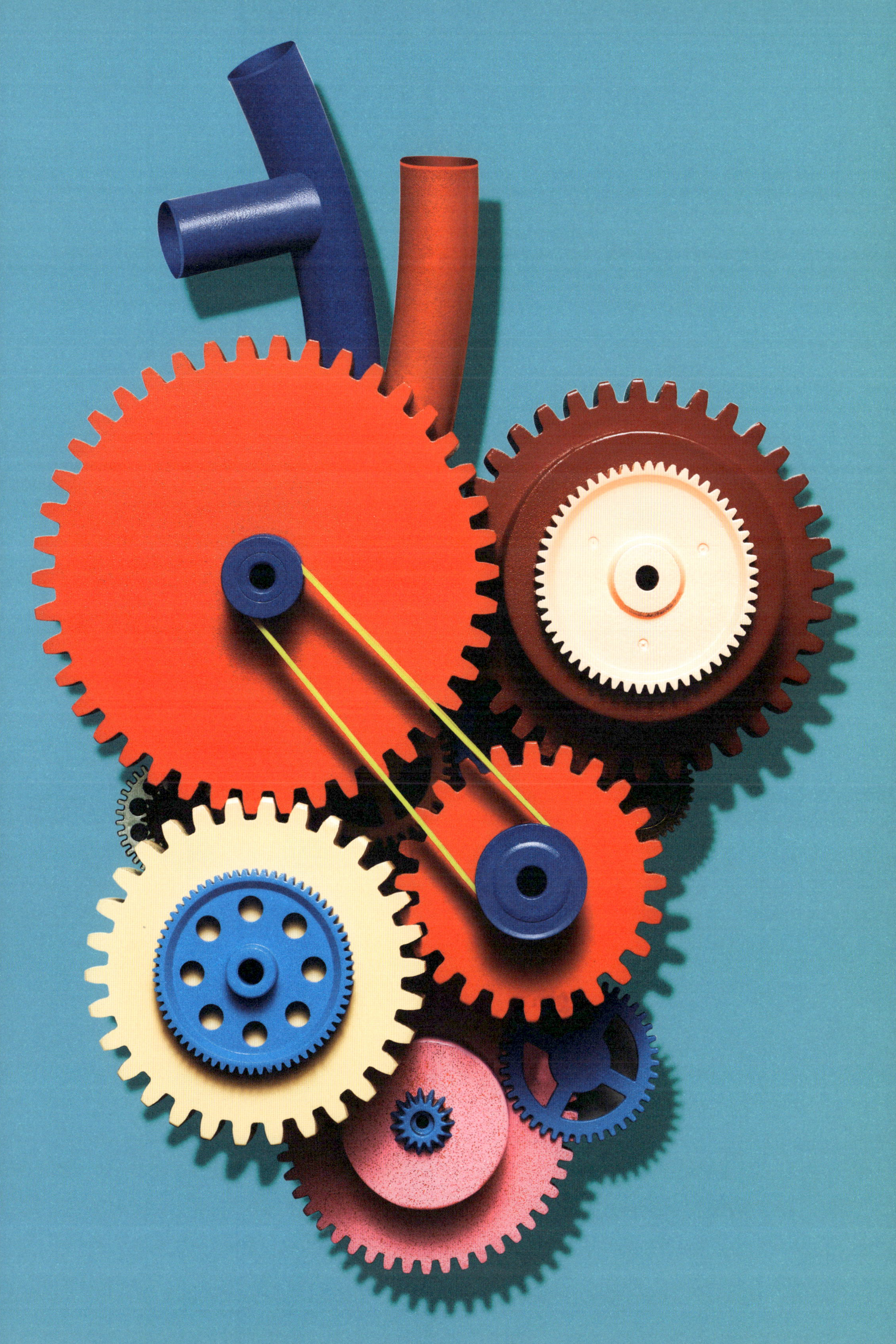

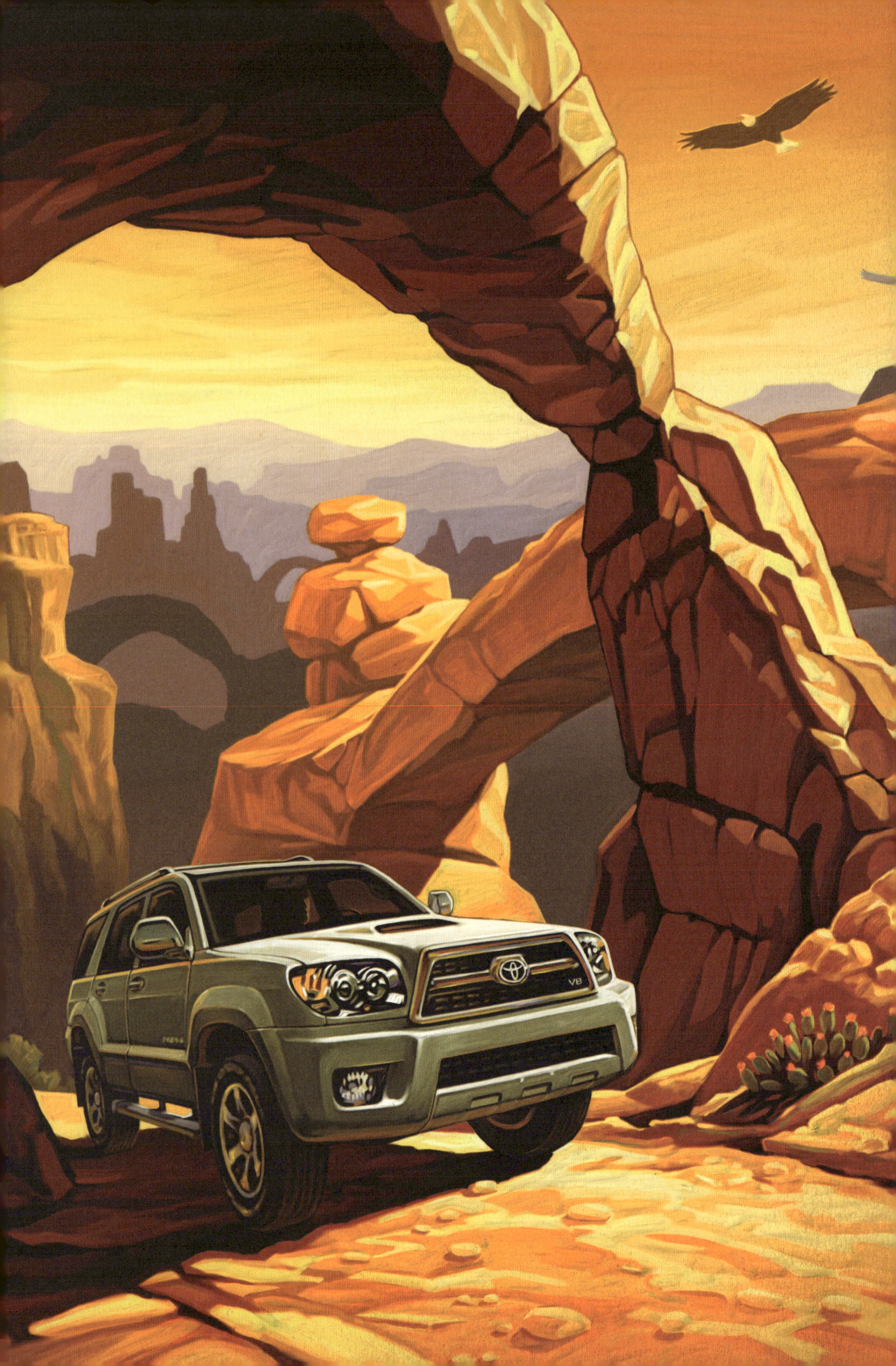

# GRAPHIC DESIGN, AS MUSIC AND FASHION, IS A ZEITGEIST PHENOMENON.

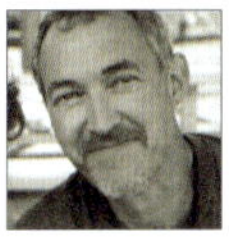

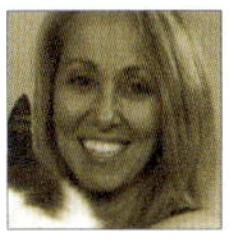

**Fons Hickmann,** *Graphic Designer & Co-founder, Fons Hickmann M23*

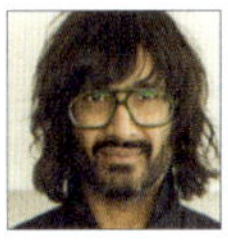

*(Opposite page) Saatchi LA; Art Director: Conan Wang; Illustrator: Jeff Foster; Toyota 4 Runner campaign*

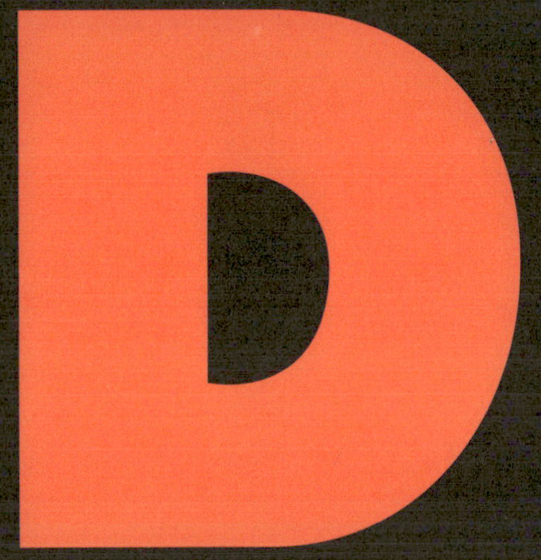

DESIGN

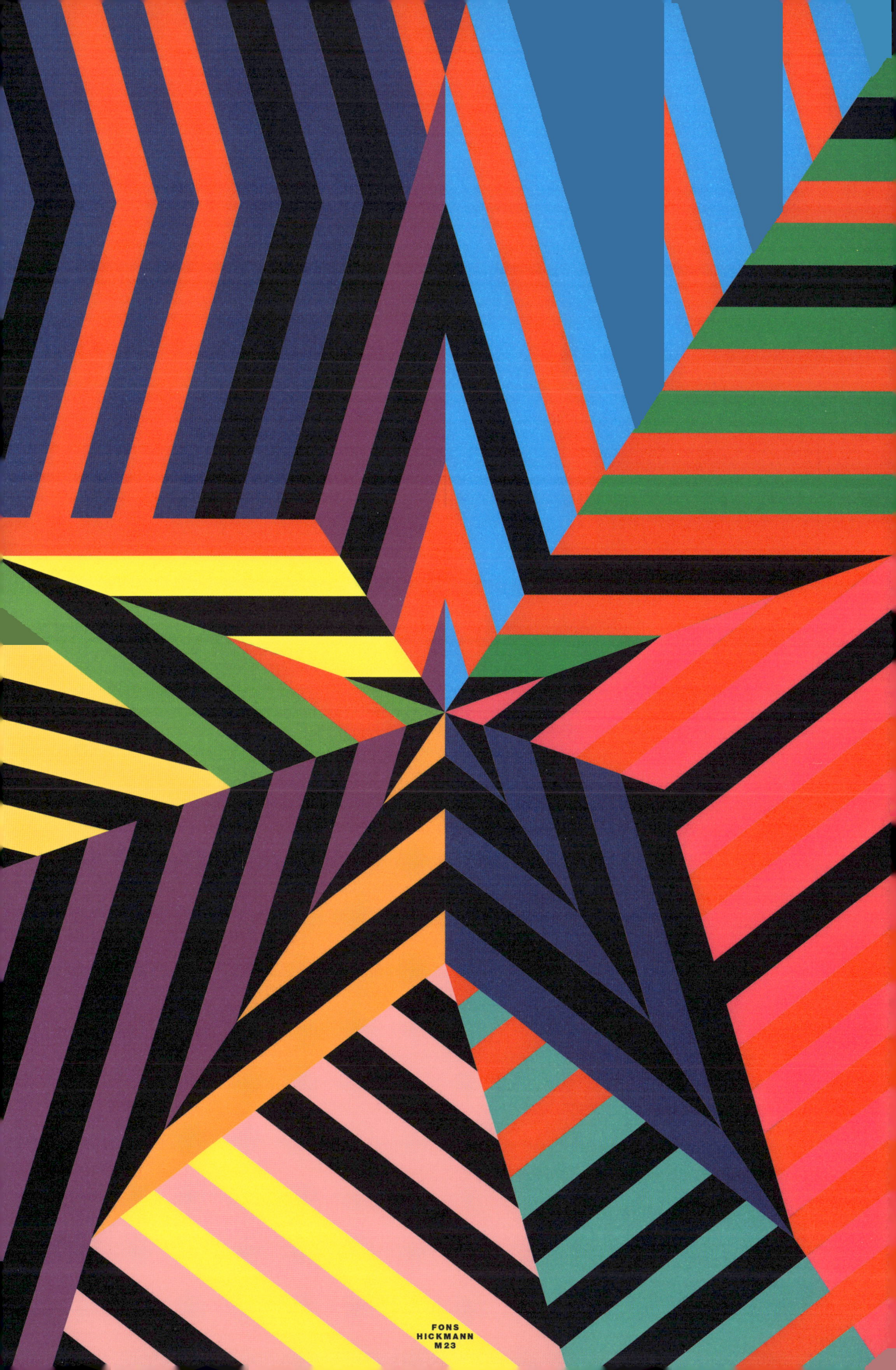
FONS
HICKMANN
M 23

FONS HICKMANN AND HIS DESIGN STUDIO CREATE A BALANCE BETWEEN THE IVORY TOWER AND EVERYDAY LIFE. THEY PROVIDE AESTHETICS AND EMOTIONALITY TO THE PRESENTATION OF SCIENCE.

**Christian Martin,** *Head of Communications, Einstein Foundation Berlin*

FONS' CREATIVE USE OF THE LETTERFORM IN PRESENTING ICONIC IMAGES IS BOTH EXCITING AND STIMULATING. HIS TYPOGRAPHIC ART COMMUNICATES BY MAKING THE READER THINK.

**Carol Wahler,** *Executive Director, Type Directors Club*

FONS IS AN IMPORTANT FIGURE IN THE INTERNATIONAL POSTER SCENE. HE DESIGNS POSTERS THAT SHOW US THAT OUR PROJECT HAS A STRONG IMPACT BEYOND LUCERNE.

THROUGH HIS EXTRAORDINARY WORK, HE SPURS THE LOCAL SCENE TO GROW BEYOND ITSELF.

**Erich Brechbühl,** *Graphic Designer, Neubad Graphic Design Pool*

FONS CREATES POSTERS THAT ARE DECEPTIVELY COMPLEX BOTH VISUALLY AND PERCEPTUALLY. TO BE ABLE TO CONVEY AN IDEA WITH SUCH IMPACT AND ECONOMY IS THE SIGN OF A TRUE MASTER.

**Erin Wright,** *Co-founder, Posters Without Borders*

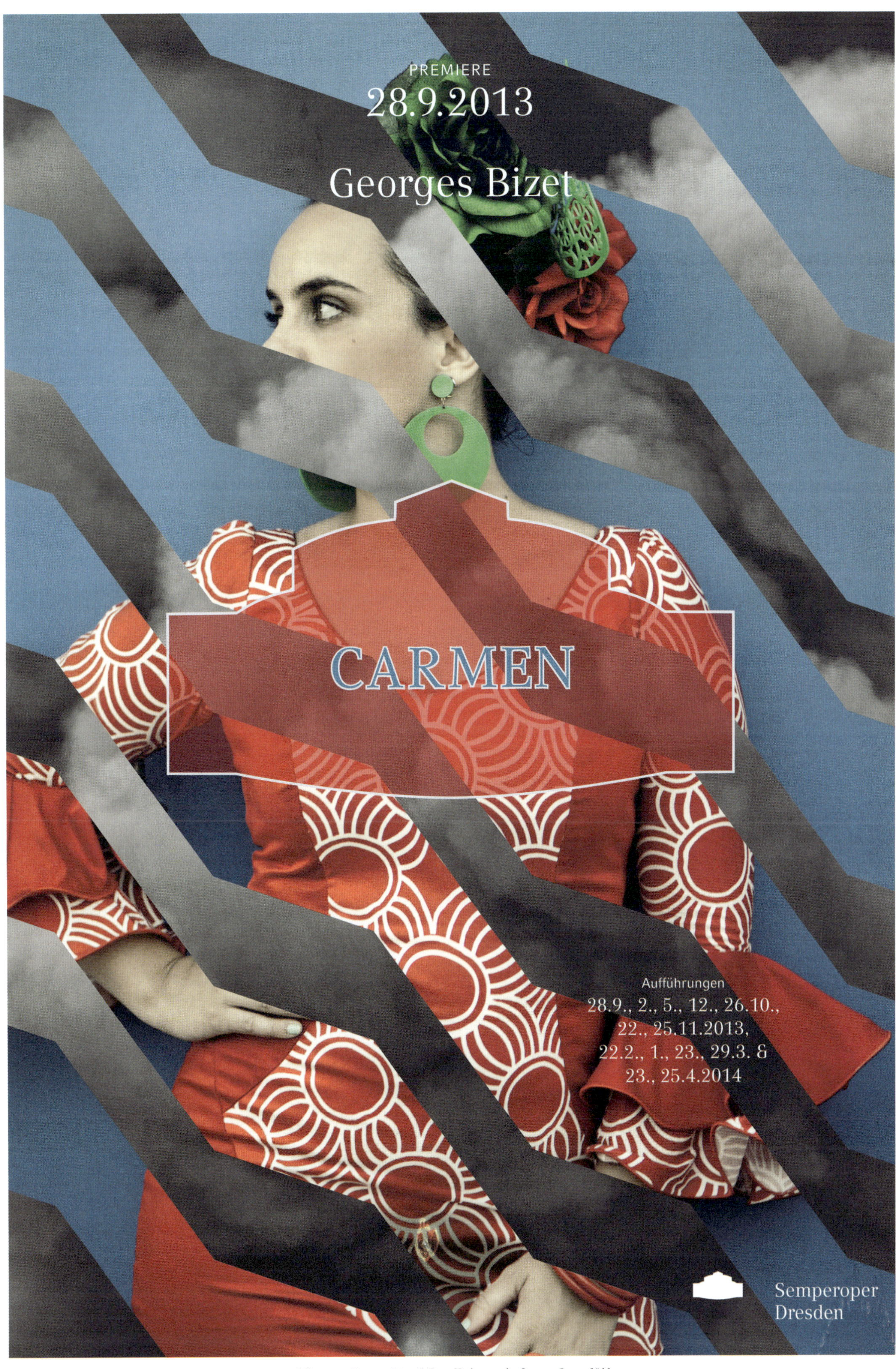


*"Carmen - Georges Bizet," Fons Hickmann for Semper Opera 2013*

# Introduction by Uwe Loesch, Poster Designer

In ancient Roman religion, "Fons" was the God of springs. Thus, it is no miracle that Fons Hickmann who carries the claim on refreshing inspiration already in his name is a cascade of bubbling over ideas and impertinences for over twenty years; as a gifted graphic designer, as a teacher in famous academies and universities worldwide, as an author of pamphlets worth reading, as an engaged fighter for the rights and duties of the Family of Man, as a lover and aficionado—of art! What otherwise?

IT IS OFTEN ONLY THROUGH HIS DESIGNS THAT I UNDERSTAND WHAT IS IMPORTANT ABOUT MY THOUGHTS AND HOW SOMETHING CAN BE SEEN.

HIS POSTER DESIGNS HAVE ALWAYS LED TO AN EXTENSION OF THE ORIGINALLY PLANNED AND HAVE IMPROVED SIGNIFICANTLY.

**Thorsten Nolting,** *CEO, Diakonie Düsseldorf*

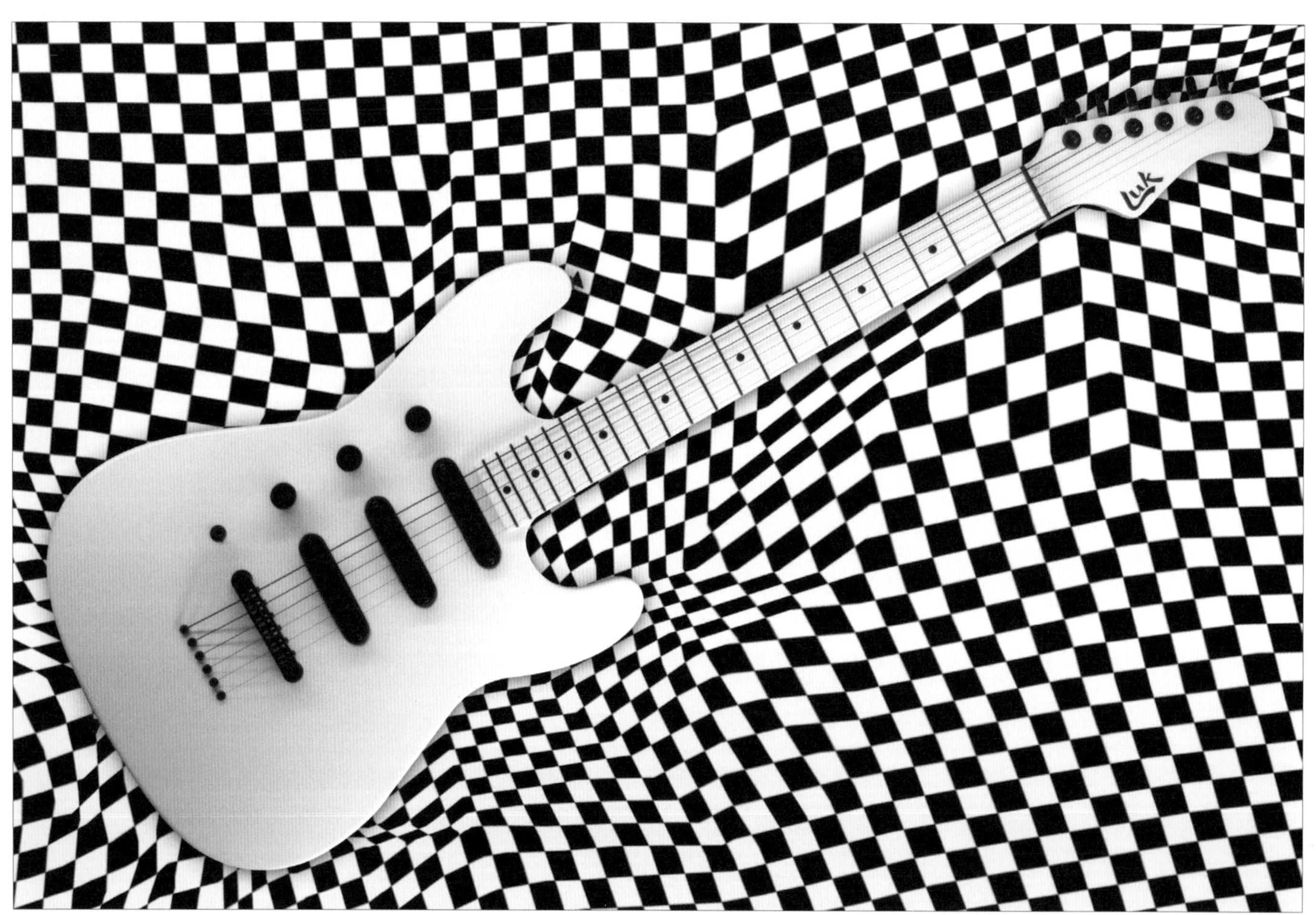

*"The White Onyx Guitar," Luk Guitars 2016*

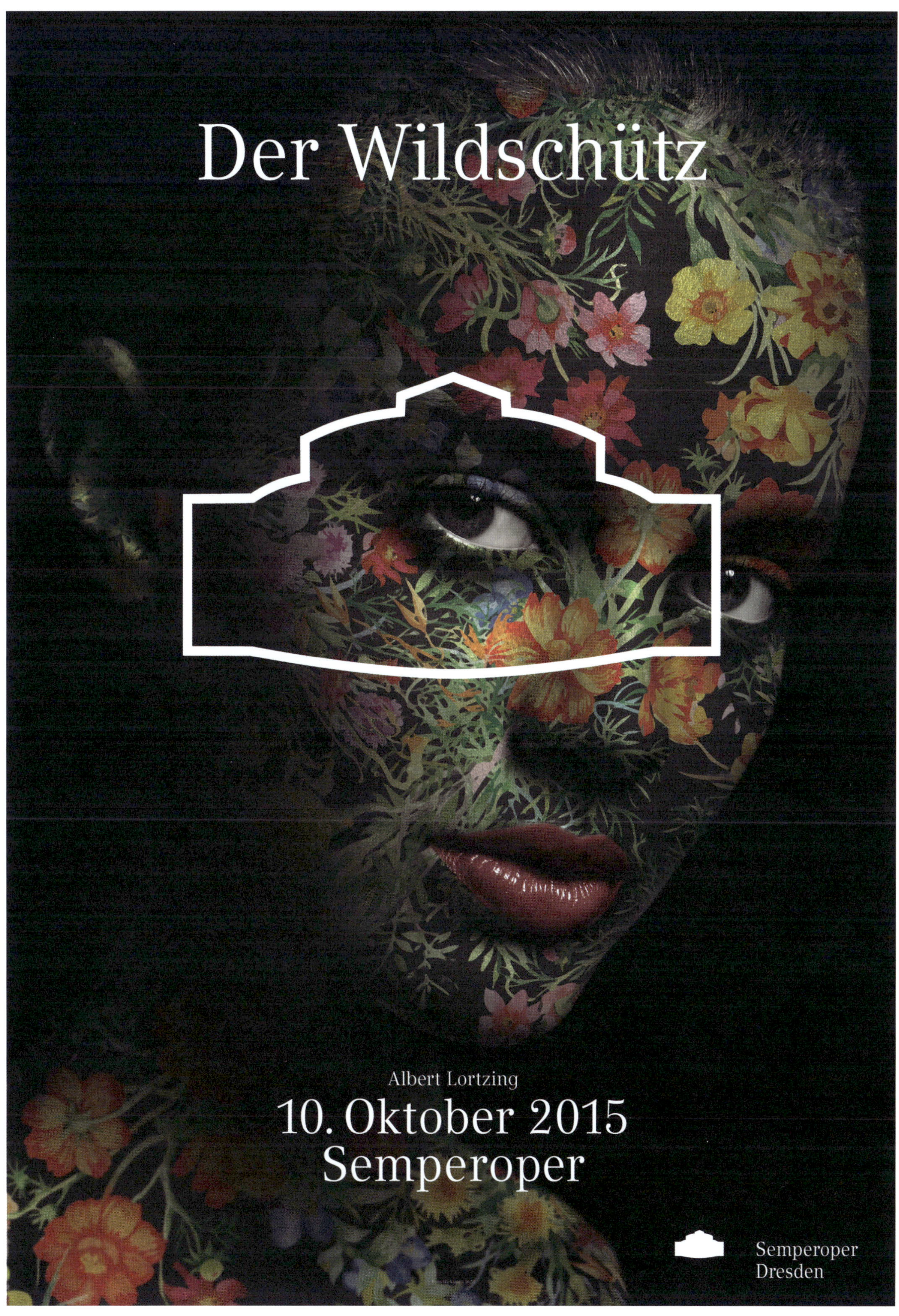


*"The poacher." Fons Hickmann for Semper Opera 2015*

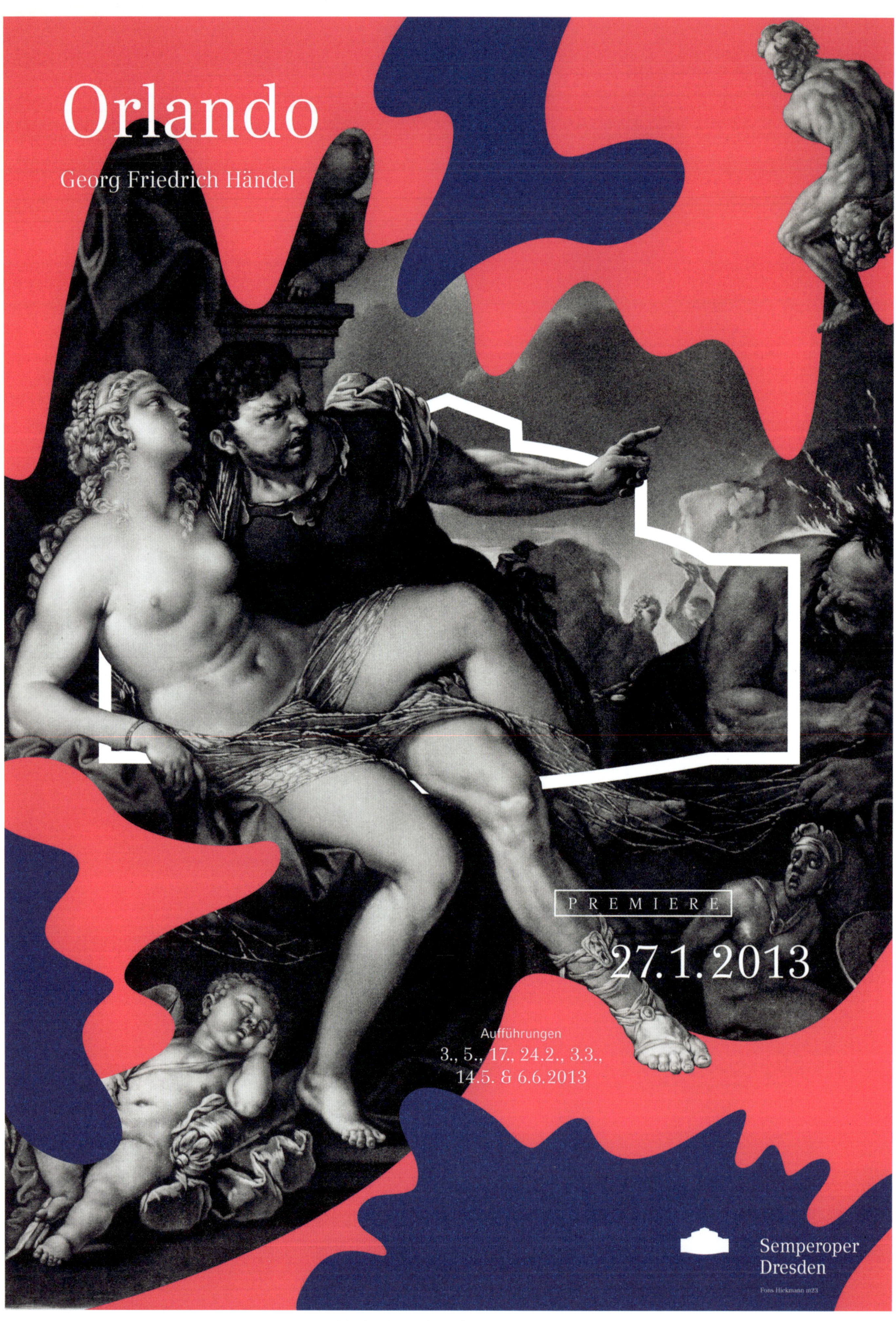


"Orlando," Fons Hickmann for Semper Opera 2013

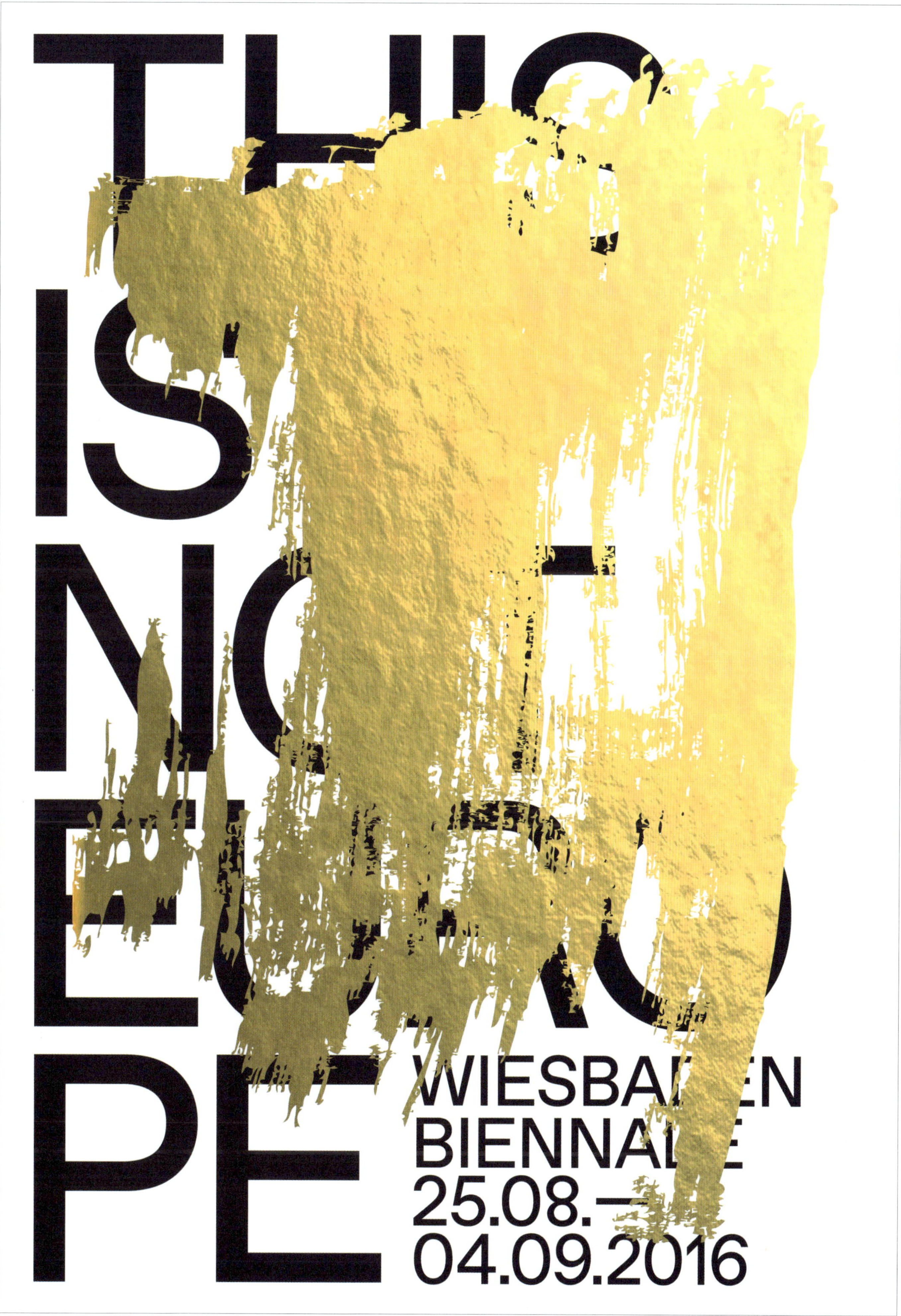


*"This is not Europe," Fons Hickmann for Wiesbaden Biennale, Performing Arts 2016*

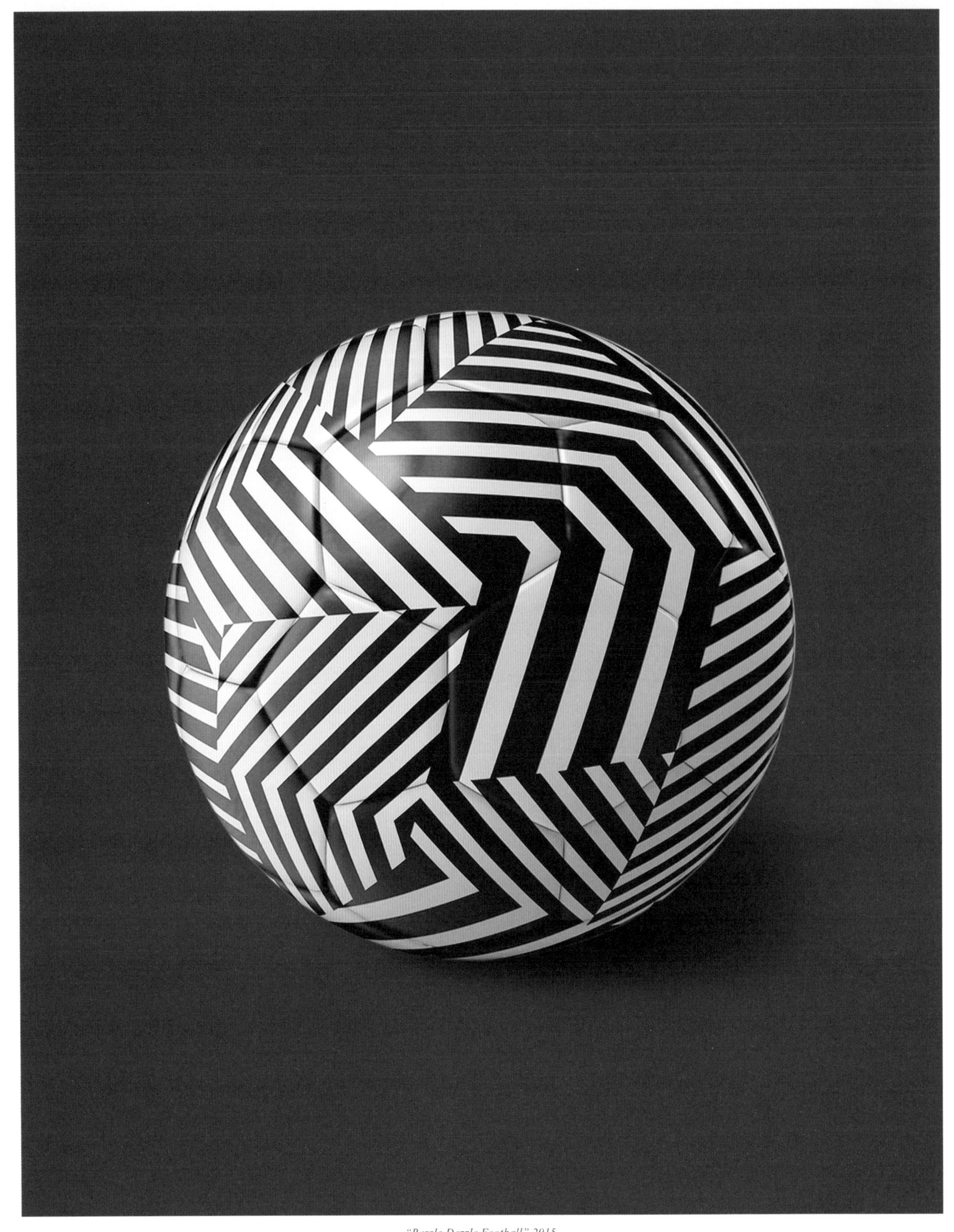

*"Razzle Dazzle Football" 2015*

# LIFE CONSISTS OF LIGHT AND SHADOW, UPS AND DOWNS, LOVE AND SUFFERING, AND A REAL CHARACTER CAN ONLY EMERGE OUT OF THIS CONTRAST PARADIGM. **Fons Hickmann,** *Graphic Designer & Co-founder, Fons Hickmann M23*

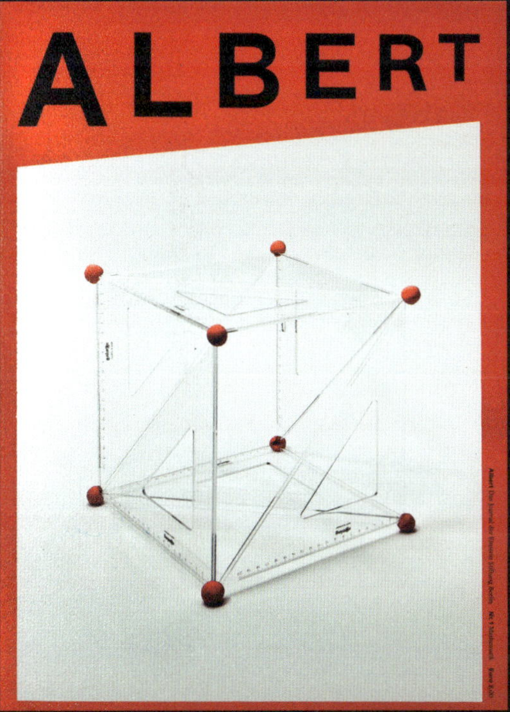
ALBERT

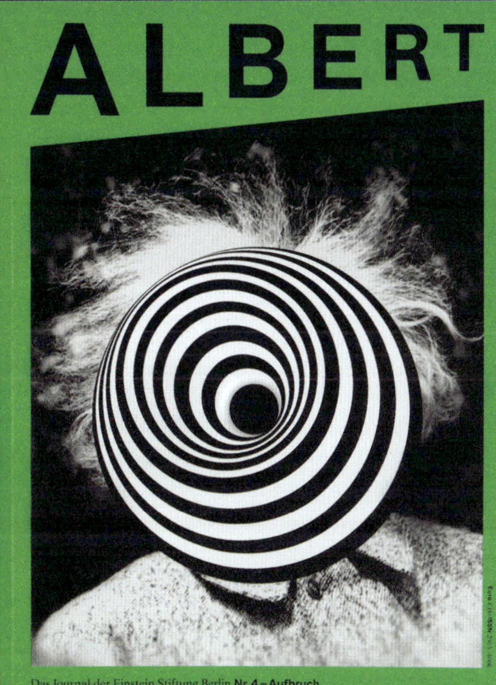
ALBERT
Das Journal der Einstein Stiftung Berlin Nr. 4 – Aufbruch

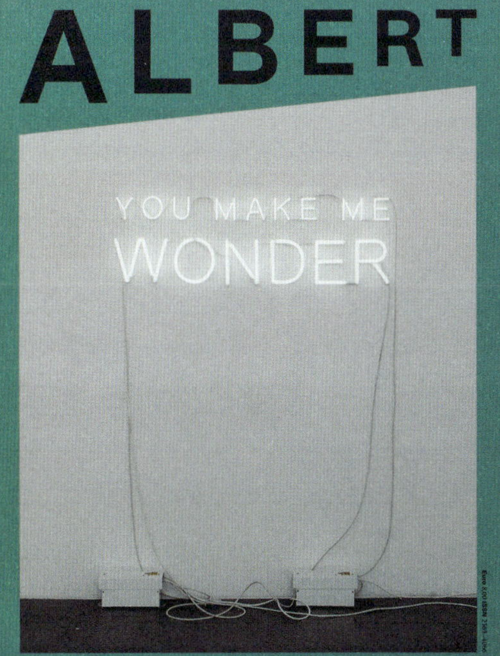
ALBERT
YOU MAKE ME
WONDER
Das Journal der Einstein Stiftung Berlin Nr. 2 – Neurowissenschaften

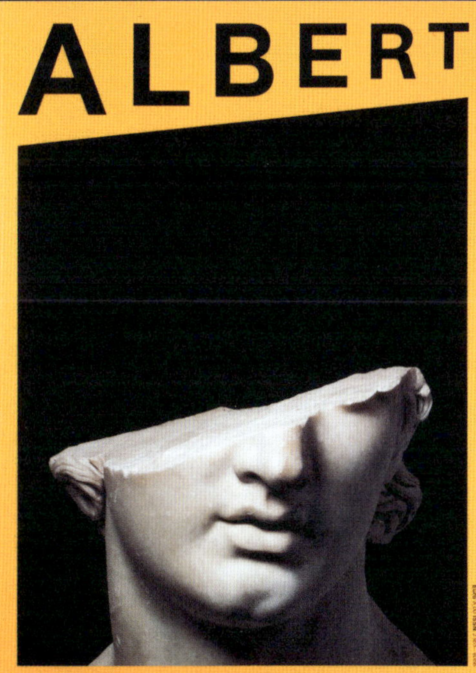
ALBERT
Das Journal der Einstein Stiftung Berlin Nr. 3 – Altertumswissenschaften

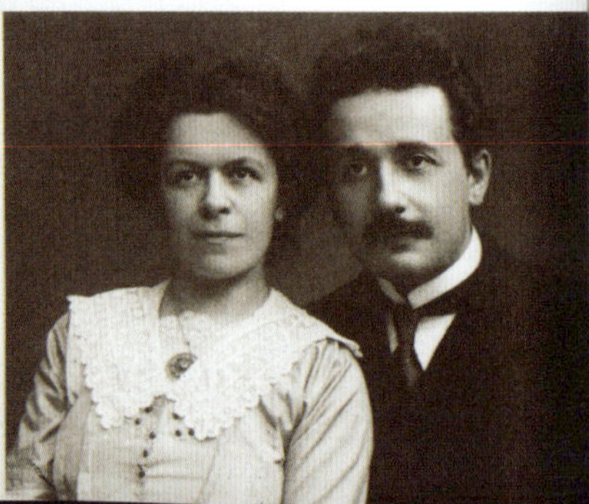

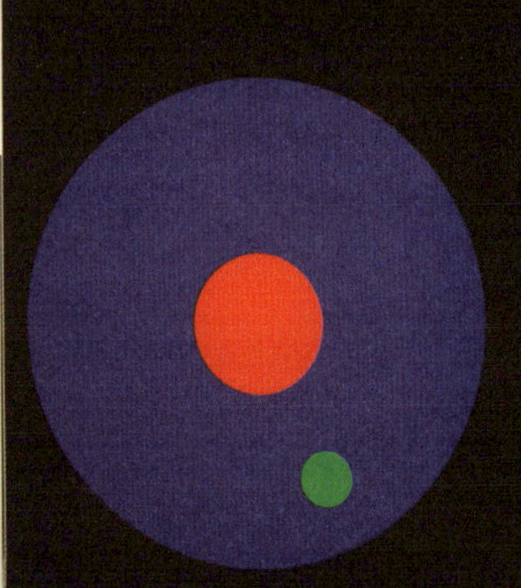

*"ALBERT magazine,"* Fons Hickmann for Einstein Foundation, 2016 – 2019

*How/when did you first fall in love with design?*
Before I fell in love with design, I had a few other "love affairs." It all started with studying photography, then art and media theory, followed by a bit of philosophy and German philology, yet my one and only true love was graphic design. 'Til this day and 'til death do us part. All things considered, I still sometimes ask myself if football hadn't been a better option...

*Who is or was your greatest mentor?*
I studied under designer Uwe Loesch, illustrator Wolf Erlbruch, and artist Dieter Glasmacher. Among the many things I had learned, the most important was the understanding of what boundaries mean. If you stay within your boundaries, your workflow will be governed by the feeling of security and ease. When you cross those boundaries and move over to the unknown, to Terra Inkognito, you will probably learn a lot more, but also expose yourself to many an unexpected danger. If you are a curious person, and I am one, then you will be dying to know what is there on the other side. And what you might find there can be excitingly beautiful and horrifyingly different at the same time.

*You mentioned in an interview with novum, that you are also inspired by the good, the bad, and the ugly. What is it about the aesthetic of the ugly, the devious, the disgusting that attracts you?*
I always find it disturbing when design is reduced only to a nice form since it is worlds away from how things are in real life. Life consists of light and shadow, ups and downs, love and suffering, and a real character can only emerge out of this contrast paradigm. It would have been more than naive to think of us humans as either being good or bad, positive or negative, since we all to a certain extent carry this ambiguity in us. The Kintsugi technique from the Japanese ceramic art is a good example for that. According to its philosophy, if say a porcelain bowl breaks to bits, it is not thrown away, but put together using a golden binding mass. The accidental cracks and fractions that occurred in the process are not hidden but rather emphasised and are there to give the object a special individual character. I consider this to be a beautiful metaphor for life.

*Who among your contemporaries today do you most admire?*
I find the graphic collective that originated around Neubad Luzern very fascinating. Since some time, events, concerts, and performances at the venue are being advertised with posters created by a number of various graphic designers. These posters are very experimental and contemporary in their style and the only existing creative guideline for them is using b/w format. I think right now this is the place where the most up-to-date graphic design comes to life and where the new and bold visual trends emerge. https://neubad-plakate.tumblr.com

*Where did the name of your studio (m23) come from?*
Because blood needs exactly 23 seconds to circulate the human body. Because the human being loses 23 grams of body weight when he dies. Because there are 23 people including the ref on the field during a football game. Because humans have 23 spinal disks and pass 23 chromosomes onto their descendants, and last but not least because the house number of my studio is 23.

*Where do you seek inspiration?*
Either under extreme pressure or utter relaxation.

*Would you consider yourself a political artist?*
Everything is political, even disliking politics in general or politicians in particular makes it still a political statement. What I support through my work for NGOs is the fact that they advocate for the preservation of the environment and promotion of human rights. They fight for life so that it remains worth living. I respect such activism and am always willing to help. I believe, however, it should be the responsibility of politicians to promote gender equality and focus on environmental protection. When they do the opposite and take advantage of the power given to them only to get rich at the expense of others, it's embarrassing and contemptible.

*How important is football in your life? Is there a decent crossover between football and graphic design or are they separate passions?*
Everything in my life exists in a symbiotic relationship. It echoes both in my work and spare time, on both private and professional levels or in design and sports. I used to have a football team with my students, now we play table tennis. Life is fluid, we flow like a river, merge, and part again. Football is a passion as chaos and order meet there. Every match has the same basic onset conditions and yet it's always different. Football is a perpetuum mobile that constantly renews itself.

*As a teacher, how would you say the minds of students and the way in which they learn or approach a project have evolved over the decades?*
Graphic design, as music and fashion, is a Zeitgeist phenomenon. We are in a constant transformation, be it in on the level of society, in politics, or merely our own lifestyle. Students change all the same and that's what makes the job of a professor so interesting and exciting.

*What would you change if you had to do it all over again?*
"If I could start again. A million miles away. I would keep myself. I would find a way." I love this Nine Inch Nails song covered by Johnny Cash. It seems like this is one of the biggest desires of any human being, to start over again and do everything differently. I guess when it comes to my profession, I would do everything exactly as I did up until now, since my job brings me true joy. I would be more careful though when it comes to love.

*Who would you like to see featured in the next Graphis Journal?*
My students.

**Fons Hickmann m23** www.m23.de
*See his Graphis Master Portfolio on graphis.com.*

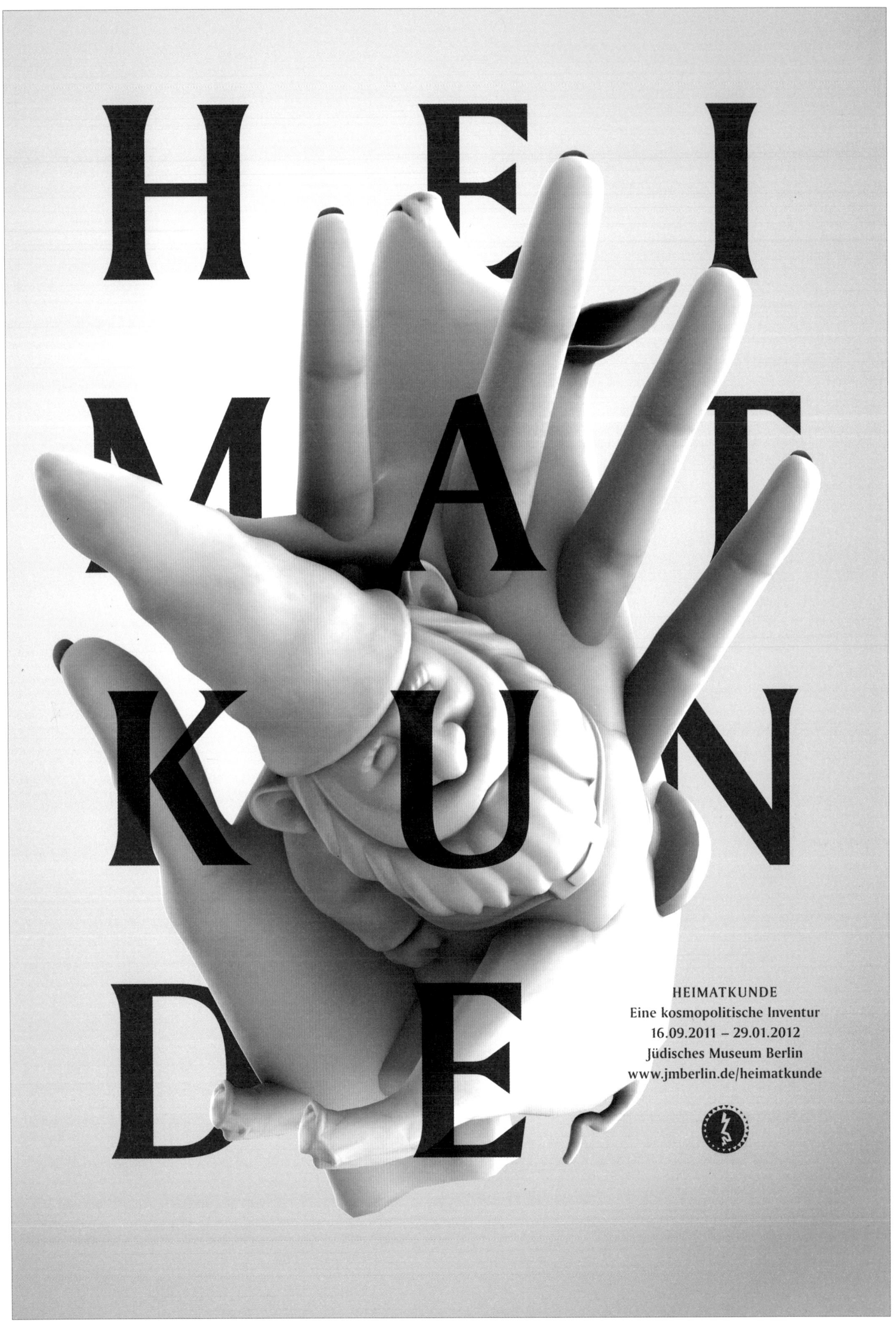


*"Heimatkunde," Jewish Museum Berlin, 2012*

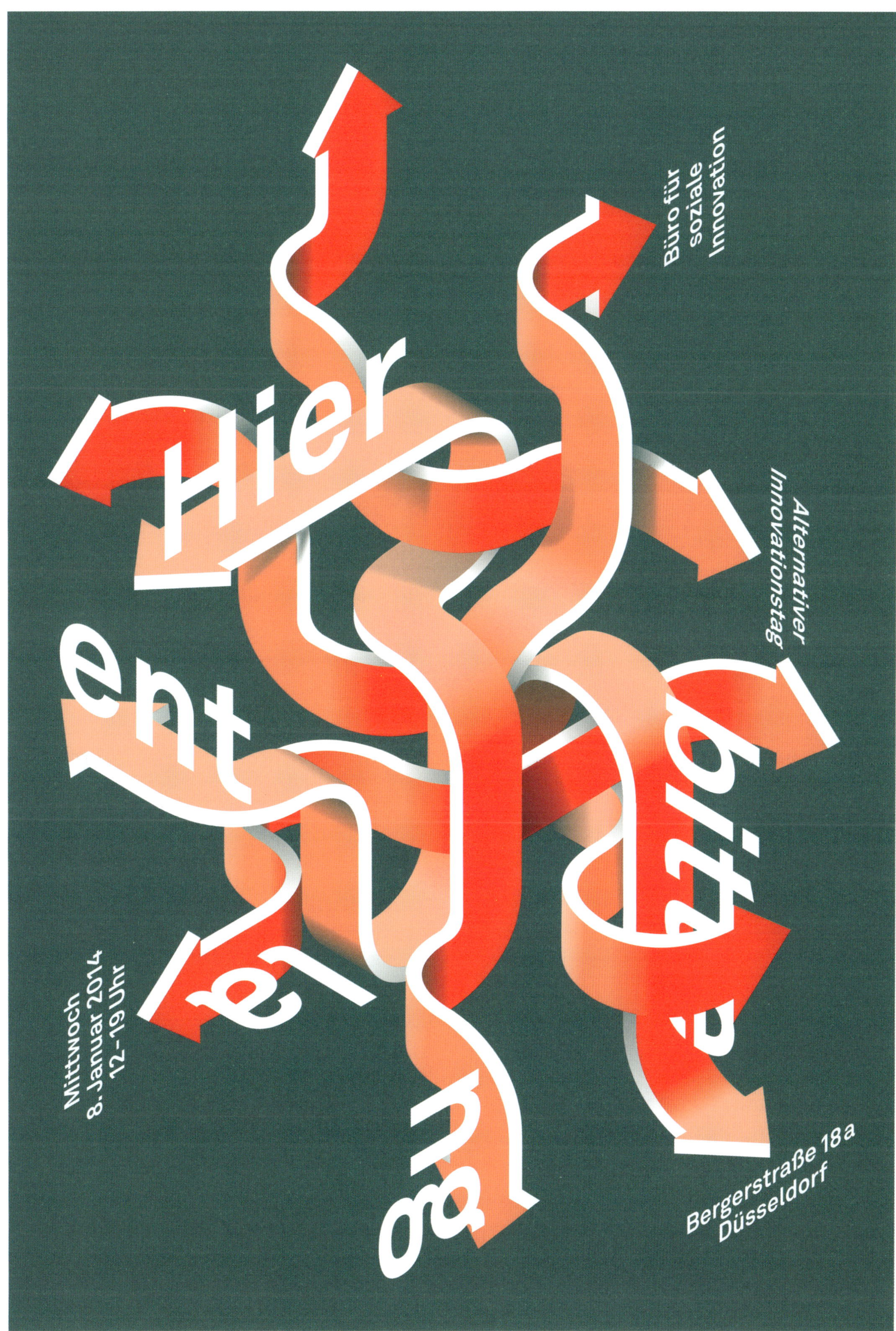

Hier
ent
Büro für
soziale
Innovation
Alternativer
Innovationstag
Mittwoch
8. Januar 2014
12–19 Uhr
Bergerstraße 18a
Düsseldorf

CHIII DESIGN IS A YOUNG DESIGN AGENCY, WHOSE WORK IS REMARKABLE. THEIR USE OF ILLUSTRATION AND AN ARTISTIC APPROACH IN THEIR DESIGNS ARE WORTH NOTING.

THEIR WORK IN GRAPHIC DESIGN IS SIMPLE YET MEMORABLE. THEY ARE ONE OF THE EMERGING DESIGN FIRMS IN MACAU.

**Kenneth Ho,** *Founder & Design Director, WWAVE DESIGN LTD.*

AS A SEASONED GRAPHIC DESIGNER, NONO LEONG IS KNOWN FOR HIS COMPOSURE AND DEFTNESS. WITH HIS DECADES-LONG CAREER IN THE FIELD, NONO HAS DEVELOPED A DISTINCT STYLE THAT IS ELEGANT, SIMPLISTIC, AND POIGNANT.

**Kent IEONG Chi Kin,** *Programming and Outreach Activities Coordinator of the 27th Macao International Music Festival*

CHIII DESIGN USES SIMPLE AND POWERFUL IMAGE TECHNIQUES TO EXPRESS THE ARTWORK. THEY MAKE GOOD USE OF THE IDENTITY OF THE DESIGNER TO HELP THE CUSTOMERS WITH CULTURAL AND COMMERCIAL PROJECTS.

WE ARE VERY GRATEFUL FOR THEIR EXCELLENT WORK, WHICH ENHANCES THE INTERNATIONAL RECOGNITION OF DESIGN IN MACAU.

**Tramy Lui,** *Creative Director, TICK.DESIGN LTD.*

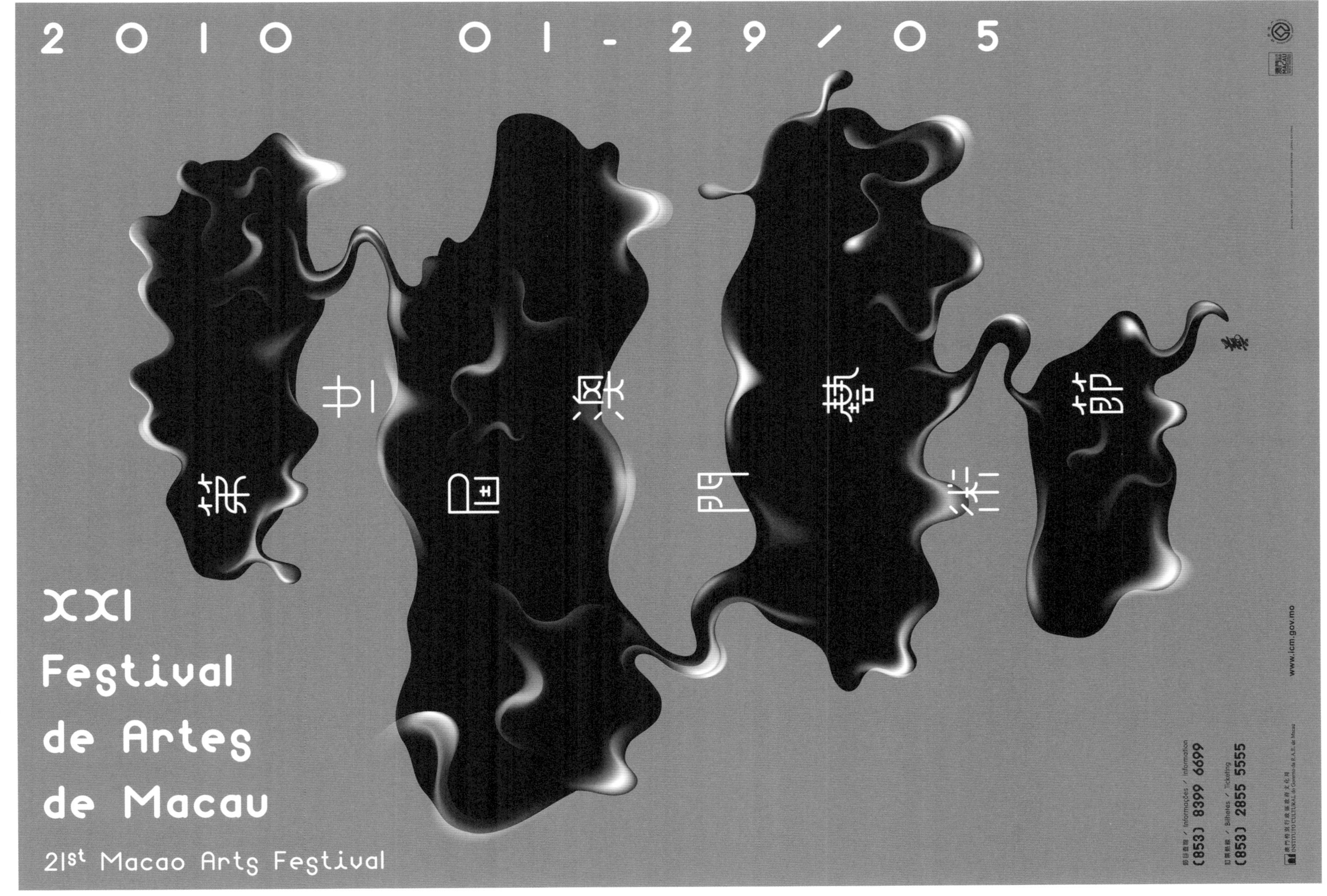


*21st Macao Arts Festival, designed by Nono Leong*

# Introduction by **Tommy Li Tommy Li Design Workshop**

The ratio of Tommy Li Design's project to culture and business is around 8:2. I believe that using business practices to influence society will make society understand the importance of design and improve the quality of people's lives. Mann Lao is in perfect balance in this regard. When we worked together, I felt that he was a very smart young man who knew the importance of business projects. A company with no more than a decade can achieve today's achievements and is rare in Macau, which has a population of only 600,000. And he can also rush out of Macau. I hope that Mann will stick to the principle in the future and take it to the next level, because what he does today is not only to represent Macao, but also to represent many Chinese designers. I believe he can influence many young designers in the future.

USING SLEEK AND GRACEFUL LINES IN BALANCED COMPOSITION, NONO ATTEMPTS TO VISUALIZE THE "UNVISUALIZABLE," AND BRING TO THE FOREFRONT THE INTANGIBLE CREATED BY SENSATION AND MUSIC.

**Kent IEONG Chi Kin,** *Programming and Outreach Activities Coordinator of the 27th Macao International Music Festival*

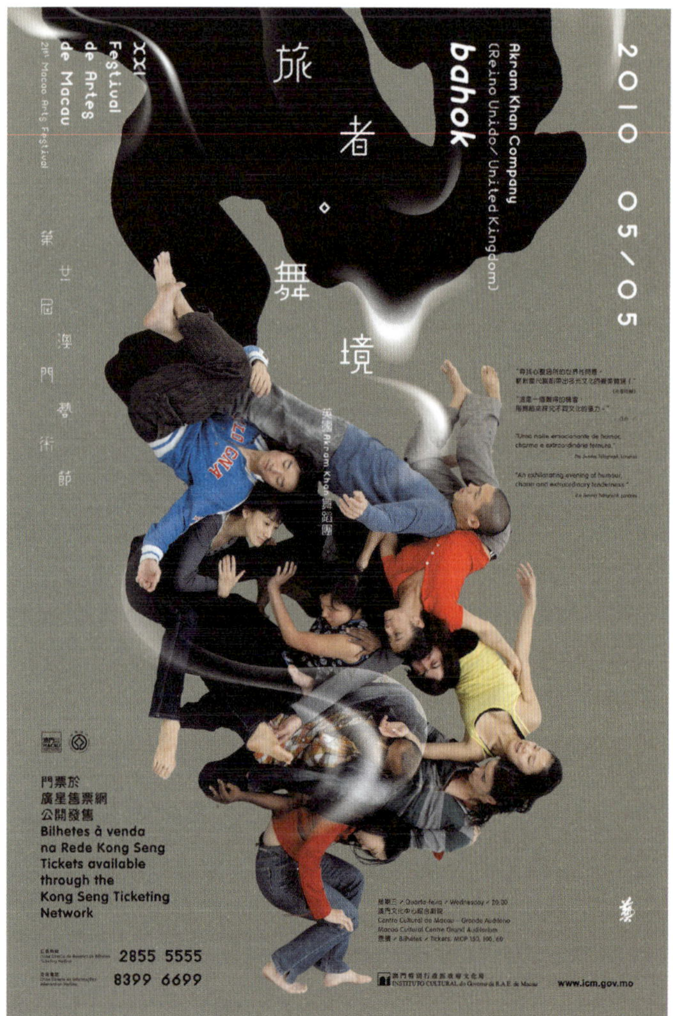


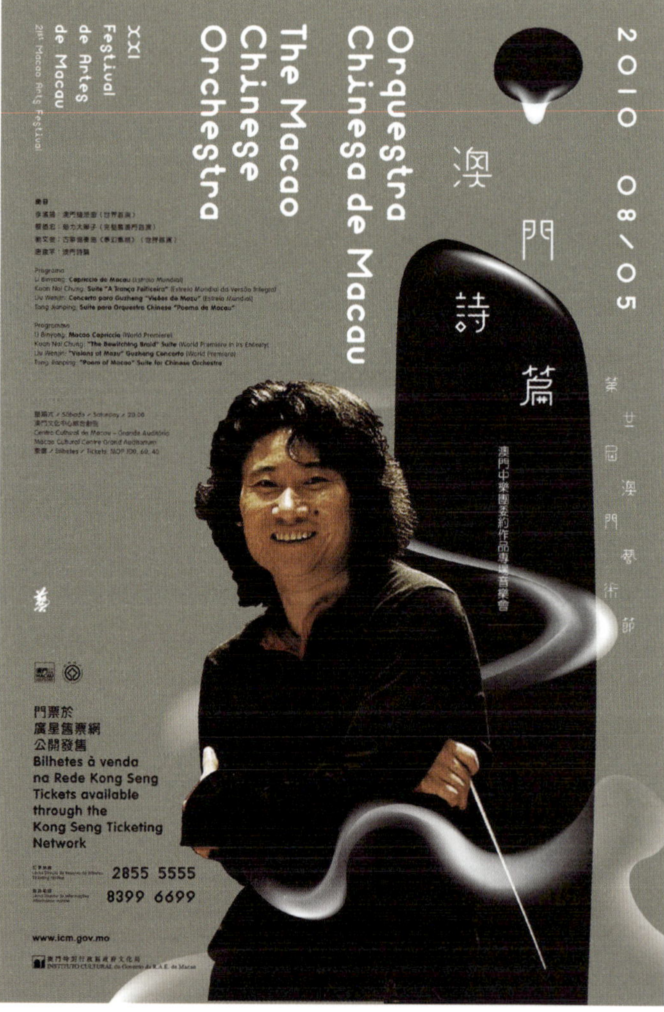


*(Left) 21st MAF, Bahok, designed by Nono Leong / (Right) 21st MAF, The Chinese Macao Orchestra, designed by Nono Leong*

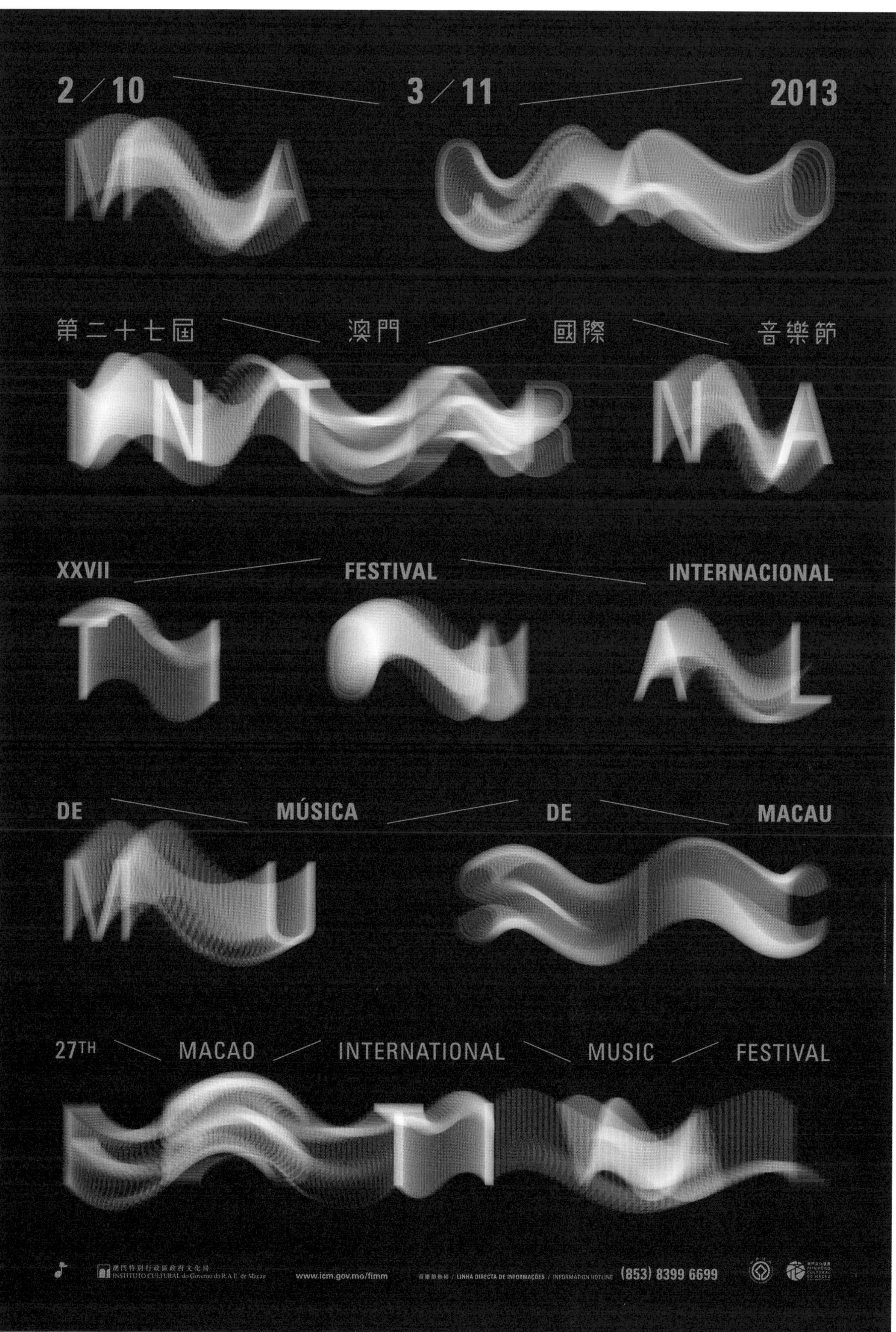


*27th Macao International Music Festival, designed by Nono Leong*

25

*What is your work philosophy?*
**Mann Lao:** To promote the importance of design, to influence and change society.
**Nono Leong:** Passion, Concentration, and Responsibility.

*Who is or was your greatest mentor?*
**ML:** Tommy Li.
**NL:** Victor Hugo Marreiros. He is a well-known artist and designer in Macau.

*How did you start Chiii Design?*
**ML:** When I came back from Lisbon, I decided to start my own studio before I reached age 30 with my partner Nono Leong Chi Hang.
**NL:** When Mann Lao and I found each other with passion and vision in design, we decided to start up our own studio.

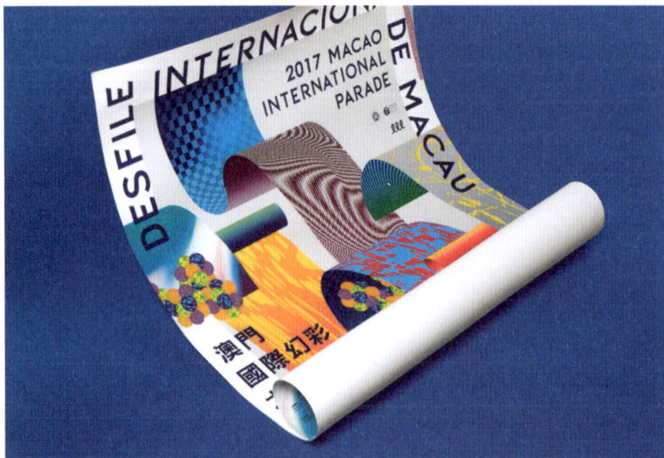


*2017 Macao International Parade, designed by Nono Leong*

*Can you explain the meaning of the name, "Chiii?"*
**ML:** Chiii Design was originally founded by me and two other friends. Each of us have got 'Chi' in our Chinese name, so we decided to name the studio 'Chiii' with three 'i's. Of course, we've still got Nono Leong Chi Hang and me, as the two founders remain for now.
**NL:** Both of the founders of "Chiii" were named "Chi" in Chinese: Mann LAO Wa Chi and me, Nono LEONG Chi Hang. We are looking forward to meeting more awesome 'I's to join our studio. When we join hands, it is "Chiii."

*Can you talk about your approach to integrating commercial elements with arts and culture?*
**ML:** Functionality is the main concern in commercial design; as for cultural design, aesthetics would be the bigger issue. It seems like they don't go along well, however, our approach is basically to catch the soul and find a balance in both.

*What is your most difficult challenge you've had to overcome?*
**ML:** To open up an overseas market beyond Macau.
**NL:** In terms of time management, 2016 was the most challenging time in my life. When the studio grew rapidly that year, it was very difficult for me to handle tons of work while preparing for my personal big project, a wedding.

*Who among your contemporaries today do you most admire?*
**ML:** There are too many, definitely many in my country and other regions who are doing very well, even better than me and it's hard for me to name each of them.

*Who have been some of your favorite people or clients you have worked with?*
**ML:** Whitestone Gallery from Japan.

*What are the most important ingredients you require from a client to do successful work?*
**ML:** They should have the same determination.
**NL:** It is very important to have our clients' trust in us. Communication is greatly essential. The more we know about their thoughts, the more efficient we can make successful work.

*What is your greatest professional achievement?*
**ML:** The power of which we can influence the commercial design market in Macau and overseas as a Macau design studio.

*What is the greatest satisfaction you get from your work?*
**ML:** The ability to visualize how our works fit in different cities all over the world and how they transform societies.
**NL:** Recognition for our designs is the greatest satisfaction in work. When I hear someone say "I like your design!" it makes my day.

*What part of your work do you find most demanding?*
**ML:** Solving the problem.

*What interests do you have outside of your work?*
**ML:** Sports, Sports and sports!
**NL:** I enjoy driving my classic Mini and Vespa during when I have free time.

*Where do you seek inspiration?*
**ML:** I find inspiration through the communication with clients, friends, and colleagues.
**NL:** Design is like a reasoning game to me, so I need a silent and peaceful place for thinking and inspiration.

*Where do you see yourself and Chiii Design in the future?*
**ML:** I found this question very interesting. How things go will never align with what we have expected. That's why life is so fascinating and I always look forward to the challenges that come up each day.

*What aspect of graphic design do you most enjoy?*
**NL:** I like minimalist design, so I enjoy working on branding or logo design.

*Who were some of your greatest past influences?*
**NL:** Victor Hugo Marreiros, who was my supervisor for more than a decade before I started up my own business. He influenced me a lot. What I have learned from him is to respect and appreciate other designers.

*What do you value most?*
**NL:** Freedom.

*What would be your dream assignment?*
**NL:** I have designed four collections of stamps issued in Macau. However, I wish that one day I will have designed something that everyone in Macau will use or something that can represent Macao.

**Chiii Design** www.chiiidesign.com

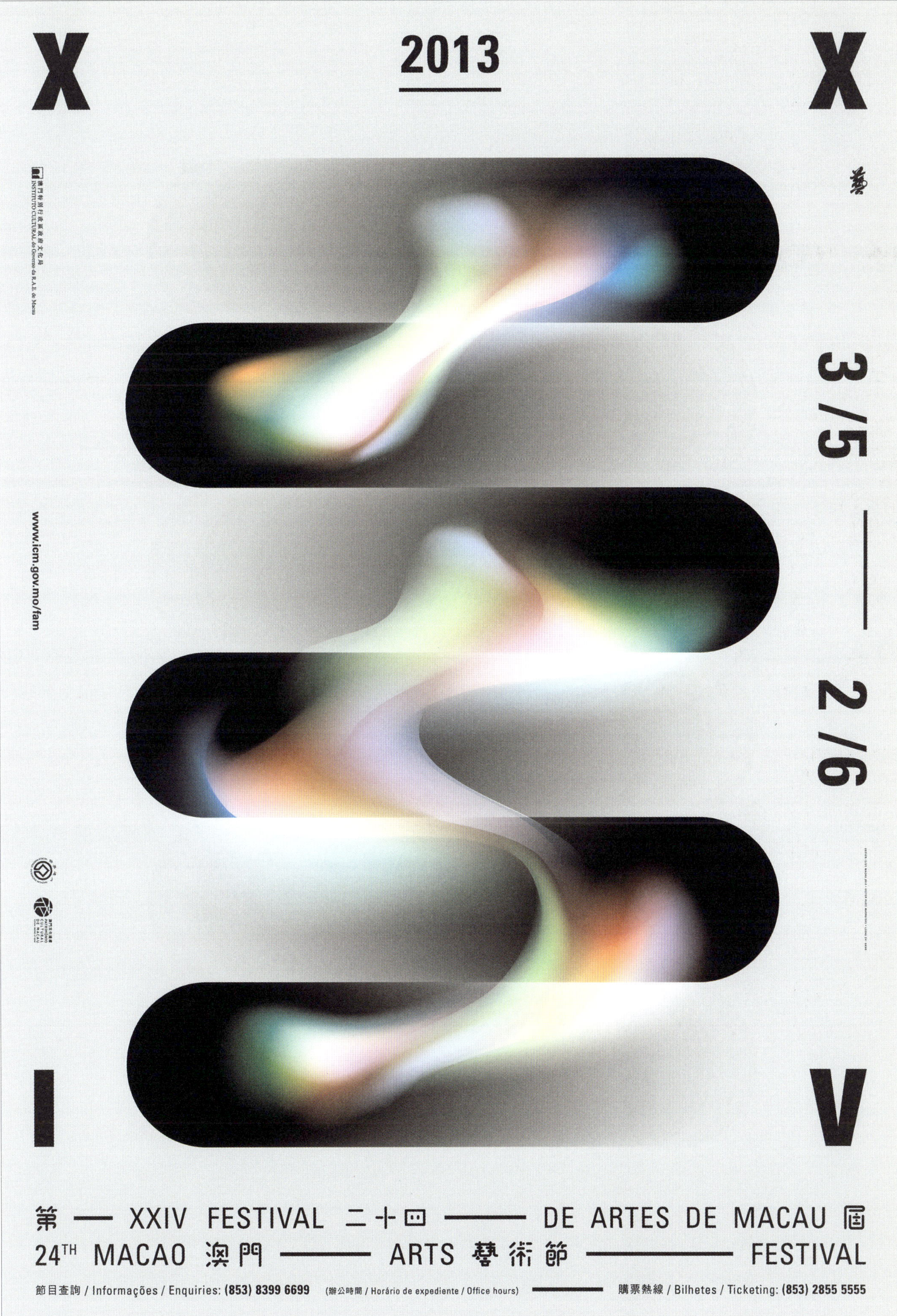


*24th Macao Arts Festival, designed by Nono Leong*

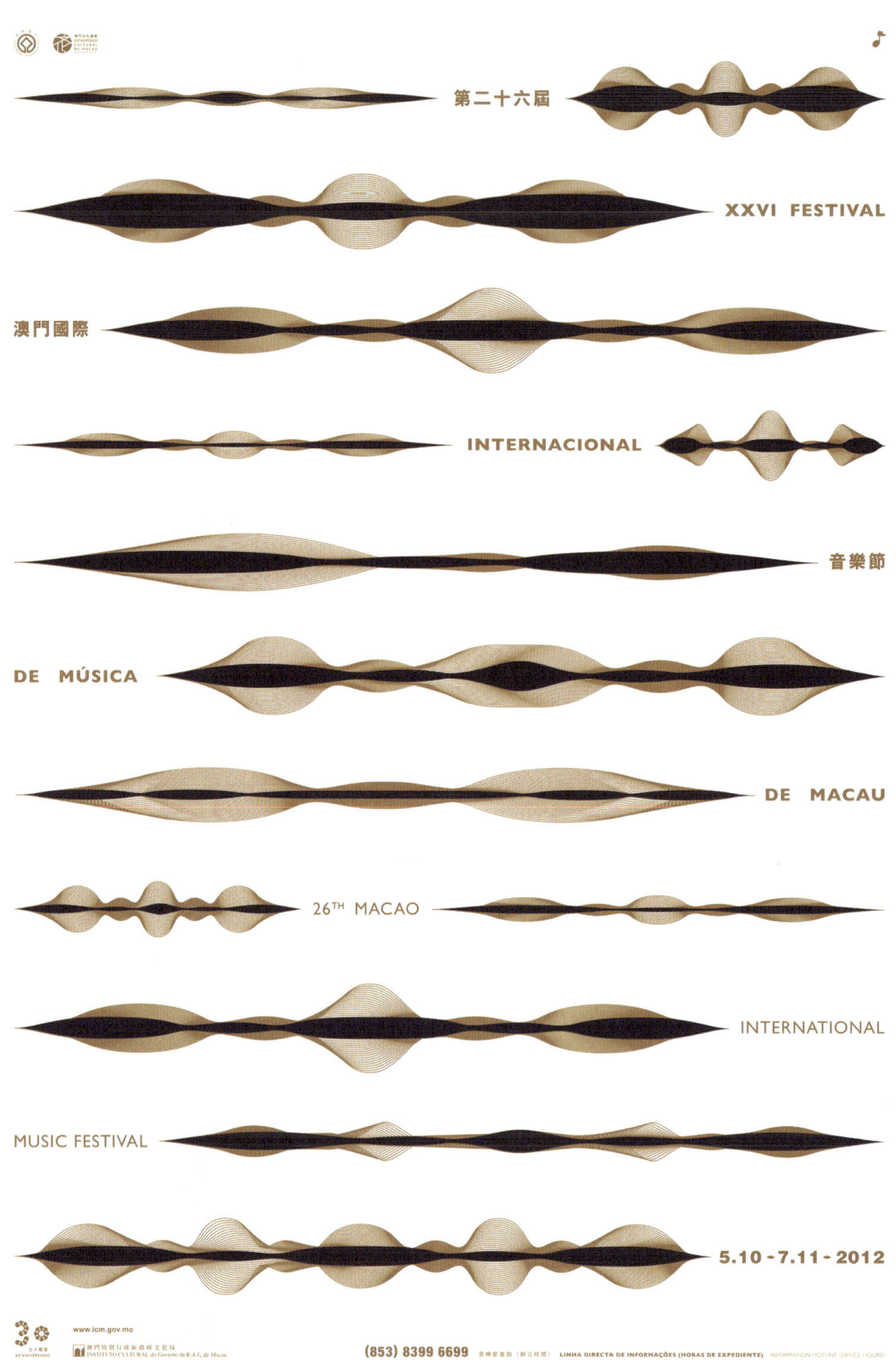


26th Macao International Music Festival, designed by Mann Lao

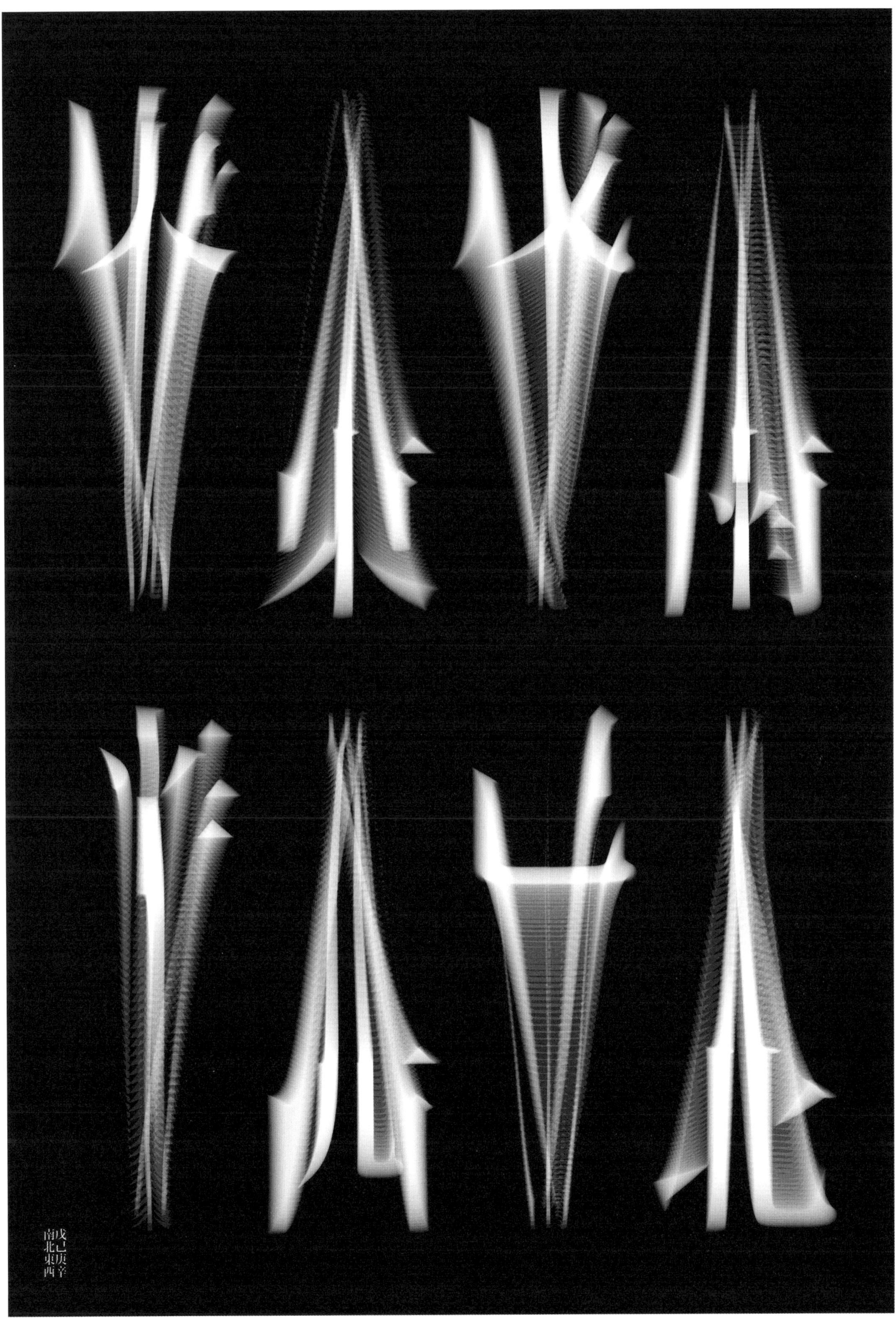



*POEM+ Design Exhibiton, designed by Nono Leong*

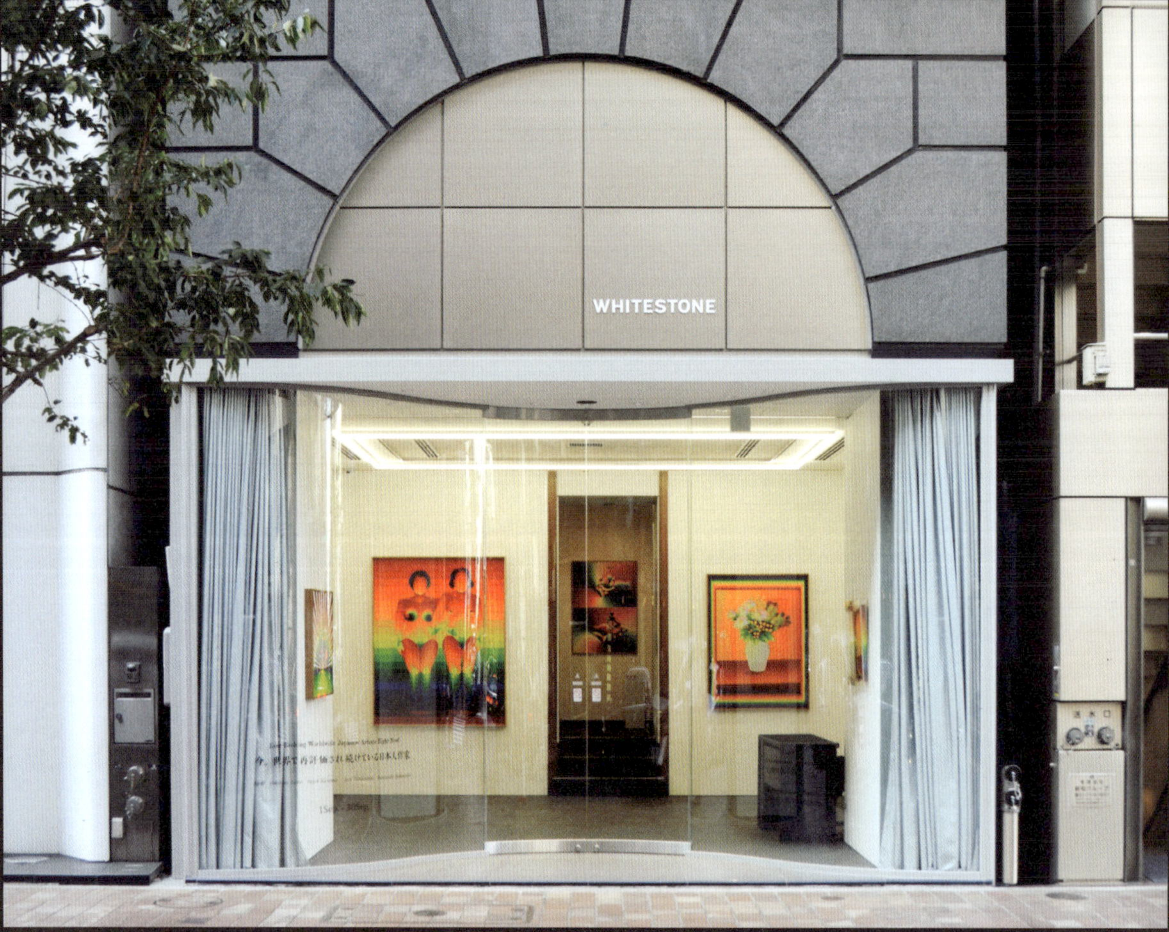

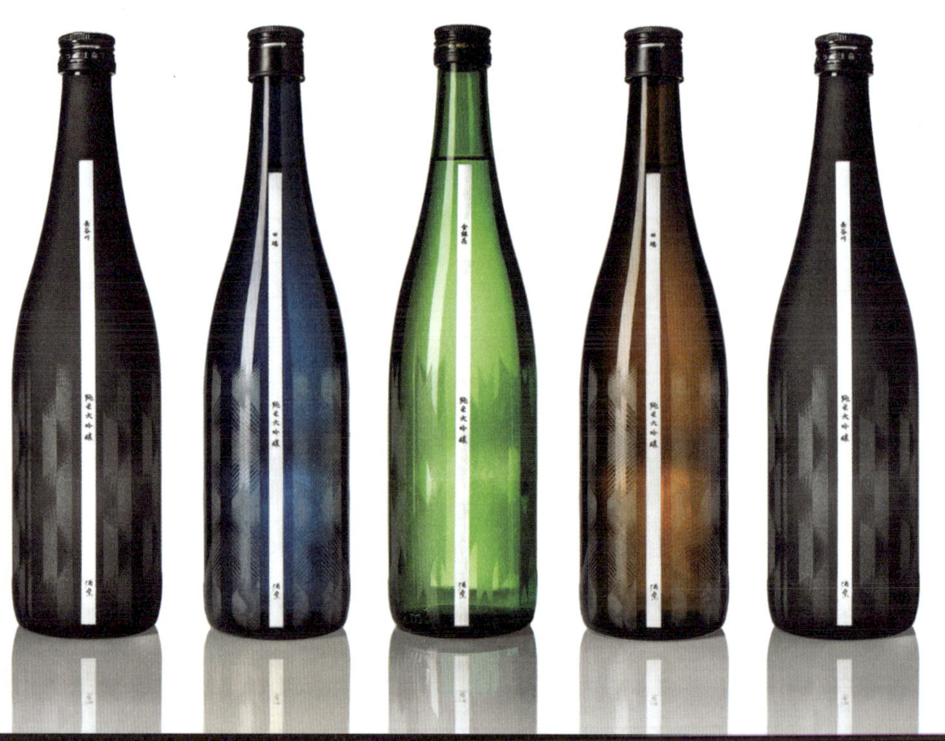

*(Top) Whitestone Gallery, designed by Nono Leong, Mann Lao / (Bottom) The Sakeraku, designed by Nono Leong, Mann Lao*

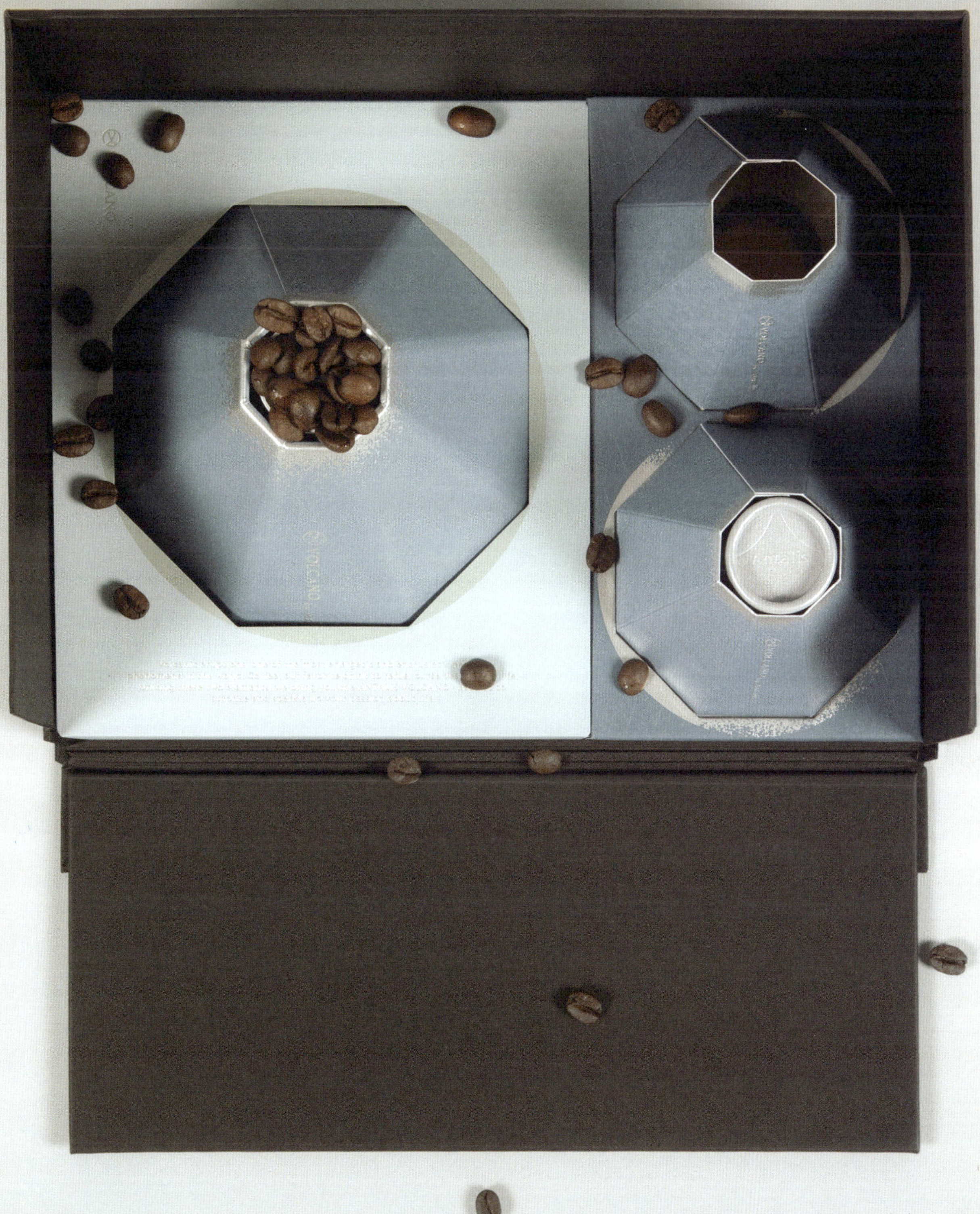

*The Volcanic Coffee, designed by Dan Ferreira, Nono Leong, Mann Lao*

I REMEMBER LOSING A JOB I WANTED (A COVER FOR THE NEW YORK TIMES MAGAZINE'S DESIGN ISSUE) TO JENNIFER. IT WASN'T FUN. AND IT WAS CLEAR THAT HER SOLUTION WAS MORE JOYFUL, RADICAL, AND ELEGANT. IT'S GOOD TO LOSE THAT WAY.

**Stefan Sagmeister,** *Designer & Art Director*

MORLA'S PATH TO DISTINCTION IS MARKED BY ORIGINAL, PROLIFIC IMAGE-MAKING, AND AN AUTHENTIC RESPECT FOR HER CLIENTS. SHE'S NOT A GIFTED "WOMAN DESIGNER." THE LABEL WON'T STICK. SHE IS A DESIGNER'S DESIGNER.

**Michael Vanderbyl,** *Designer*

JENNIFER CHALLENGES THOSE AROUND HER TO APPROACH DESIGN AS SERIOUSLY AS SHE DOES, ALL WHILE IGNORING THE TRADITIONAL BOUNDARIES BETWEEN MEDIA, DISCIPLINES, ETC. SHE IS A CHALLENGER AND A VISIONARY.

**Max Batt,** *Interaction & Visual Designer*

HER WORK HAS THE ABILITY TO ASTOUND PEOPLE WITH ITS UNIQUE APPROACH TOWARDS GRAPHIC DESIGN, JUXTAPOSING THE TRADITIONAL AND FAMILIAR WITH THE INNOVATIVE AND SLEEK IN EXTREMELY EYE-CATCHING WAYS.

**Agustin Plancarte Fexas,** *Designer*

HER WORK IS AN EXAMPLE OF SAN FRANCISCO'S MOST INFLUENTIAL GRAPHIC DESIGN TODAY. AS LONG AS I HAVE KNOWN JENNIFER, HER WORK ENDLESSLY INSPIRES AUDIENCES AROUND THE WORLD.

**Thomas McNulty,** *Brand & Package Design Consultant*

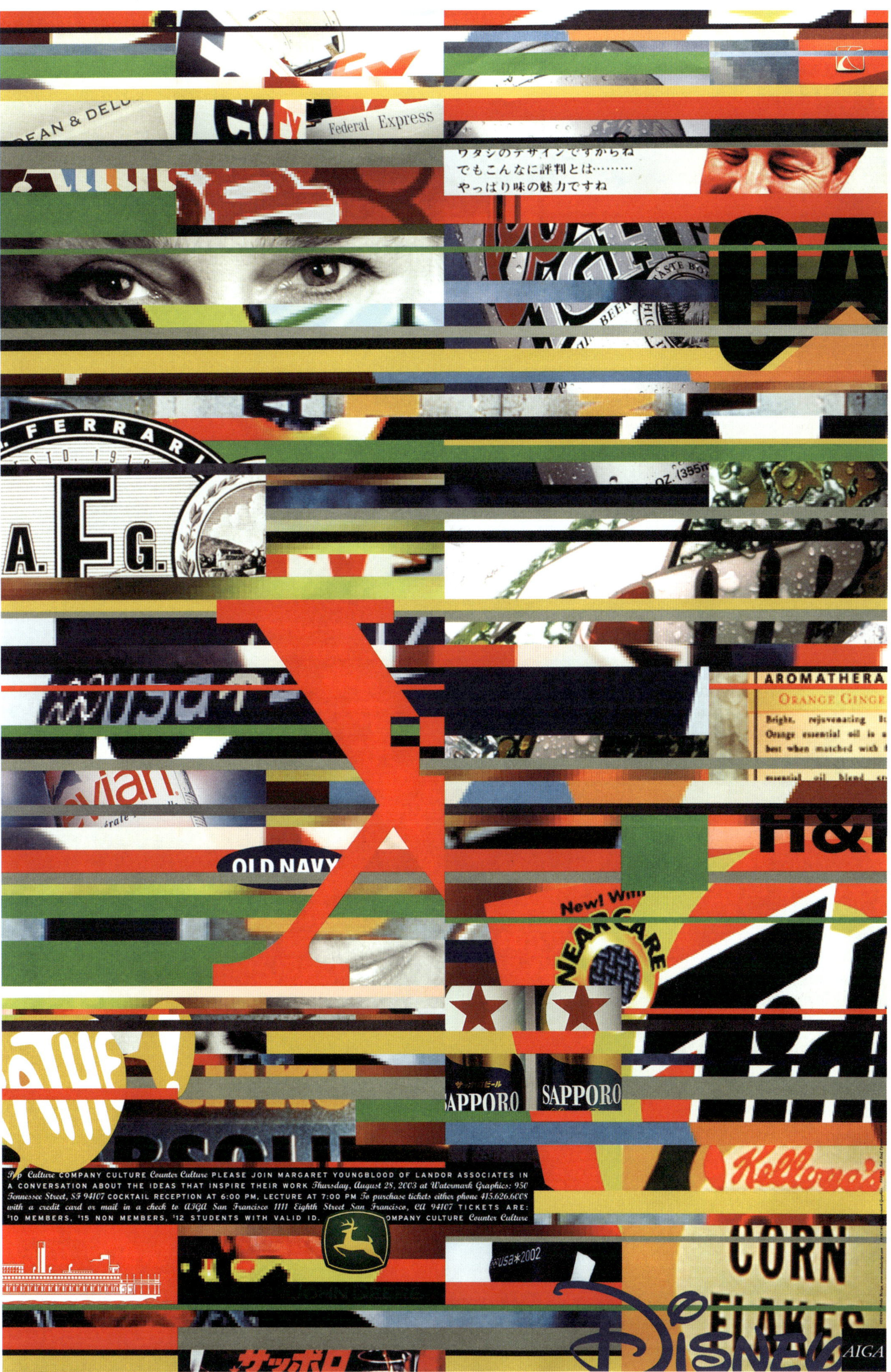

*"AIGA Landor Lecture Poster;"* 2003; Client: AIGA; 20" x 30"; Creative Director: Jennifer Morla; Designers: Jennifer Morla, Brian Singer

I remember encountering Jennifer's work for the first time while I was working on a coffee project in San Francisco with Primo Angeli. Immediately, I noticed her beautiful Bay Area way to handle typography. Her feminine touch not only in choosing chromatic element, but her elegance in reaching the synthesis of the message with the power of clarity. We finally met years later, while we were both in the Jury for the Design section at Cannes Lions 56th International Advertising Festival. She was as a person exactly as her work; lively, exuberant, but strong and to the point, with a classy sense of elegance and style. It takes a lot of skills to navigate with such approach in fully diverse fields, whether she creates corporate identity, web design, videos, posters, or a publication's project.

JENNIFER IS A TRUE "ORIGINAL" THAT OFFERS A UNIQUE BLEND OF STYLE AND MEANINGFUL DESIGN. I APPLAUD JENNIFER FOR HER TALENT AND CONTRIBUTION AS AN INDUSTRY LEADER.

**Thomas McNulty,** *Brand & Package Design Consultant*

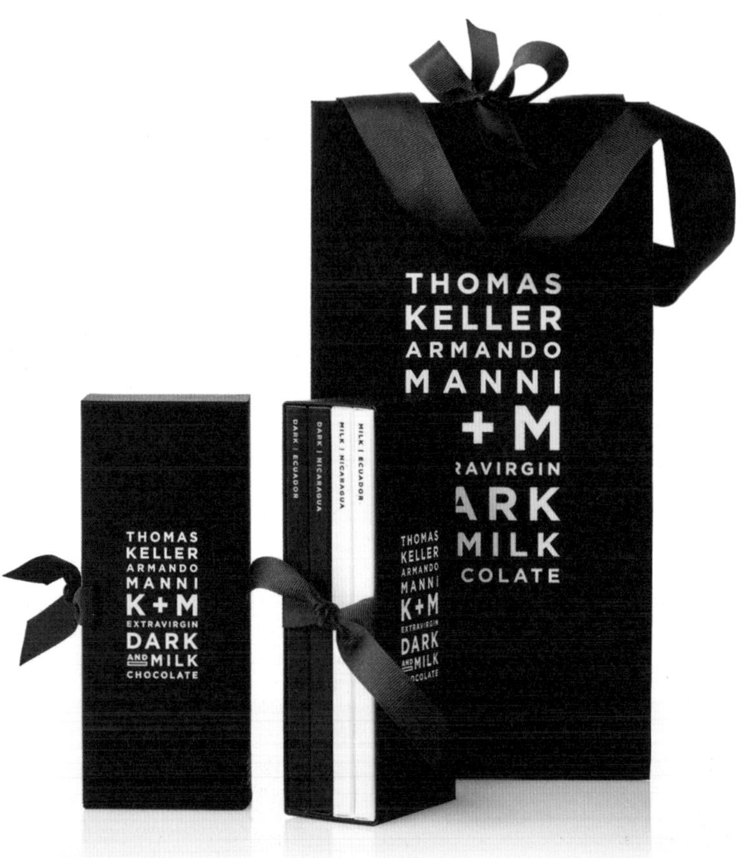


*"Thomas Keller: K+M Packaging;" 2017; Client: Thomas Keller Restaurant Group; 2.75" x 6.75"; Creative Director: Jennifer Morla;*
*Designers: Jennifer Morla, Reymundo Perez III; Photographer: Eric Zepeda*

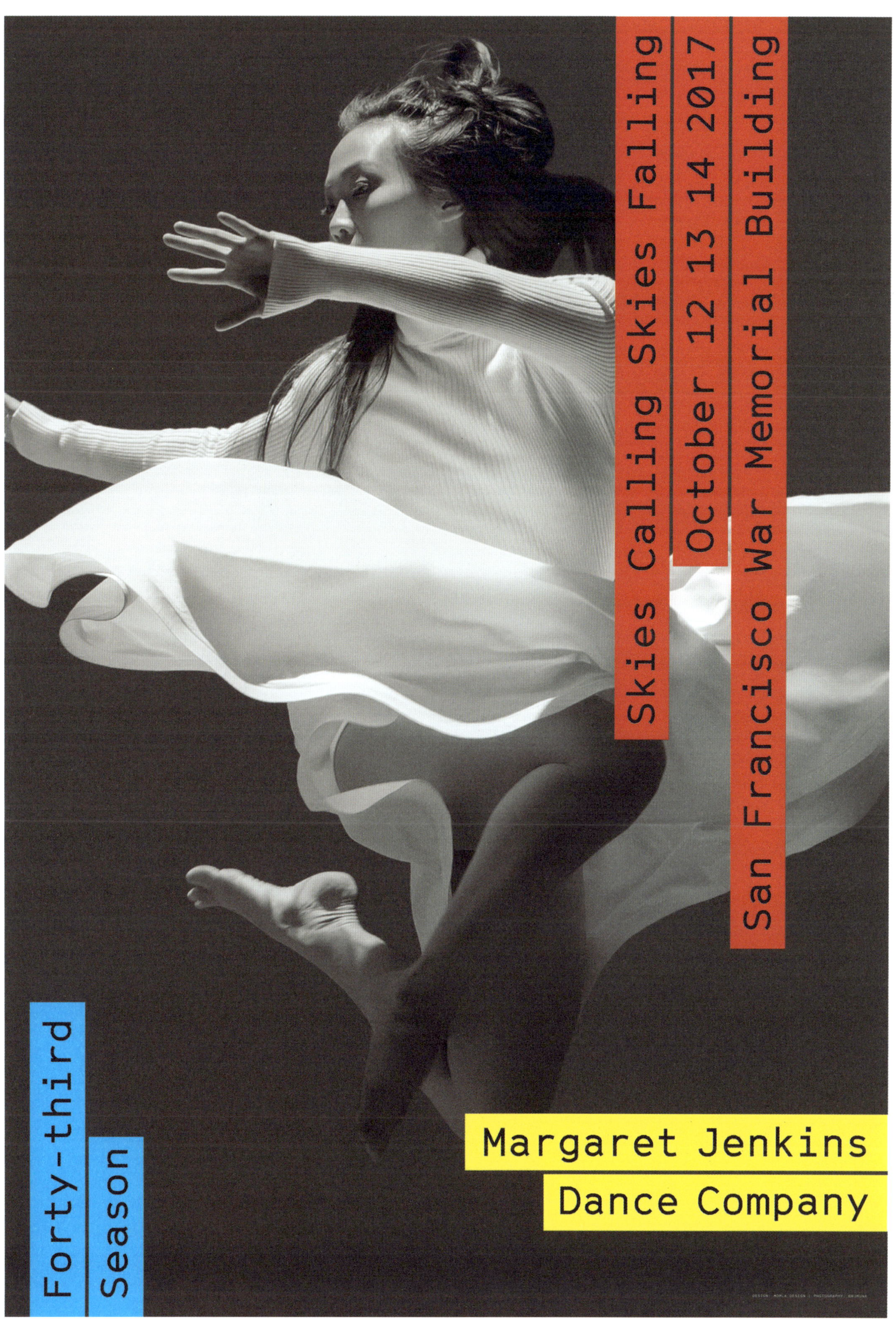


*"MargaretJenkins Dance Company Posters;" Client: Margaret Jenkins Dance Company; 28" x 40"; Creative Director: Jennifer Morla;*
*Designers: Jennifer Morla, Reymundo Perez III; Photographer: RJ Muna*

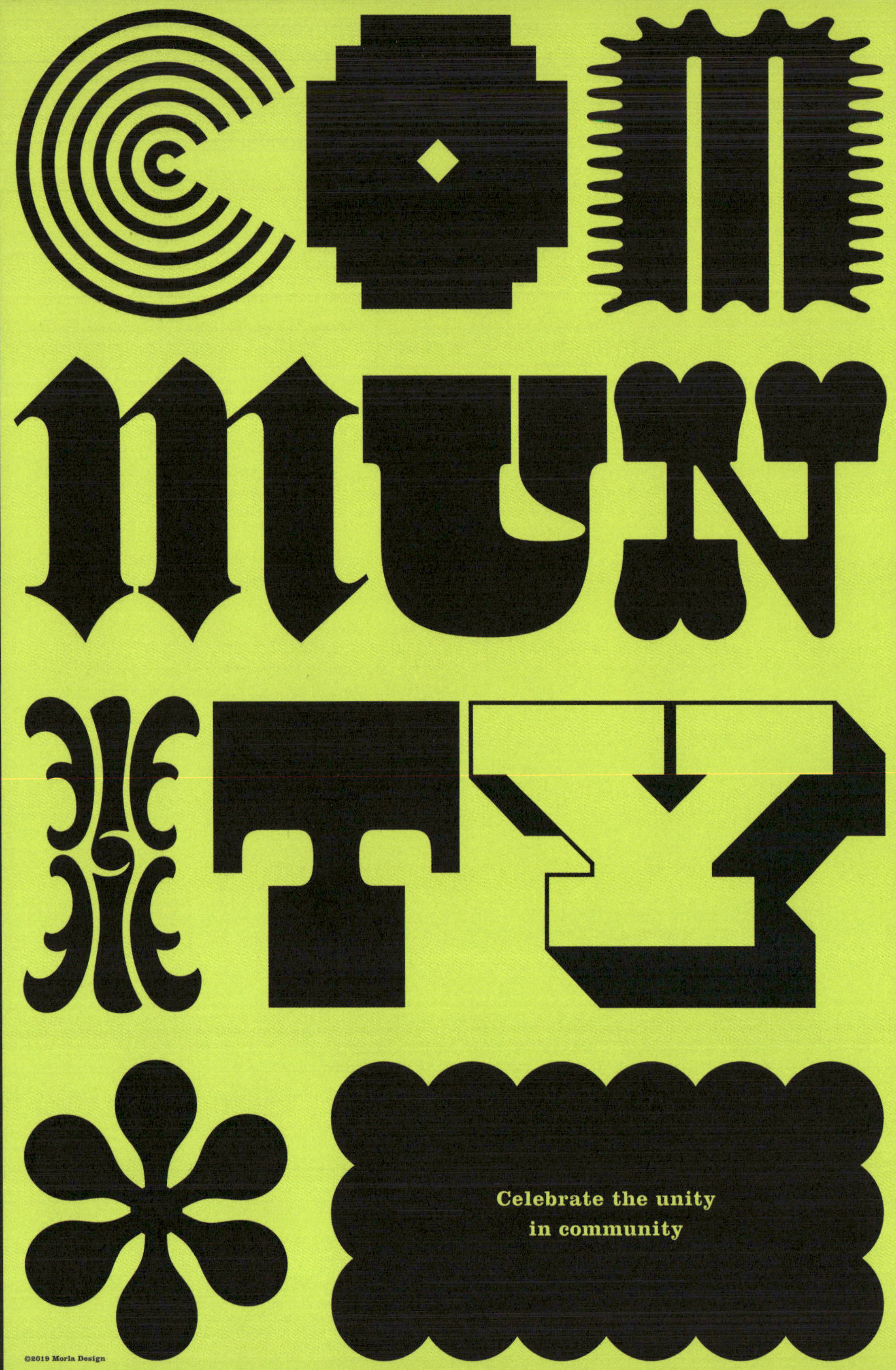

COMMUNITY
Celebrate the unity
in community
©2019 Morla Design

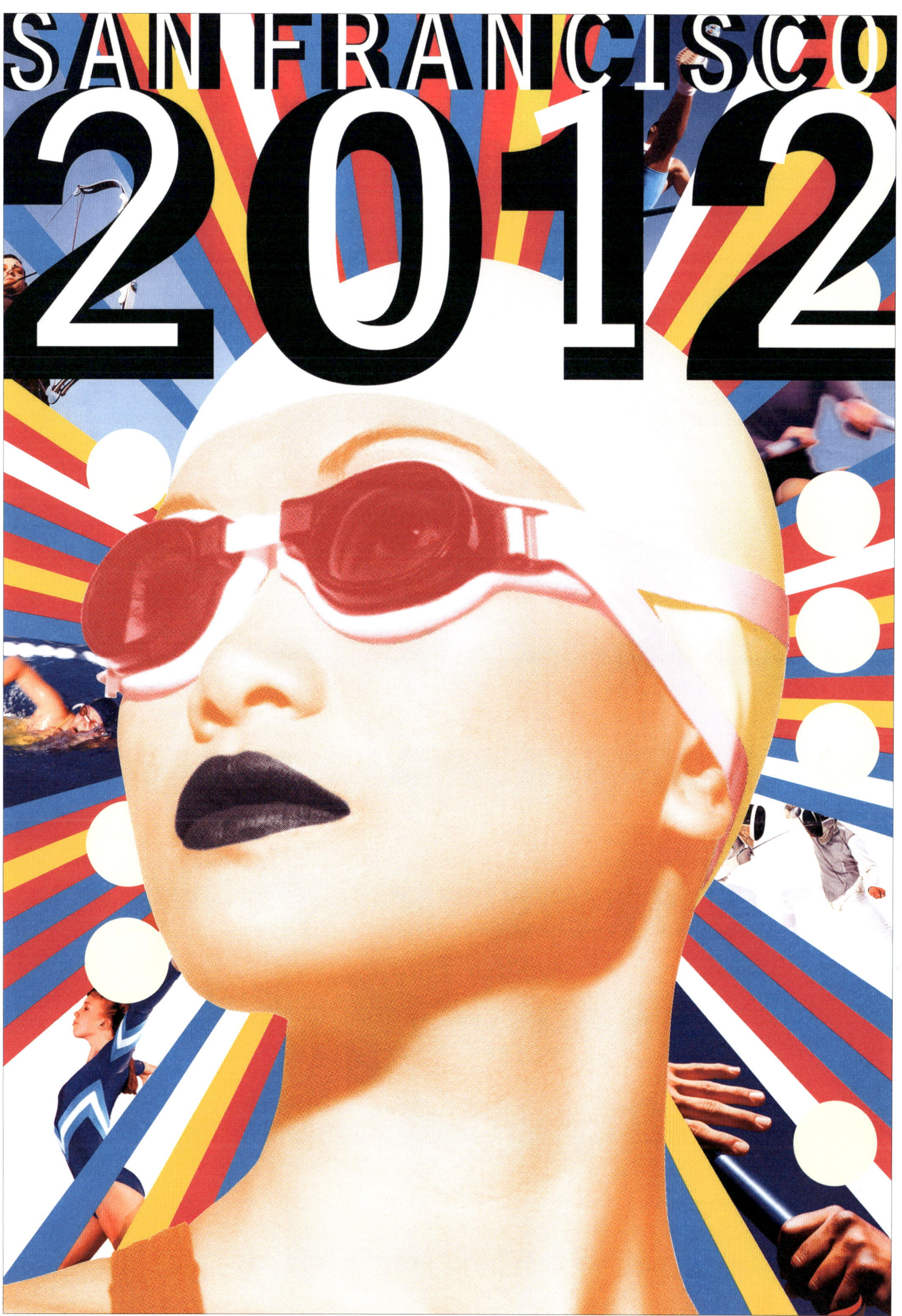


*"Olympic Bid Poster;" 2002; Client: Bay Area Sports Organizing Committee; 24" x 36"*
*Creative Director: Jennifer Morla; Designers: Jennifer Morla, Hizam Haron; Photographer: Jock McDonald*

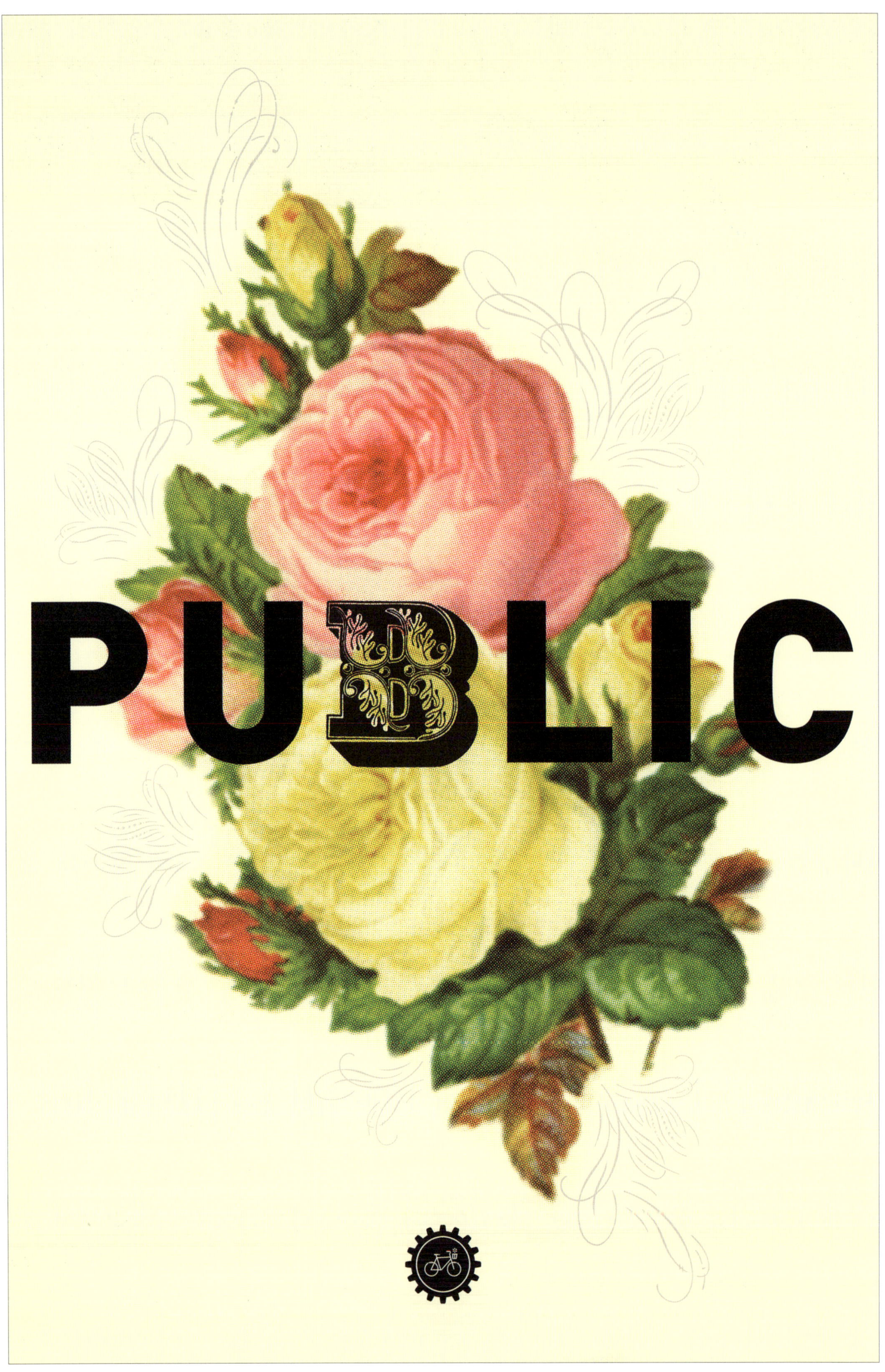


*"Public Bikes Poster;"* 2012; Client: Public Bikes; 40" x 60"; Designer: Jennifer Morla

*What inspired or motivated you into your career?*
My mother and her sister, Mary and Phoebe.

I grew up in Manhattan. My aunt was an editor at Condé Nast in the 1960s, and as an eight-year-old, it was a thrill to visit the art department: white Formica surfaces, stylish professional women, Breuer chairs, Irving Penn photos scattered on a lightbox, and hundreds of Magic Markers on a lazy-Susan carousel perched atop the designer's drawing board. I imagined someday being an adult and working in an art department just like it.

My mother, an art history major in college, would take me on outings to the Met, the Frick, and, an early favorite of mine, the Guggenheim Museum. It was quite unlike any other museum or building in the city- white, curvaceous, modern. And what nine-year-old doesn't love to skip down a spiraling six-story ramp? Wright's masterpiece opened my eyes to the wonders of architecture.

A few years later, I wandered into the design wing of the Museum of Modern Art. I was surprised that everyday Russel Wright dishware (what I had breakfast on every morning!), stereo speakers, and graphic Russian Constructivist posters were, along with Matisses and Picassos, were a part of the museum's collection. Prior to that memorable visit, I thought I would be an artist when I grew up, but after that visit, I knew I would be a designer.

*What is your work philosophy?*
How can I design smarter, more truthfully, and less wastefully?
How can I incorporate more humanity in my work and touch people's lives in a way that resonates meaningfully?
How can I create a compelling visual narrative in which the solution doesn't turn into a stylistic conceit?

*Who is or was your greatest mentor?*
I did not have a mentor guiding me through my design career. When I was thinking of moving to San Francisco in 1975, I met with a few established designers with studios in the Bay Area. My meeting with the graphic design pioneer, Marget Larsen, was memorable and inspiring. Marget's work encompassed environmental graphics, packaging, identity, and advertising. Always innovative, her massive scale signage and packaging are as relevant today as they were 45 years ago when I had the honor of spending the afternoon with her. Marget's fearlessness in embracing the spectrum of design mediums has been a guiding light for me throughout my career.

*Who among your contemporaries today do you admire?*
Stefan Sagmeister for his courage to create risk-taking, 100% honest design solutions. Michael Vanderbyl for expanding the scope of "graphic" design to include designing furniture, textiles, and showrooms with the same sophistication and attention to detail as all of his print work. And Paula Scher for her ability to instill humanity in her work.

*What are the most important ingredients you require from a client to do successful work?*
A good client tells you the problem, not the solution. They trust your ability to strategically design the right approach by giving you the time to question assumptions. They are not beholden to the cliches of their industry and are willing to take the risk of looking different.

*What advice would you have for students starting out today?*
As a designer, I draw to get my thoughts down quickly. These quick sketches allow me to evaluate any number of solutions in the beginning of the design process, as they take enough shape on the page that I can decide which have value and which don't. They are an invaluable tool in articulating ideas, whether to young designers in my studio or to help a client visualize an approach.

I don't believe in concepting design solutions on the computer. I find going directly to screen at this initial phase is restrictive and laborious. Design software requires too many superfluous decisions that are detrimental to exploring ideas in the early stages. I encourage both students and interns alike to instead sketch their design options, allowing for more time to ideate both content and form before moving their concepts into a digital workspace.

*What interests do you have outside of your work?*
I painted when I was a young adult and I rediscovered my love for the medium around 20 years ago. Using my custom mixture of oil, wax, linseed oil, and marble dust, I typically paint 5-by-7-foot abstract canvases, primarily in black and white. I rarely use color. There are so many aspects of painting large canvases that I enjoy, such as the muscle it takes to mix a gallon of wax and paint, the joy of working without a specific end goal, and the act of creating with no problem to solve. It is the antithesis of graphic design.

*Where do you seek inspiration?*
Conceptual artists often provide insight as to how I approach design. While attending art school as an undergraduate in the early '70s, I saw a piece by conceptual artist Sol LeWitt that struck me as profoundly beautiful. A vast number of penciled dots radiated out in a ring from a dense black center on a large sheet of paper, the dots dissipating outwards, the image transitioning from black to gray to white. The title was something like *Trying to Hit the Center of the Paper with a Pencil One Million Times with My Eyes Closed.* Standing in front of it, enamored by the artist's intent, I learned a key lesson: Reconsider how to create beauty.

*See her Graphis Master Portfolio on graphis.com.*
**Morla Design** www.morladesign.com

# WHAT NINE-YEAR-OLD DOESN'T LOVE TO SKIP DOWN A SPIRALING SIX-STORY RAMP? WRIGHT'S MASTERPIECE OPENED MY EYES TO THE WONDERS OF ARCHITECTURE.

**Jennifer Morla,** *President and Creative Director of Morla Design*

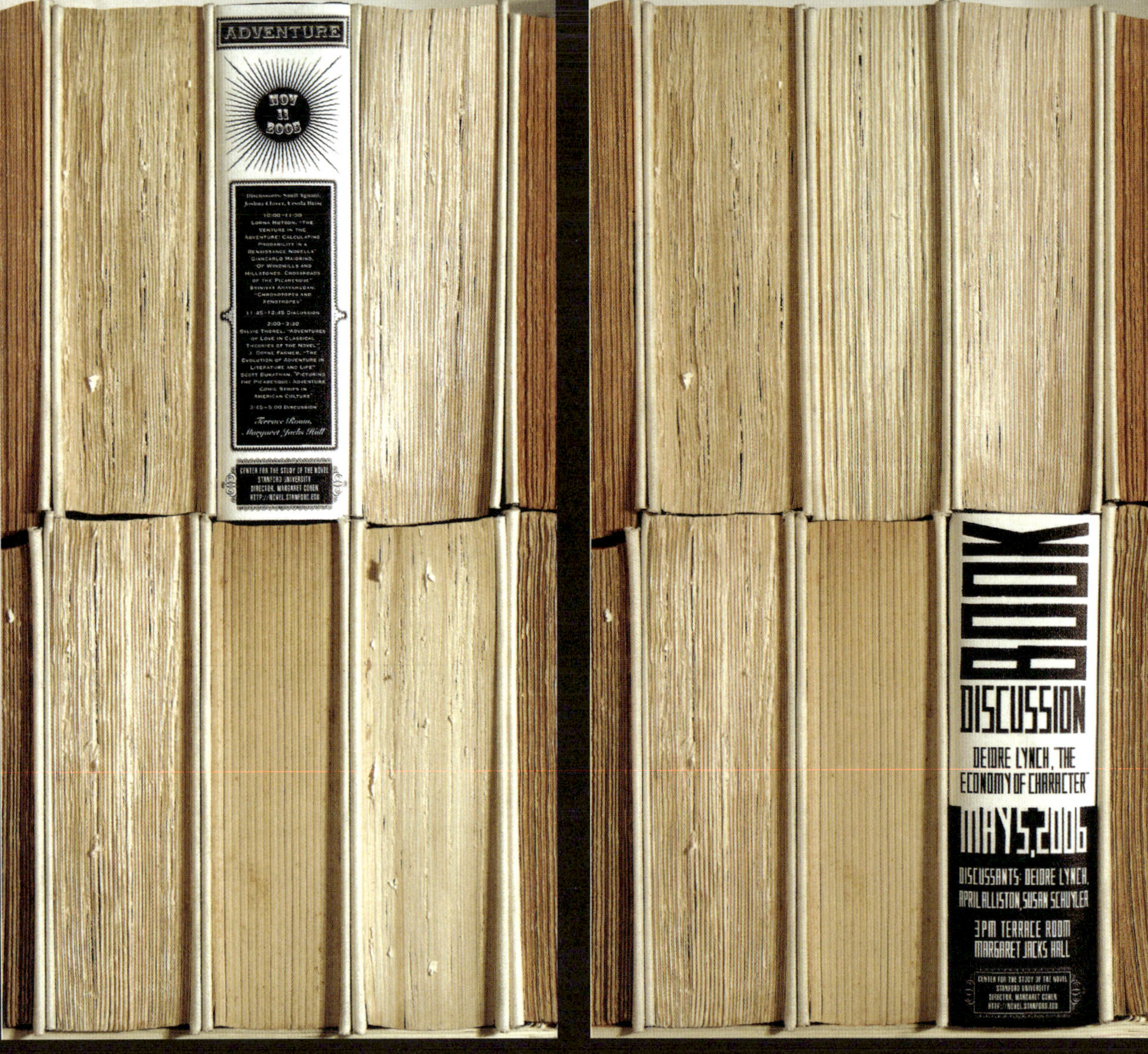



*(This spread) "Stanford Literature Lecture Posters;" 2005; Client: Stanford University; 20.5" x 37"; Creative Director: Jennifer Morla*
*Designers: Jennifer Morla, Bryan Bindloss; Photographer: Bryan Bindloss*

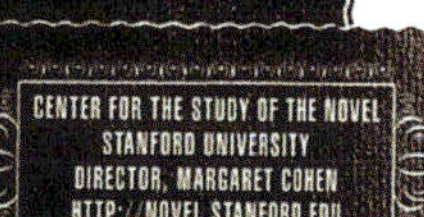
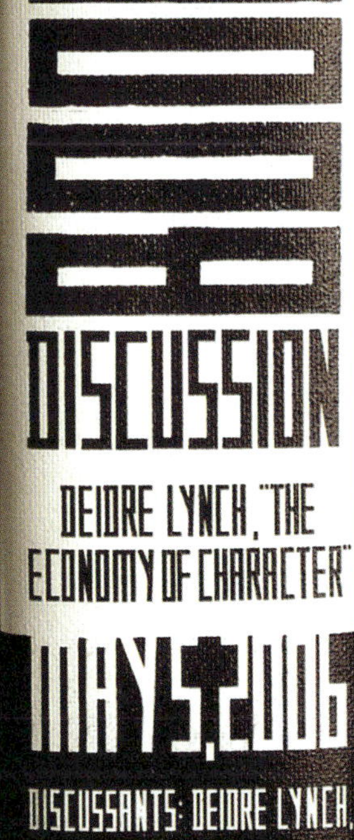


CENTER FOR THE STUDY OF THE NOVEL

STANFORD UNIVERSITY

DIRECTOR. MARGARET COHEN

EVENTS 2005–2006

CENTER FOR THE STUDY OF THE NOVEL
STANFORD UNIVERSITY
DIRECTOR, MARGARET COHEN
HTTP://NOVEL.STANFORD.EDU



ADVENTURE

NOV 11 2005

Discussants: Sunil Agnani, Joshua Clover, Ursula Heise
10:00–11:30
Lorna Hutson, "The Venture in the Adventure: Calculating Probability in a Renaissance Novella"
Giancarlo Maiorino, "Of Windmills and Millstones: Crossroads of the Picaresque"
Srinivas Aravamudan, "Chronotopes and Xenotropes"
11:45–12:45 Discussion
2:00–3:30
Sylvie Thorel, "Adventures of Love in Classical Theories of the Novel"
J. Doyne Farmer, "The Evolution of Adventure in Literature and Life"
Scott Bukatman, "Picturing the Picaresque: Adventure, Comic Strips in American Culture"
3:45–5:00 Discussion

Terrace Room, Margaret Jacks Hall

CENTER FOR THE STUDY OF THE NOVEL
STANFORD UNIVERSITY
DIRECTOR, MARGARET COHEN
HTTP://NOVEL.STANFORD.EDU



ILLUSTRATION

JANUARY 13, 2006
DISCUSSANTS:
NANCY ARMSTRONG,
LESLIE CAMHI, KATE FLINT,
CHRISTOPHER PRENDERGAST,
WILLIAM SCHAEFER,
RICHARD TERDIMAN

10:00–11:30
EMILY APTER,
"KAPITAL: THE NOVEL
(MADAME BOVARY)"
SHARON MARCUS,
"THE FASHIONABLE
FEMALE GAZE"

11:45–12:45 DISCUSSION

2:00–3:30
ANNE HIGONNET,
"THE CULTURE OF THE COPY:
MANET EAST/WEST"
VANESSA SCHWARTZ,
"ICONS: OVERUSED AND
UNDERVALUED IN MODERNITY'S
VISUAL ECONOMY"
ANTHONY VIDLER,
"THE AERIAL PHOTOGRAPH:
NADAR TO DEBORD"

TERRACE ROOM,
MARGARET JACKS HALL

ILLUSTRATION

CENTER FOR THE STUDY OF THE NOVEL
STANFORD UNIVERSITY
DIRECTOR, MARGARET COHEN
HTTP://NOVEL.STANFORD.EDU



IAN WATT LECTURE
on the
HISTORY and THEORY
of THE NOVEL

FEBRUARY 23, 2006

BILL BROWN
"NOVEL OBJECTS:
OBJECT RELATIONS
in an EXPANDED FIELD"

TERRACE ROOM,
MARGARET JACKS HALL
7 PM

CENTER FOR THE STUDY OF THE NOVEL
STANFORD UNIVERSITY
DIRECTOR, MARGARET COHEN
HTTP://NOVEL.STANFORD.EDU



BOOK DISCUSSION

April 21, 2006

PASCALE CASANOVA,
"THE WORLD REPUBLIC OF LETTERS"

DISCUSSANTS: PASCALE CASANOVA,
FRANCO MORETTI, AAMIR MUFTI

3 PM TERRACE ROOM
MARGARET JACKS HALL

READINGS AVAILABLE IN ENGLISH DEPARTMENT

CENTER FOR THE STUDY OF THE NOVEL
STANFORD UNIVERSITY
DIRECTOR, MARGARET COHEN
HTTP://NOVEL.STANFORD.EDU



BOOK DISCUSSION

DEIDRE LYNCH, "THE
ECONOMY OF CHARACTER"

MAY 5, 2006

DISCUSSANTS: DEIDRE LYNCH,
APRIL ALLISTON, SUSAN SCHUYLER

3PM TERRACE ROOM
MARGARET JACKS HALL

ADVERTISING

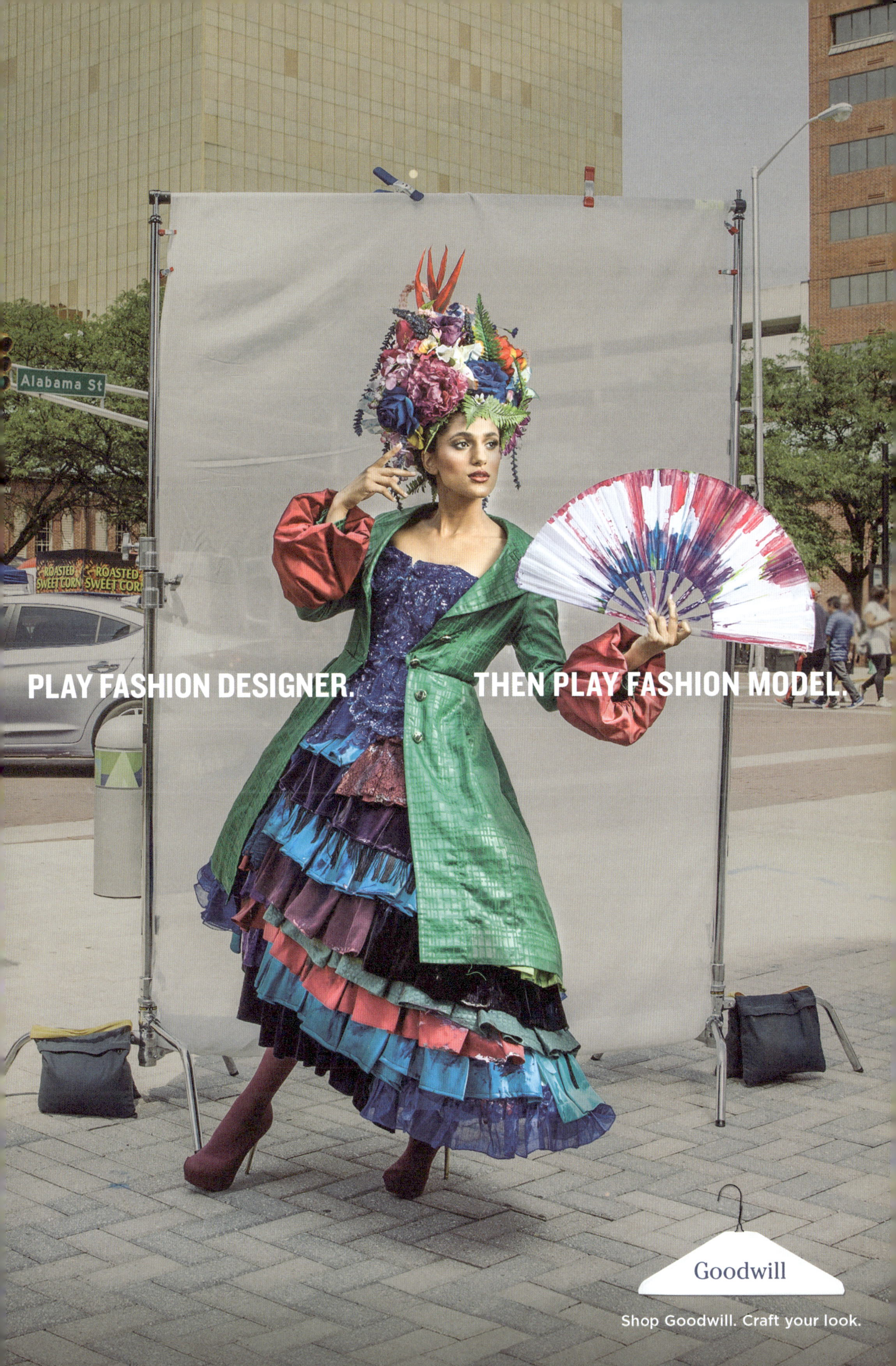

Alabama St
ROASTED SWEET CORN
PLAY FASHION DESIGNER.
THEN PLAY FASHION MODEL.
Goodwill
Shop Goodwill. Craft your look.

THE EXPERIENCE OF WORKING WITH Y&L ON OUR DIGITAL AD CAMPAIGN, FOCUSING ON MAKING YOUR OWN STYLE FROM THRIFTED FINDS, WAS A GREAT EXPERIENCE FROM THE IDEA'S CONCEPTION TO THE FINAL PRODUCT.

WE'RE FORTUNATE TO HAVE SUCH A CREATIVE AND COLLABORATIVE TEAM TO WORK WITH.

**Cindy Graham,** *Vice President, Marketing, Goodwill of Central & Southern Indiana*

Y&L IS NOT JUST A CREATIVE AGENCY, BUT A STRATEGIC BUSINESS PARTNER. THEY ARE TRUE PROBLEM SOLVERS WHO CONSISTENTLY PROVIDE OUTSIDE-THE-BOX THINKING.

THEY DELIVER BREAKTHROUGH CREATIVE WORK THAT IS CUTTING-EDGE AND ALLOWS OUR BRAND TO PUSH BOUNDARIES.

**Lucia Bayt,** *Brand Manager, Brizo Kitchen & Bath Company*

FROM CONSUMER INSIGHTS TO THE CREATIVITY THAT BREAKS THROUGH AND CONNECTS US WITH OUR TARGET MARKET, Y&L HAS BEEN COLLABORATING AT EVERY STAGE OF THE HIGH & MIGHTY BRAND'S DEVELOPMENT AND LAUNCH.

IT REALLY IS A TRUE STRATEGIC PARTNERSHIP, FOCUSED ON BUILDING SOMETHING MEANINGFUL.

**Tim Ferguson,** *Home and Access Solutions Global Business Leader & V.P., The Hillman Group*

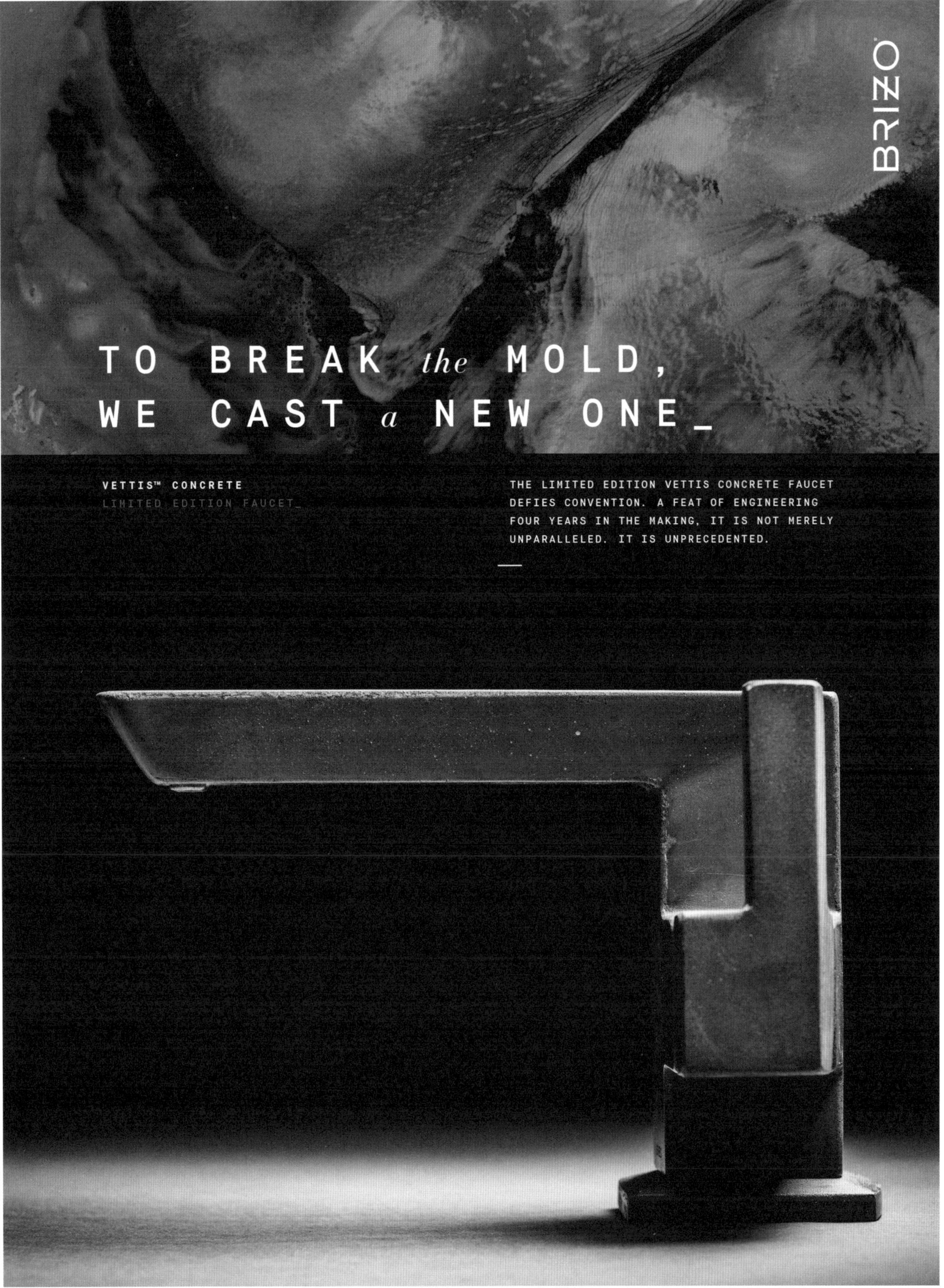


*(Page 43) 2018 - Goodwill – "Craft Your Look;" Executive Creative Director: Carolyn Hadlock; Senior Designer: Daniel Vuyovich; Senior Writer: Charlie Hopper; Videographer: Sam Mirpoorian; Motion Designer: Sara Frucci; Chief Strategy Officer / President: Tom Denari; Account Manager: Sydney Jameson; Editorial Partner: Pattern Magazine; Editor / Photographer: Polina Osherov; Stylist: Julie Valentine; Artist: Beck Jones*

*(Above) 2018 - Brizo – "Vettis Concrete;" Executive Creative Director: Carolyn Hadlock; Group Creative Director: Trevor Williams; Creative Director: Scott King; Associate Creative Director: Dan Shearin; Writer: Jane Brannen; Designer: Mitchell Brown; Account Director / VP of Account Management: Nick Prihoda; Account Supervisor: Sara Walker; Account Manager: Adair Dorsett; Photographer: Nils Ericson; Visual Effects: Susi Sie*

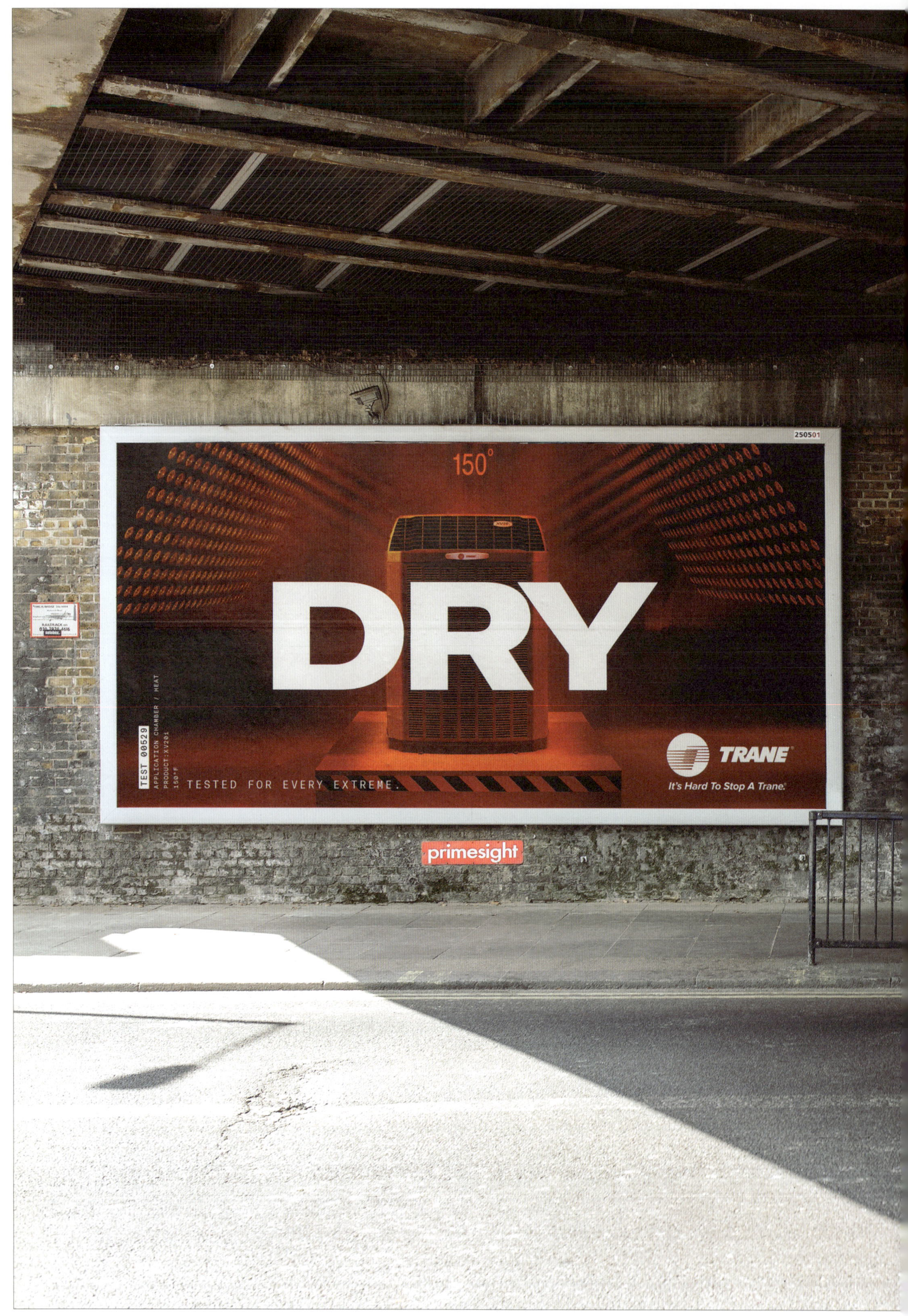


*2018 - Trane – "Relentless Testing;" Executive Creative Director: Carolyn Hadlock; Group Creative Director: Bryan Judkins; Senior Writer: Deidre Lichty; Associate Creative Director: Dan Shearin; Account Director / VP Marketing: Brad Bobenmoyer;*

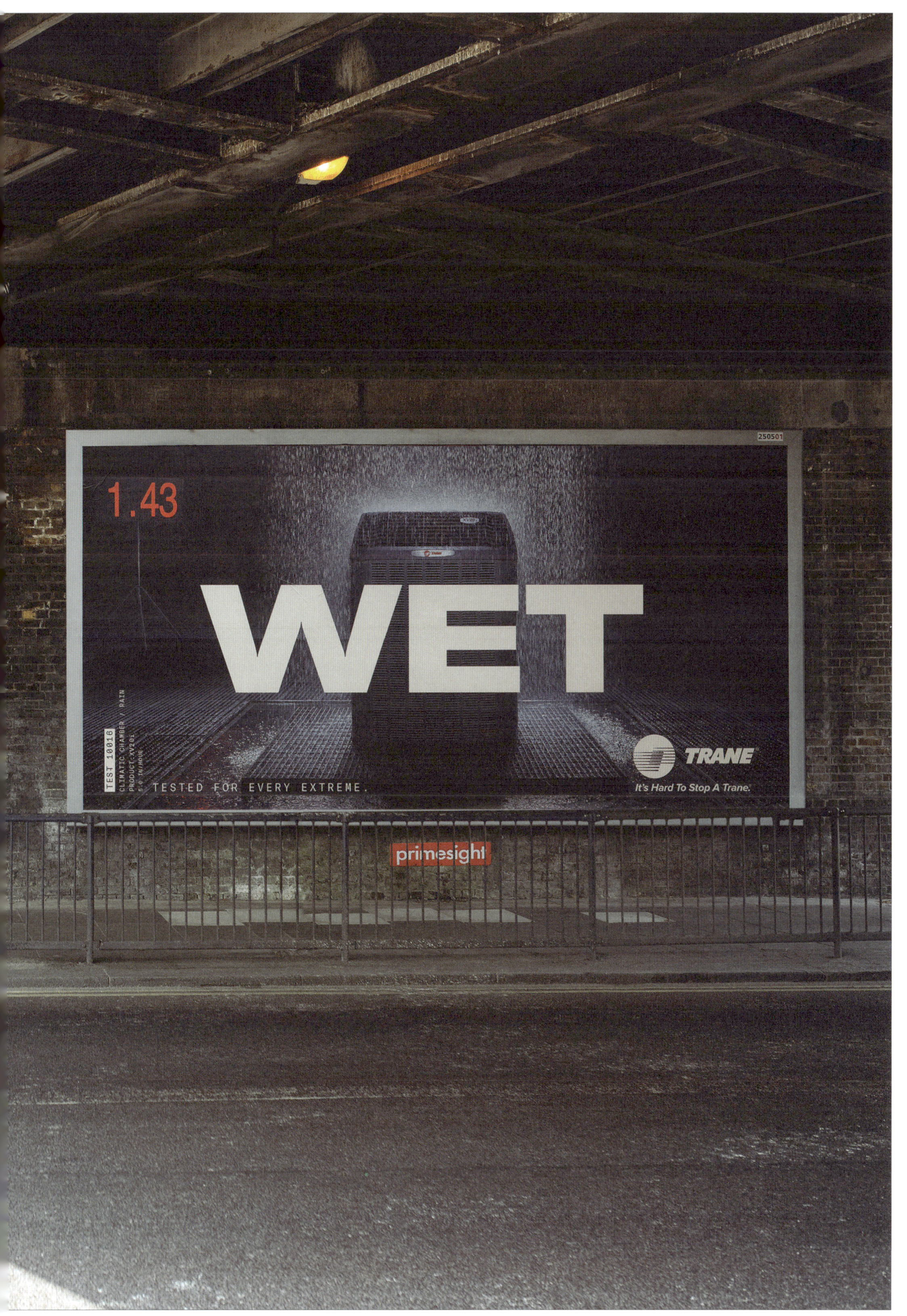


*Associate Account Director: Jacqueline Hacker; Account Supervisor: Cory Schneider;*
*Account Manager: Catherine Watson; Photographer: Joe Wright; Executive Producer: Amy Jo Deguzis*

# Introduction by **Kari St. Clair** Indiana Farm Bureau Insurance

Indiana Farm Bureau Insurance has worked with Young & Laramore since 2010 as our Agency of Record. We are very fortunate to have a team of creative minds working alongside us to develop memorable content in the saturated insurance advertising space. It's hard to believe it's been nearly 10 years since Young & Laramore conducted consumer research which resulted in the creation of our tagline 'Stop Knocking on Wood.' We thank them for their efforts in continuing to evolve this concept through the years to bring our brand up to where it is today.

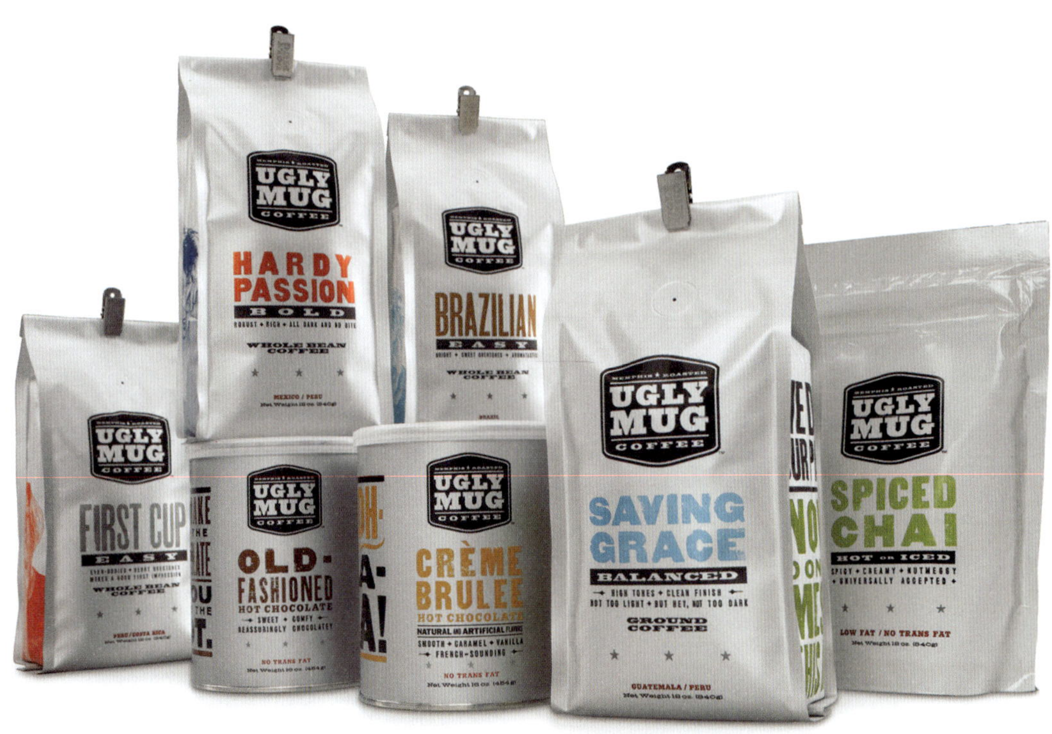


*2008 - Ugly Mug Coffee – "Oh What a Beautiful Morning;" Creative Director: Charlie Hopper; Associate Creative Director / Writer: Bryan Judkins; Associate Creative Director / Art Director: Trevor Williams; Chief Strategy Officer / President: Tom Denari; Account Supervisor: Margit Fawbush; Account Manager: Christian Mehall; Designer: Yee-Haw Industries; Photographers: Harold Lee Miller & Gary Sparks*

*What inspired or motivated you into your career?*
In the early '90s, you didn't go into advertising. You ended up in advertising. Portfolio schools didn't exist. It was a job (not a career) where misfits went and those who weren't academic overachievers ended up. I ended up in advertising by starting college as a nursing student. Once I figured out that I couldn't see people in pain, I shifted to graphic design. Two years into the program, I was kicked out. I was told I had no talent and that I was wasting my parent's money. That did it, gauntlet thrown. I went to art school and four years later, I graduated with a BFA and a suit of steel.

*What is your work philosophy?*
To make it safe to be scary. It's the environment I thrived in as an Art Director and one that I've tried to create as a Creative Director. The best work comes from play. It's effortless. That only happens with a great deal of effort from all departments and an agency philosophical backbone. The moment that falls apart, it's impossible to do great work.

*Who is or was your greatest mentor?*
Agency founder, David Young. Most people get developed by their mentors. I think I was forged by mine. As a philosophy major, he had an intellectual rigor that was not for the faint of heart. He's tall, big, and bombastic. I'm the complete opposite. But I learned early that what he said was more important than how he was saying it. He was fearless, demanding, and believed in me. It infused a confidence in me that I still tap into.

*What is it about Advertising that you are most passionate about?*
I love its potential. Some people hate its ever-changing nature, but I believe that's its superpower. The fluidity creates opportunity for experimentation and happy accidents.

*What is your most difficult challenge you've had to overcome?*
My inner voice. Though David instilled confidence in me, and my partners continue to have faith in me and my talents, I'm my biggest critic. I often worry that I'm not doing it right or well. By the way, my partners, and David will be surprised to

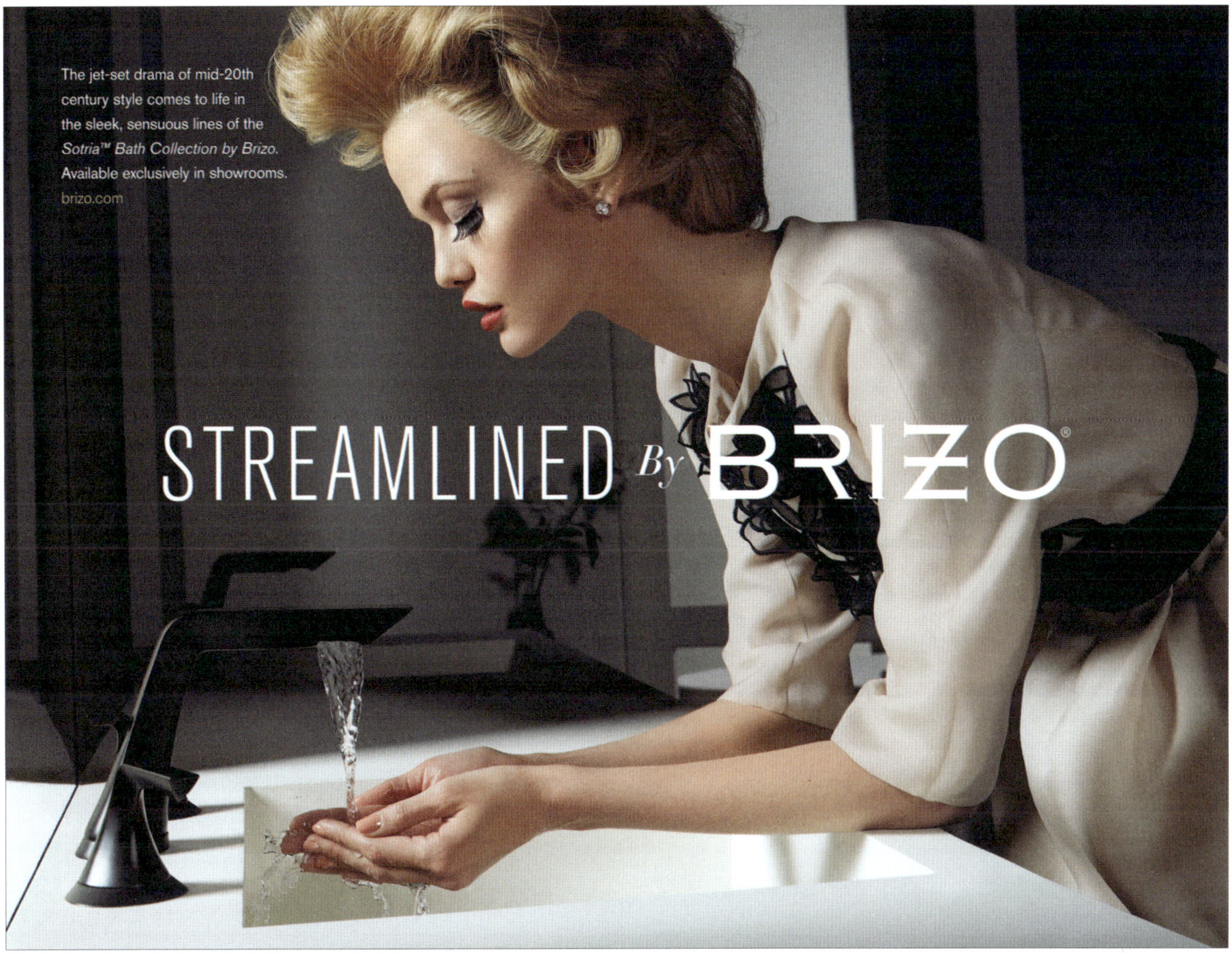

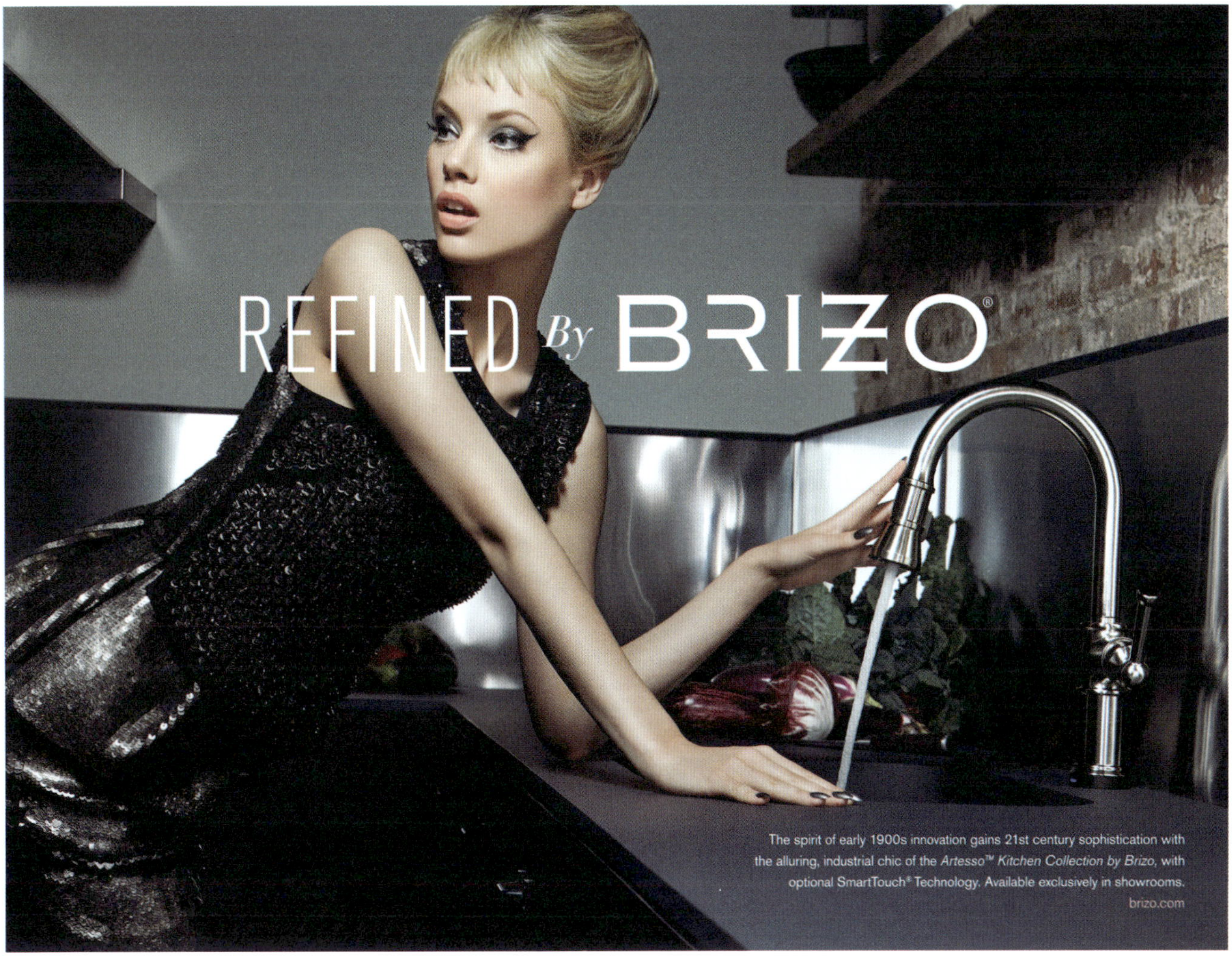

*2015 - Brizo – "by Brizo;" Executive Creative Director: Carolyn Hadlock; Group Creative Director: Trevor Williams; Senior Writer: Scott King; Writer: Sarah Holcombe; Designer: Mitchell Brown; Chief Strategy Officer / President: Tom Denari; Account Director: Nick Prihoda; Senior Account Manager: Sara Walker; Photographer: Greg Lotus; Stylist: Cannon Media Group; Models: MUSE Model Management (Sotria: Jennifer Pugh, Artesso: Luize Salmgrieze)*

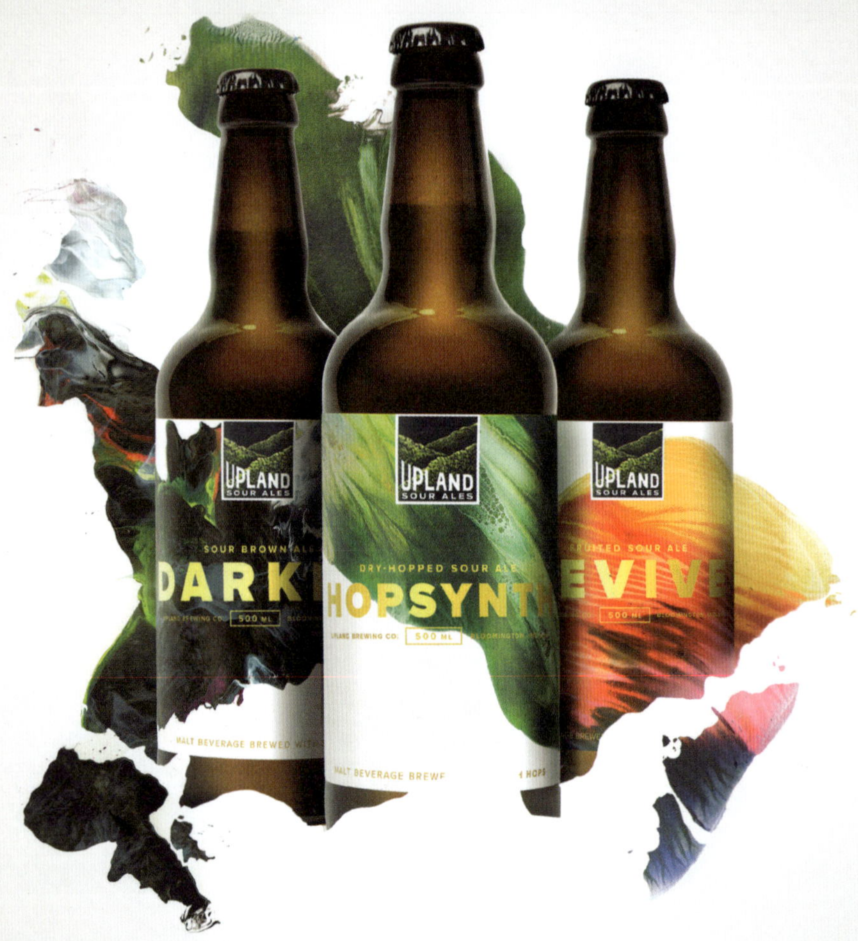


WHAT IS **WILD** CANNOT BE **TAMED.**

ONLY BOTTLED.

UPLAND SOUR ALES | BLOOMINGTON, INDIANA

PLEASE DRINK RESPONSIBLY

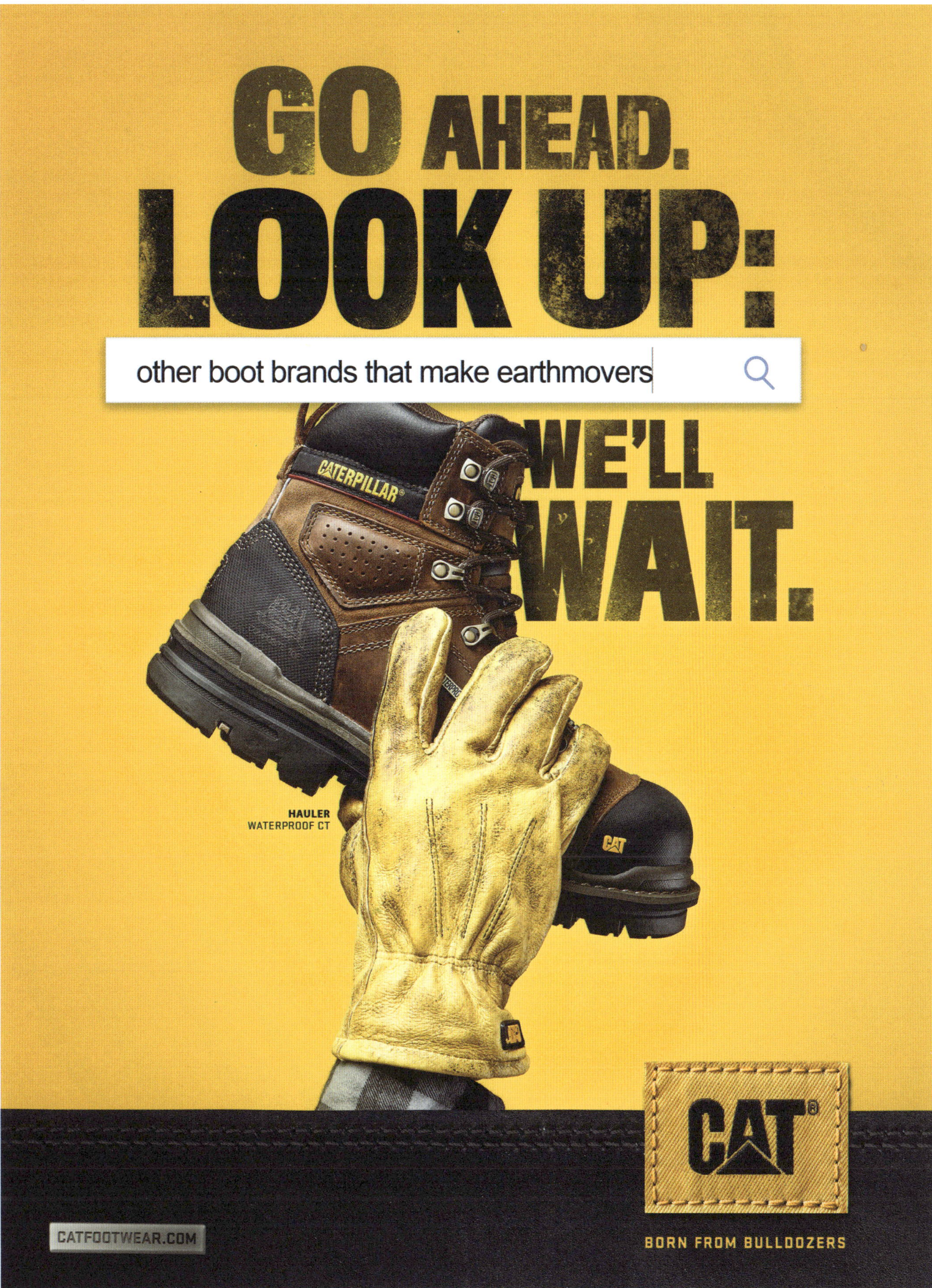


*2017- Cat Footwear – "Built From Bulldozers" 2018; Executive Creative Director: Carolyn Hadlock; Group Creative Director: Bryan Judkins; Associate Creative Director: Scott King; Associate Design Director: Zac Neulieb; Writer: Aidan McKiernan; Chief Strategy Officer / President: Tom Denari; Account Director / VP Marketing: Brad Bobenmoyer; Account Supervisor: Cory Schneider; Photographer: Dean Van Dis*

read this because I hide it really well. The positive part is that it keeps me honest and scrappy.

*Who were some of your greatest past influences?*
I love art. I mean, I love art. Every time I visit a city, the first thing I do with my downtime is find a museum. My mom was an art docent when I was little, and she used to drag me and my brothers through exhibits and practice her tour on us. We were endlessly bored and a poor audience, but I realize now that she subconsciously planted a seed in me to see the world differently. I love Klee, Picasso, O'Keefe, Renoir, Basquiat, Miro, and Seurat. I can literally feel myself soaking up the way they paint and sculpt as I walk through the galleries.

*Who among your contemporaries today do you most admire?*
Six years ago, I submitted a proposal to the One Club in NYC for a Creative Leaders Retreat; a 3-day getaway where people like me in smaller agencies and markets could meet creative directors we admired. I was able to meet a few of them in an intimate environment and learn firsthand from their tribulations and their trials. I have always loved W+K, any of their offices. Susan Hoffman was kind enough to spend an afternoon with me. I learned more from her than I would have reading non-stop for a year. BBH London was my first love when I was a student. Still admire the hell out of them. I love Rethink and Sid Lee in Canada, and Droga5. I tend to gravitate towards culture and philosophy more than the latest campaign. If you have those two things, you'll do good work.

*What would be your dream assignment?*
Most people would say Nike, Apple, or Coke, but I actually think I'd be trapped by their iconic status. I'm a big fan of the underdog where you can be on the offensive, not defensive. Defending ground can dilute the work. I also love inventing brands and then advertising them. Category or industry doesn't matter as much as opportunity. Some of my favorite work that the agency has created wasn't ever an assignment. It was an untapped opportunity.

*Who have been some of your favorite people or clients you have worked with?*
Two very different clients come to mind. One is creating the luxury fixtures brand, Brizo, for the Delta Faucet company. It was over a decade ago and the first foray into fashion in the home category. We legitimized our space in fashion by partnering with fashion designer Jason Wu, which is still intact today. It was a unique strategy and helped Brizo compete with category behemoth Kohler.

The second one was when a group of Carmelite cloistered nuns approached us to do a recruiting campaign for them. How do you say no to a group of nuns? They were fascinating, smart, extremely well-educated, funny, and passionate about healing the world through contemplative prayer. We created a website for them, praythenews.com, that ended up becoming a global destination to process the news through the lens of contemplative prayer. It was featured in several mainstream media outlets and The Today Show came to Indianapolis to do a story about them.

*Was Young & Laramore always a full-service agency? If not, what prompted the expansion?*
No. We started as a small design boutique because we were founded by a poet and a painter. At that time, most of the clients were local and almost everything was made in house; il-

lustration, photography, airbrushing, yes airbrushing and lettering. We became an advertising agency overnight when we won the Steak'n Shake pitch in the early 90s. In 1998, when we started EchoPoint Media, our media division, we became a legitimate full-service agency. And we've never looked back. David Young used to say it was better to be a generalist. He would quote Maslow's law of the instrument where if the only tool you have is a hammer, you will treat everything as a nail. Having the agility to solve the problem in a multitude of ways is one of our core strengths.

*What are the most important ingredients you require from a client to do successful work?*
Trust in intuition. In themselves, and in us.

*What is it like to work from downtown Indianapolis?*
Indianapolis is a city on the rise. Our culinary scene is getting national attention and companies like Salesforce are choosing the city for their regional headquarters because you can have quality of life, but also leverage national opportunities since we're centrally located. I'm from here and have loved seeing the acceleration, but many of our clients aren't based here. Many employees of the agency aren't originally from here either and love it. Many graduates tend to seek the coast, but quickly realize that geography doesn't ensure great work.

*What is the greatest satisfaction you get from your work?*
Making something happen against all odds.

*What part of your work do you find most demanding?*
Building trust. It takes patience and persistence to earn trust. But it pays off every time.

*What professional goals do you still have for yourself?*
Make Y&L a nationally sought out agency. I've always said the ultimate power is the ability to say "No." That only comes with leverage from doing amazing work for good clients. Also, to make Indianapolis a creative destination. That was David and Jeff's original vision and I'd like to help make it happen.

*What advice would you have for students starting out today?*
Don't look to the industry for inspiration. Don't try to figure out the system. Hack the system. Be interested and interesting. Oh, and please make sure that you check the salutation before you send a note. I've received way too much cut and paste names on cover letters.

*What interests do you have outside of your work?*
If my work is to see the world differently, and I believe it is, then I have no outside interests.

*What would you change if you had to do it all over again?*
I probably wouldn't have gone to art school. I'd have just flown to the agency I wanted to work at and offered to work for free. Hell, I'd even pay them to let me work for them.

*Where do you seek inspiration?*
From beauty in art and nature. And my kids.

*How do you define success?*
Doing what you love to do and getting paid well for it.

**Young & Laramore** www.yandl.com

## 1. SLOW KNOCK: POOL

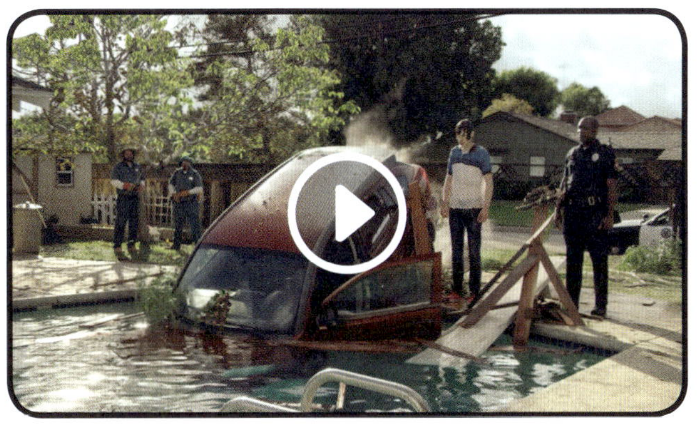

**Client: IFBI**

## 2. RELENTLESS TESTING

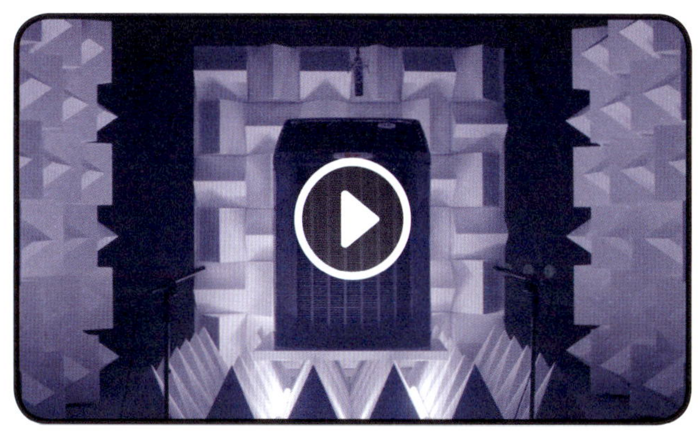

**Client: Trane**

## 3. BIG BOX VS. SMALL BOX

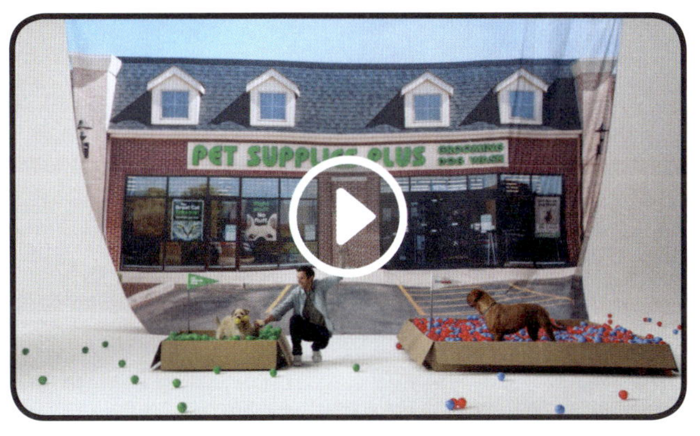

**Client: Pet Supplies Plus**

## 4. I COULD HAVE SAVED THIS ONE

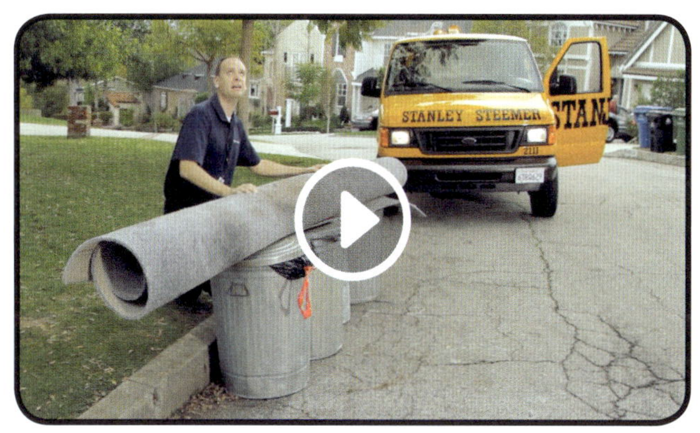

**Client: Stanley Steemer**

## 5. DOORMAT

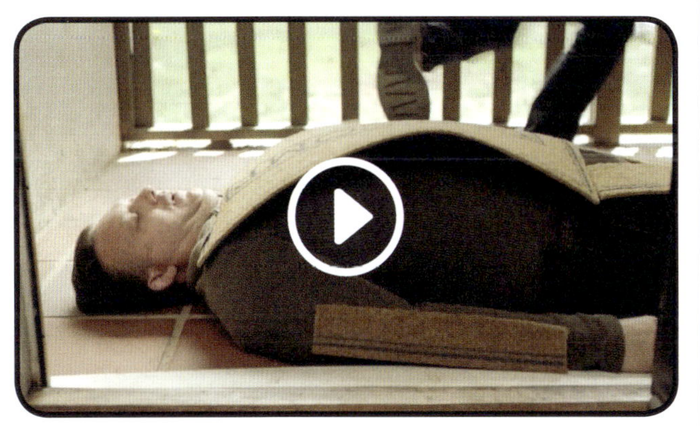

**Client: Schlage**

## 6. HANGXIETY

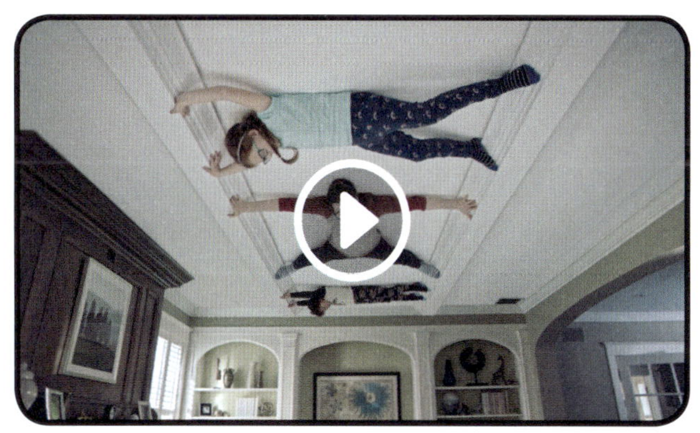

**Client: High & Mighty**

**1.** *2014 - Indiana Farm Bureau Insurance – "Slow Knock: Pool;" Executive Creative Director: Carolyn Hadlock; Creative Director: Trevor Williams; Senior Art Director: Brian Thibodeau; Writer: Sarah Holcombe; Brand Action Strategist: Taylor Schaffer; Chief Strategy Officer / President: Tom Denari; Account Director / VP Marketing: Brad Bobenmoyer; Account Manager: Sara Walker; Agency Producer: Char Loving; Production Company: Company Films; Director: Harald Zwart; Editorial: Beast; Sound: Airstream Audio; Online / Finish: Method Studios*

**2.** *2018 - Trane – "Relentless Testing" Executive Creative Director: Carolyn Hadlock; Group Creative Director: Bryan Judkins; Senior Writer: Deidre Lichty; Associate Creative Director: Dan Shearin; Account Director / VP Marketing: Brad Bobenmoyer; Associate Account Director: Jacqueline Hacker; Account Supervisor: Cory Schneider; Account Manager: Catherine Watson; Executive Producer: Amy Jo Deguzis; Production Company: SIBLING RIVALRY Director: Joe Wright; Director of Photography: Peter Konczal; Editorial: LOST PLANET; Editor: Bruce Herrman; Original Music: Gavin Little/Echolab; Sound Design: Gavin Little/Echolab; Mix House: Lime Studio*

**3.** *2016 - Pet Supplies Plus – "Big Box vs. Small Box;" Executive Creative Director: Carolyn Hadlock; Creative Director: Bryan Judkins; Associate Creative Director: Scott King; Art Director: Zac Neulieb; Writer: Sarah Holcombe; Designer: Kyle Nordsiek; Chief Strategy Officer / President: Tom Denari; Account Director / VP Marketing: Brad Bobenmoyer; Senior Account Manager: Cory Schneider; Associate Account Manager: Sam Hanes; Agency*

*Producer: Amy Jo Deguzis; Production Companies: Thank You for Lunch, Pizza Fist 100; Producer: Barry Sonders; Director: Jeff + Pete; Editorial: Cutters LA; Editor: Adam Parker*

**4.** *2010 Stanley Steemer – "I Could Have Saved This One;" Creative Director: Carolyn Hadlock; Associate Creative Director / Writer: Bryan Judkins; Associate Creative Director / Art Director: Trevor Williams; Chief Strategy Officer / President: Tom Denari; Executive Producer: Kathy Awe; Production Company: Company Films; Editorial: Beast; Editor: John Dingfield; Color / Finish: Optimus Music: Comma*

**5.** *2014 - Schlage – "Doormat;" Executive Creative Director: Carolyn Hadlock; Creative Director: Bryan Judkins; Associate Creative Director / Writer: Scott King; Art Director: Zac Neulieb; Brand Action Strategist: Taylor Schaffer; Chief Strategy Officer / President: Tom Denari; Account Director: Brad Bobenmoyer; Senior Account Manager: Cory Schneider; Executive Producer: Amy Jo Deguzis; Editorial: Foundation Content; Editor: Nick Pezzillo; Production Company: Curator Pictures; Director of Photography: Jeffrey Waldron*

**6.** *2017 High & Mighty – "Hangxiety;" Executive Creative Director: Carolyn Hadlock Group; Creative Director: Trevor Williams; Senior Writer: Deidre Lichty; Designer: Sara Frucci; Chief Strategy Officer / President: Tom Denari; Account Director / VP Marketing: Brad Bobenmoyer; Account Manager: Sam Hanes; Executive Producer: Char Loving; Production Company: Hungry Man; Director: Dave Laden; Editorial: Beast; Editor: Angelo Valencia*

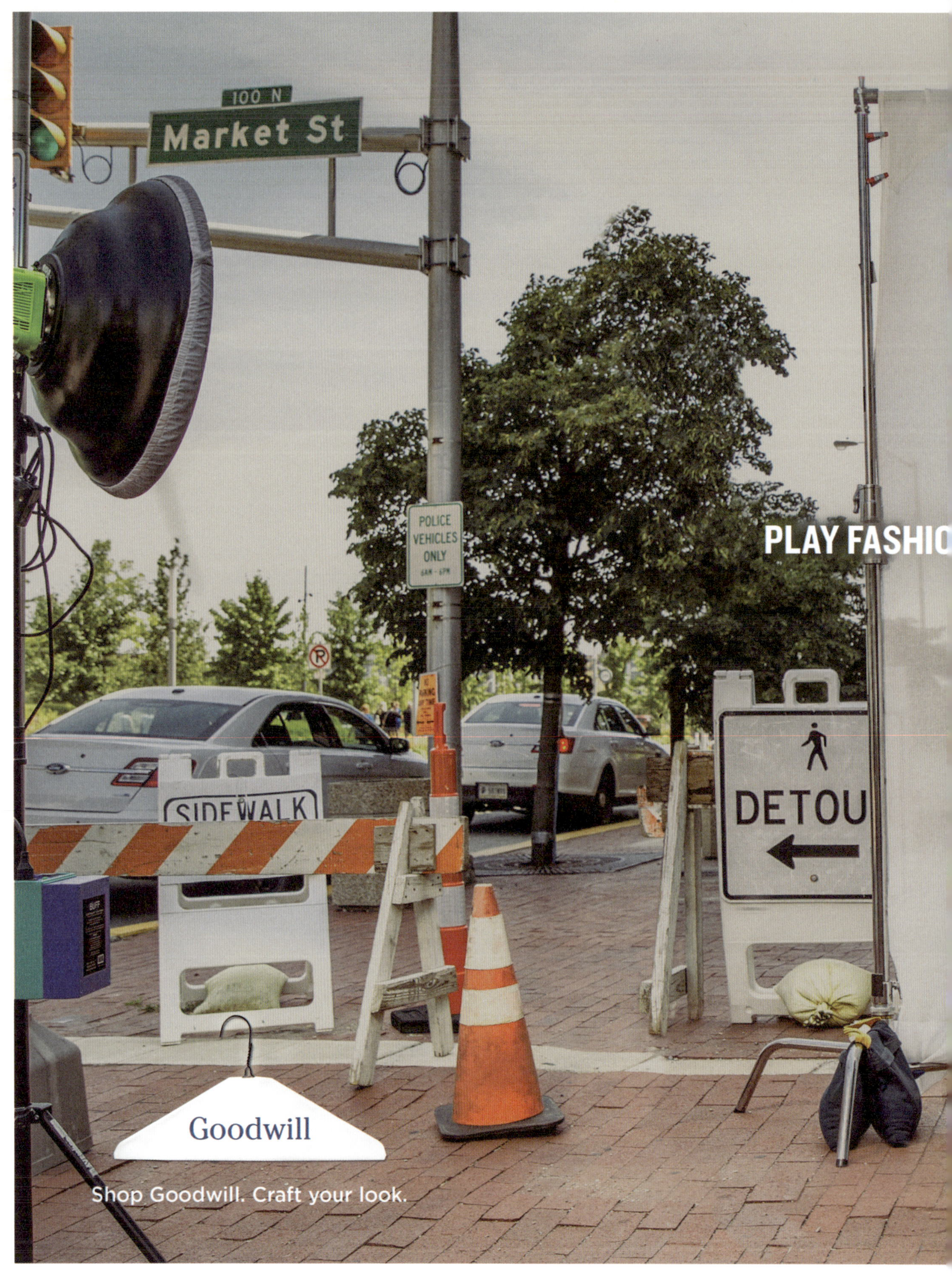

100 N
Market St
PLAY FASHIO
POLICE
VEHICLES
ONLY
6AM - 6PM
SIDEWALK
DETOU
Goodwill
Shop Goodwill. Craft your look.

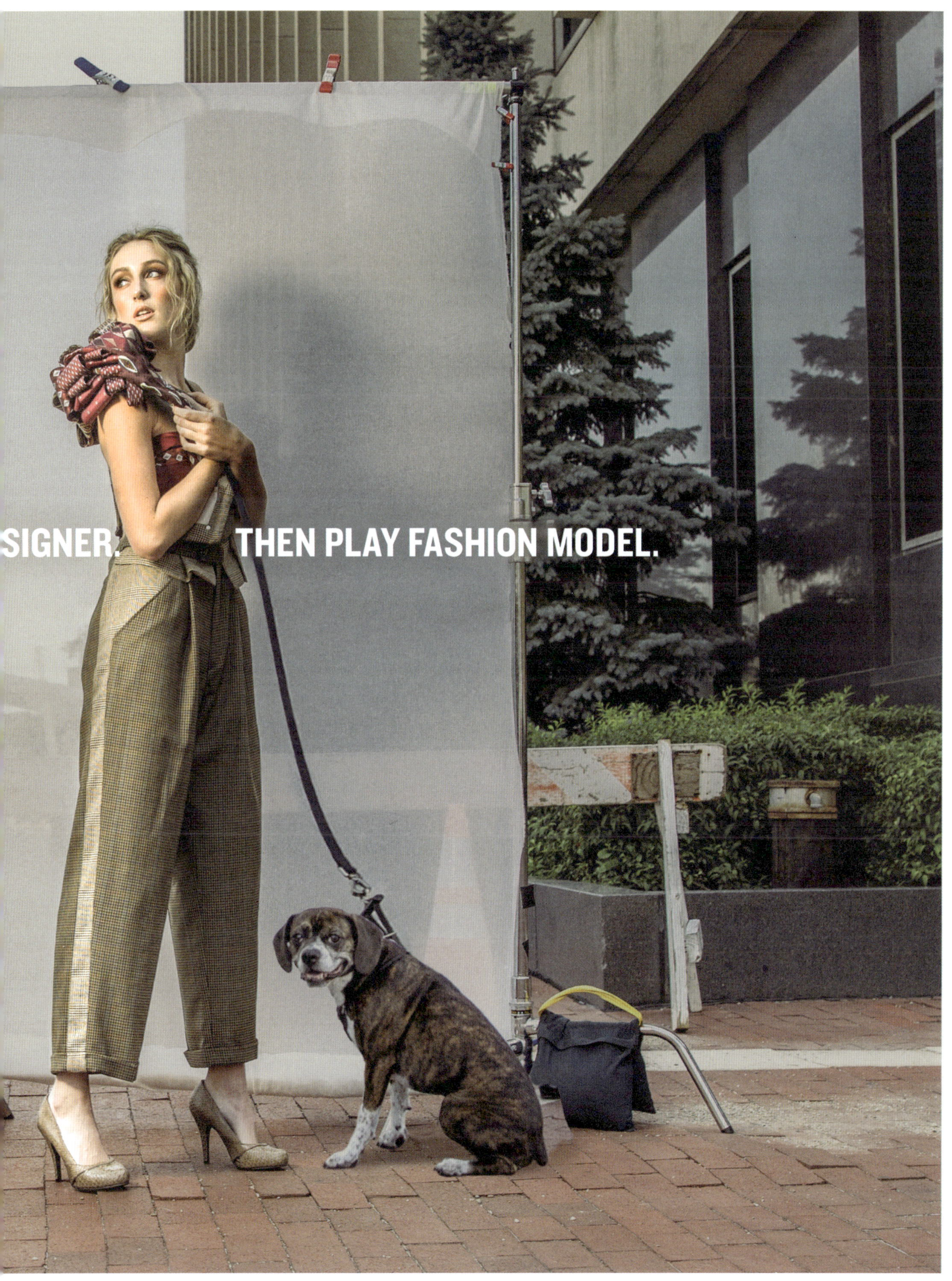


2018 - Goodwill – *"Craft Your Look;"* Executive Creative Director: Carolyn Hadlock; Senior Designer: Daniel Vuyovich; Senior Writer: Charlie Hopper; Videographer: Sam Mirpoorian; Motion Designer: Sara Frucci; Chief Strategy Officer / President: Tom Denari; Account Manager: Sydney Jameson; Editorial Partner: Pattern Magazine; Editor / Photographer: Polina Osherov Stylist: Julie Valentine; Artist: Beth Bennett

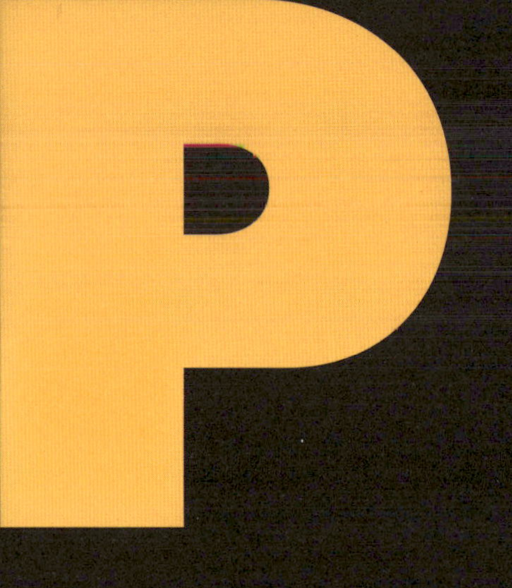

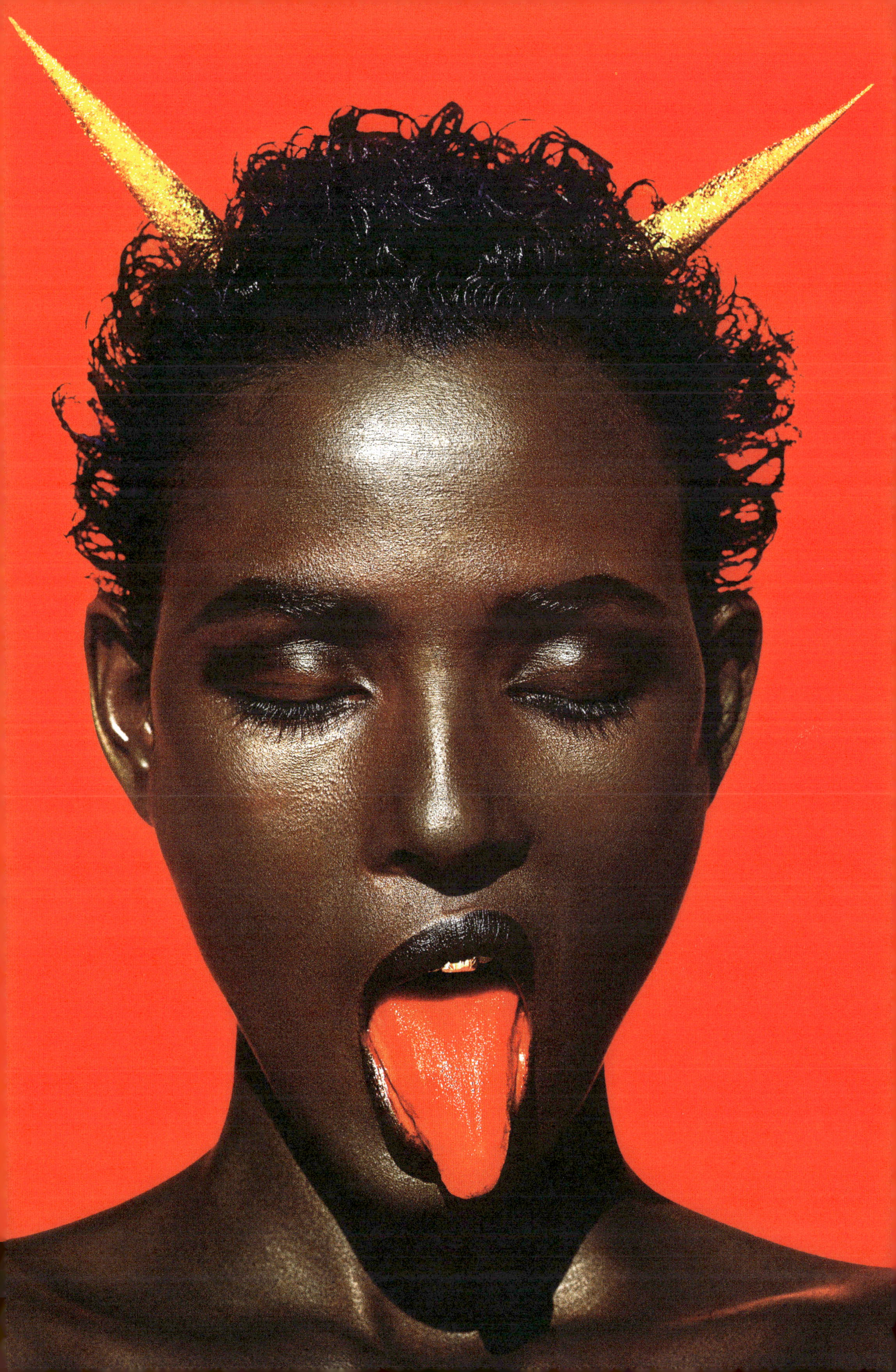

ALBERT WATSON IS UNDENIABLY ONE OF THE GREAT MASTERS OF MODERN PHOTOGRAPHY. WHAT PICASSO IS TO ART, ALBERT IS TO PHOTOGRAPHY. HIS COMPOSITION OF LIGHT MIXED WITH HIS PRECISE GRAPHIC SENSIBILITY IS UNPARALLELED.

**Freddie Leiba,** *Creative Director, Fashion Editor, and Stylist*

AS A MAKEUP ARTIST, I APPRECIATE HIS LIGHTING TECHNIQUE. HIS BLACK AND WHITE PHOTOGRAPHY HIGHLIGHTS AND CONTOURS THE FACE TO PERFECTION. WHEN I HAVE WORKED ON COLOR SHOOTS WITH ALBERT, HIS LIGHTING IS SO RICH AND COMPLEMENTARY TO MAKEUP.

I AM SO GRATEFUL TO HAVE BEEN INCLUDED IN HIS TEAM FOR 20 YEARS. IT'S BEEN QUITE AN HONOR.

**Sandy Linter,** *Makeup Artist*

I HAVE WORKED WITH ALBERT FOR MANY YEARS, DOING HAIR FOR MANY OF HIS IMAGES. HE ALLOWS ONE TO BE CREATIVE AND ENCOURAGES YOU TO EXCEL IN YOUR FIELD WHICH I FIND VERY INSPIRING.

HE IS A MASTER OF LIGHT. I ALWAYS LOOK FORWARD TO WORKING ON PROJECTS WITH ALBERT AS THEY ARE ALWAYS SO VARIED.

**Kerry Warn,** *Hair Stylist*

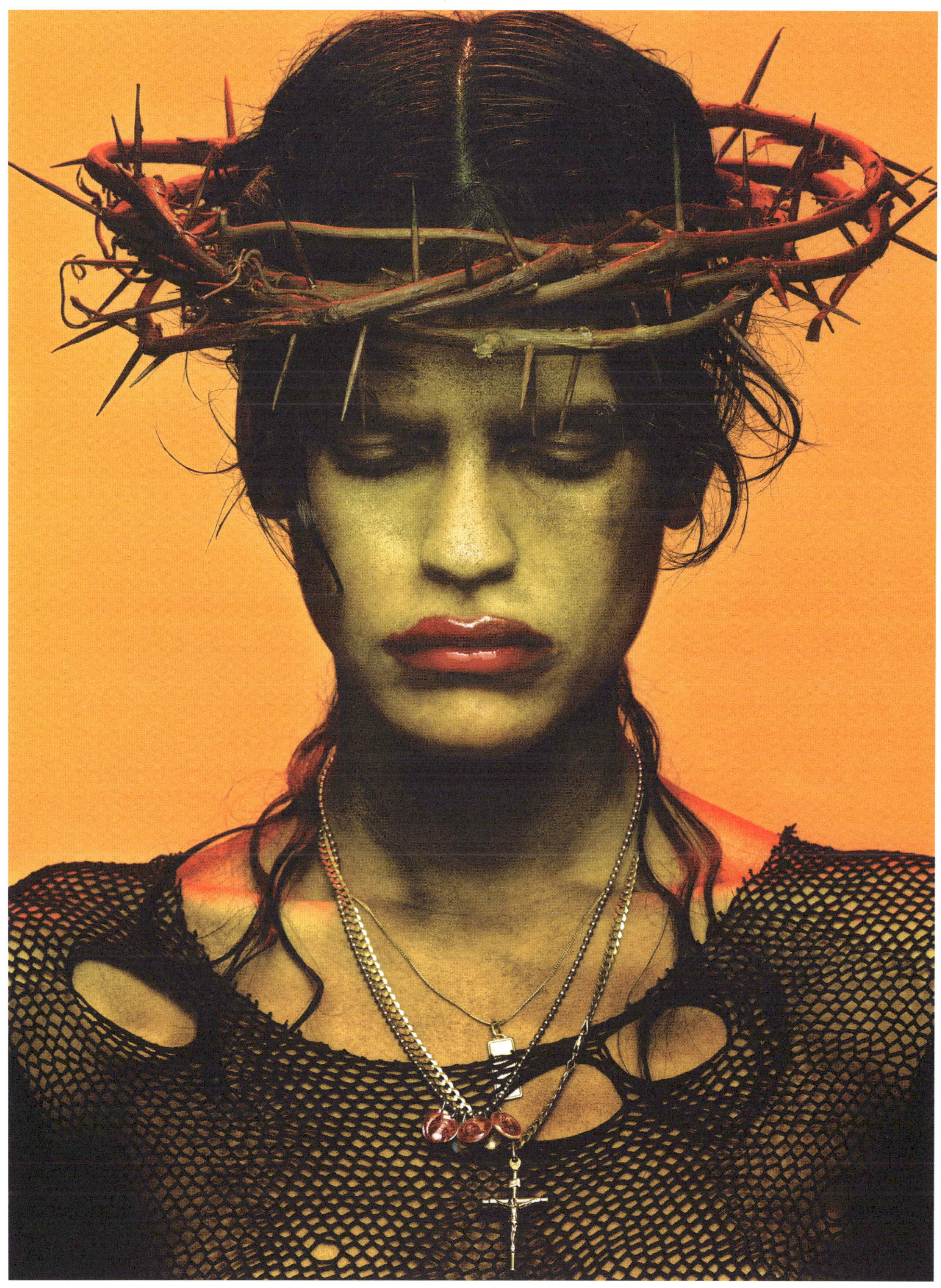

*(Page 57) Waris, Ouarzazate, Morocco, 1993 / (Above) Omahyra, Crown of Thorns, New York City, 2004*

Albert Watson might be the world's greatest living photographer. Armed with an education in graphic design and film, Albert has been breaking the rules of photography for nearly 50 years. His body of work is best described as intimidating. In a world of specialists, he has created iconic pictures in virtually every genre, including portraiture, fashion, landscapes, and still life. Even more unusually, his visual fingerprint can be seen in every image he produces. That fingerprint is an uncommon dedication to visual excellence, determined by his taste. That could mean lighting a supermodel with a sharp beam of hard light. Or focusing on a boxer's neck. Or even handing a gun to a chimp.

## THE GOOD NEWS IS THAT PHOTOGRAPHERS NEVER RETIRE AND THE BAD NEWS IS THAT PHOTOGRAPHERS NEVER RETIRE.

**Albert Watson,** *Fine Art, Commercial, and Fashion Photographer*

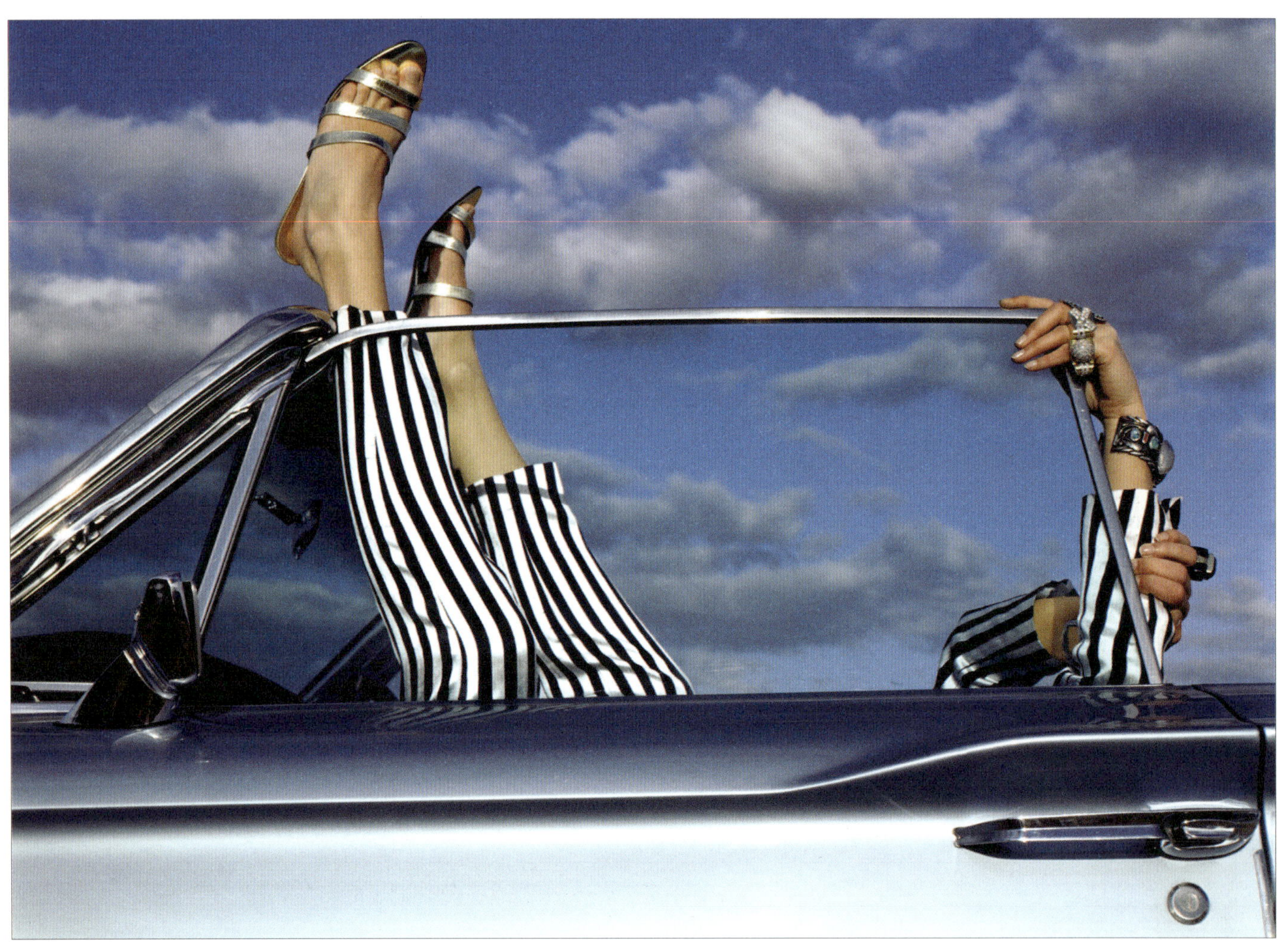

*'Feet Up,' Blumarine in vintage Thunderbird, Phoenix, 1991*

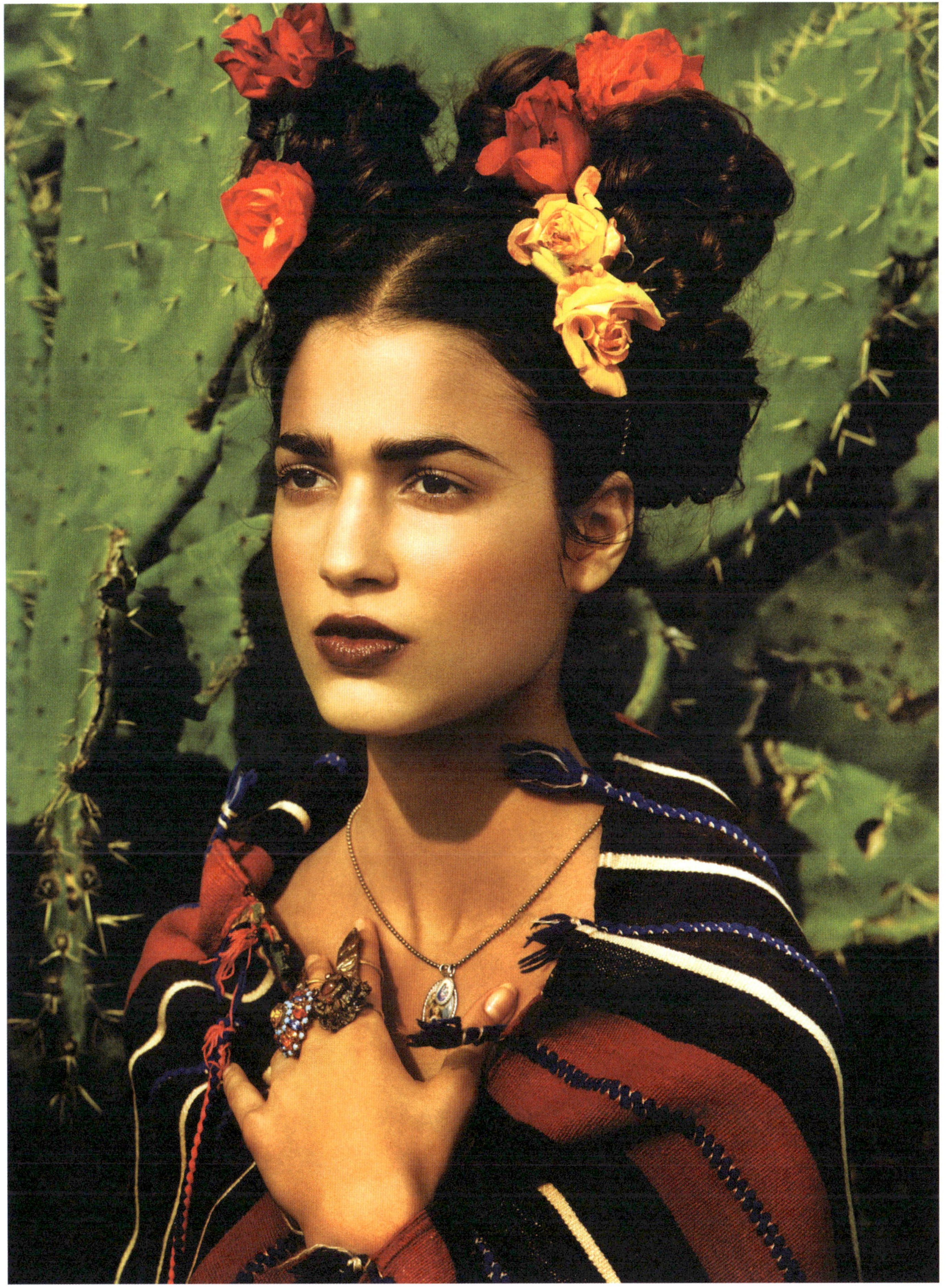

*Teresa Lourenco, 'Frida,' Marrakech, Morocco, 1998*

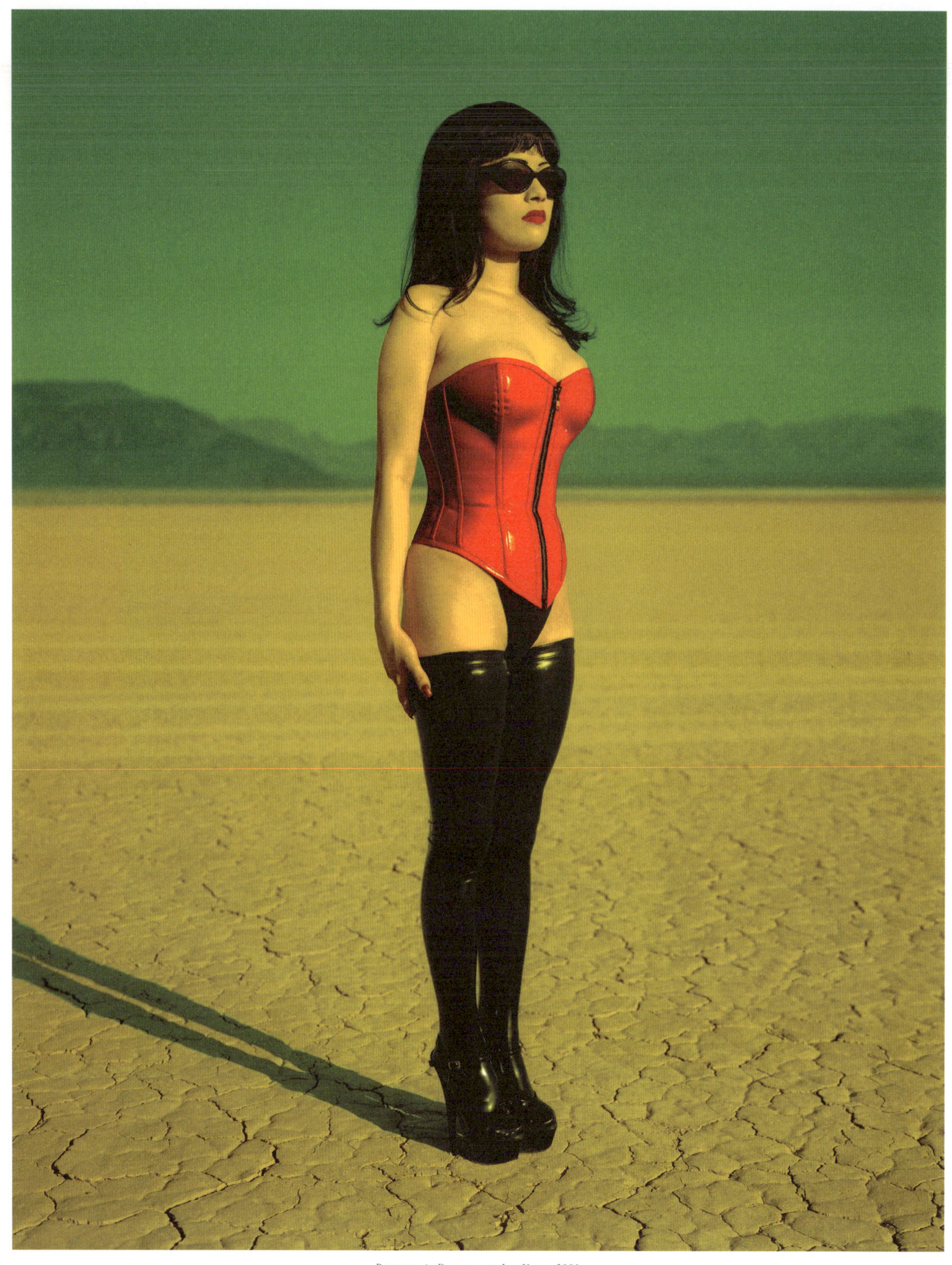

*Breaunna in Desert, near Las Vegas, 2001*

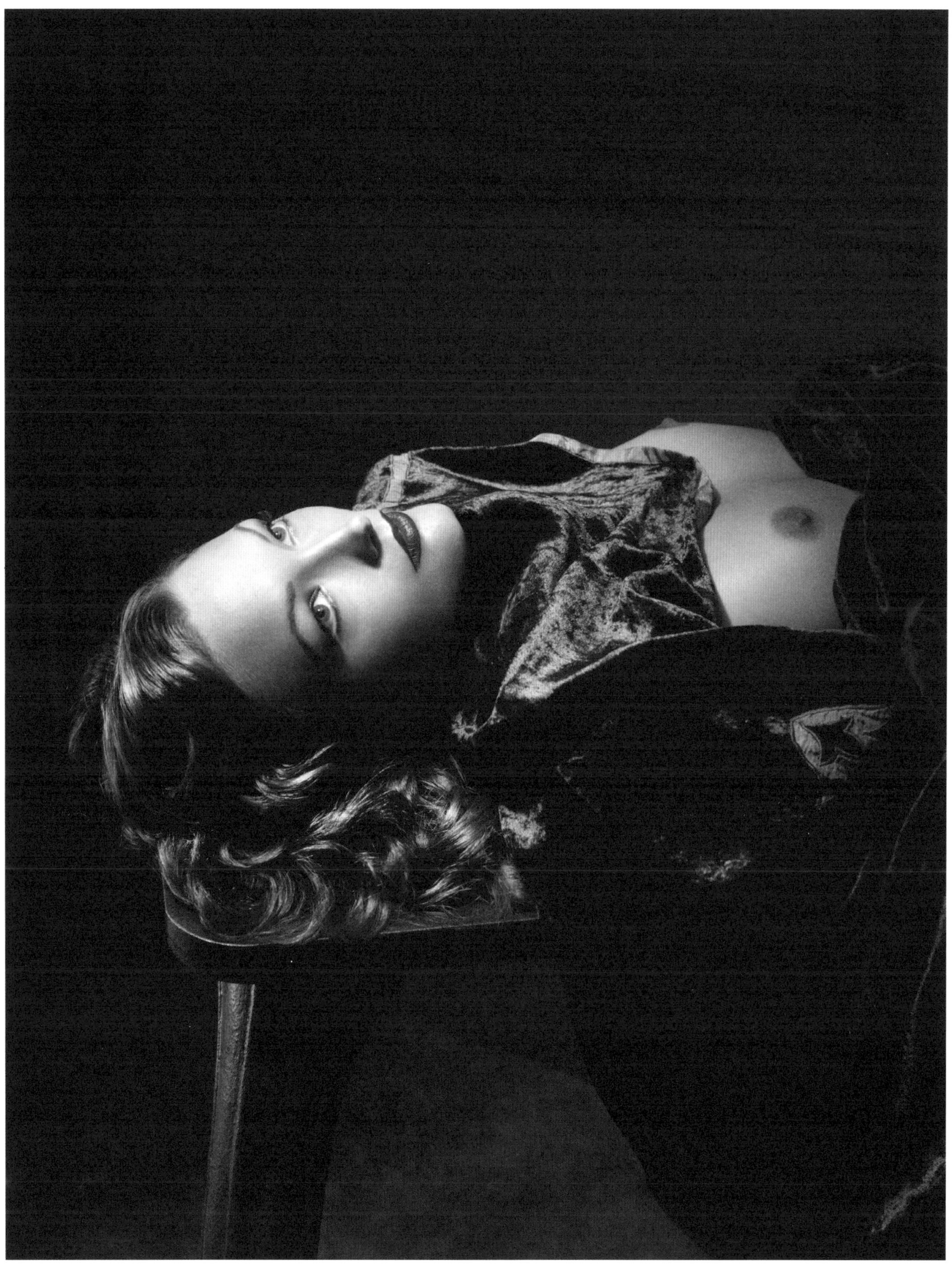

*Fanny 'Daydreaming.' New York City, 2010*

*What inspired or motivated you into your career?*
I would say that the minute I discovered photography, I was pretty obsessed with it. All the aspects of photography are the driving forces of my career. In other words, my deep passion for photography has been my motivation and driving force throughout the years.

*What is your work philosophy?*
I try my best to combine two elements together: creativity combined with absolute professionalism.

*What aspect of photography do you most enjoy?*
Although I enjoy proper work, whether or not it was done yesterday, a year ago, or two years ago, I enjoy looking at the work and criticizing it... saying whether it was good or not. I would say that the moment of taking the picture is the most enjoyable.

*Who is or was your greatest mentor?*
The very first photography teacher I had, Joseph McKenzie. I was very lucky because he was a dark room maestro and the lessons he taught me have stayed with me my whole life. Now, because of his influence, we can do everything in-house. Yet, we are completely self-contained and we don't send out prints. I would say that McKenzie was someone that certainly created a foundation for me.

*How would you describe your process?*
I would say that there's three words for that: preparation, preparation, and preparation. In other words, it is all about organization and the planning of the shoot. Not only creative planning, but planning for the mechanics of the shoot. The mechanics are how you're going to approach it, and fulfill an already established philosophy of how to use black and white, or color. Of course, you always leave some space for spontaneity. For example, sometimes you say it is definitely going to be in color, but then at the last minute you change your mind. It can be very impulsive.

*What is your most difficult challenge you've had to overcome?*
I had a lot of problems with the technical side of photography. A lot of photographers think of me as being very technical now, and say that everything I do is technically well done. I like to think that it is, but to get to this point was enormously difficult because I was not a naturally technical person. There are many photographers out there that have this technical side come very naturally. I was not one of them, so I had to overcome that. You do the best you can and I did, but it was hard work. It wasn't easy.

*Who were some of your greatest past influences?*
Painters, graphic designers, and of course five thousand photographers. I really can't say, "Oh, this was the number one person or that was the number one person." I like Russian Expressionist photographers and German Expressionists. I also like Czechoslovakian photographers such as Sudek. There are endless photographers that are inspiring, which of course helps you improve and grow.

*Who among your contemporaries today do you most admire?*
There are lots of very good photographers around today that are strong and who are trying to do interesting work. There are many that are trying to do new work. Sometimes the young photographers are a little bit lazy, I think, but there's also, amongst that, a lot of very good photographers.

*Who have been some of your favorite people or clients you have worked with?*
There's lots of people that were great to work with. I had clients like Levi's, Prada, and Blumarine (the Italian clothing company), that were great to work with. With them, I had great freedom and could do whatever I wanted. Of course, within reason, because I had to shoot the clothes, but I had a lot of freedom too. They were very good, and of course, all of the Vogue magazines were good to work with over the years. In fact, I just got back from Japan where I did 50 pages for Japanese Vogue.

*What are the most important ingredients you require from a client to do successful work?*
As I mentioned, preparation. Sure, I check that I've got all the batteries for the cameras and I make sure the cameras are tested, my lights are tested, I've got my assistants and all of that. That, in my opinion, could be as little as ten percent of the prep. It's the creative aspect I'm referring to when I talk about preparation.

*What is your greatest professional achievement?*
I think it was finally coming to grips with a lot of the technical aspects of photography that were so hard for me. It is overcoming this hurdle and then using it as a key for creativity. In other words, being technically fluent creates more possibilities. Unfortunately, there are many photographers that get sucked into photography and what they really love is the equipment. Digital was made for these guys. A new software program, a new Photoshop filter, a new something or other... it goes on and on. I was never like that. I was never having an affair with my camera.

*What part of your work do you find most demanding?*
I think it's always trying to find the creative solution. This is what it is all about now. It used to be just getting the damn thing done, you know, technically. Now I have to make sure that I truly maximize my day.

*What advice would you have for young photographers starting out today?*
Organization. This encompasses the technical side, which is a given, and it is important but not the most important. The point is to do creative planning, to think about, "What's my philosophy here? What am I doing? What is the concept? What's the idea here?"

*What interests do you have outside of your work?*
Museums, movies, galleries, and good TV. There is a lot of good TV that you can utilize for creativity.

*What do you value most?*
Right now, because I'm older, the thing that I value the most is time. Therefore, I don't do shootings now unless they're definitely worth doing. I have to make sure I'm really getting something out of it.

*Where do you seek inspiration?*
On a visual level, painters are my inspiration at the moment.

*How do you define success?*
50 years ago, I was happy when there was something on the film when it came back the next day. Now it's more complex and the success comes when the thought you have in your mind ends up in front of you after you take the picture. If all of

the effort you put into it comes through, the image you see in front of you is what you planned.

*What would you change if you had to do it all over again?*
I would do only 60 percent of the shootings that I have done. I did too many shootings. I worked for too many people. I was doing everything from fashion campaigns to movie posters to HBO posters to still life campaigns to TV commercials and I've done more than 500 TV commercials. So, basically I just did too many things.

*What would be your dream assignment?*
I'm in charge of it, it's my dream assignment.

*Where do you see yourself in the future?*
That is the most difficult question because sometimes you plan but life is like going up a mountain and you kind of get to the top and there's two ways of looking at the top… some photog-

raphers would say you never get to the top. I understand that because there's a certain amount of truth in that.
Since I'm still obsessed with photography, I see myself shooting… you just keep going. The good news is that photographers never retire and the bad news is that photographers never retire. I've got relatives who turn 65 and they retire. They say, "I've done it, I'm now retired, I'm going to go down to Florida, out on the beach." Photographers don't do that.

*Is there anything else you would like to share with us?*
In the 1960s when I was a Graphic Designer, I used to go to the library and pour over the Graphis Annuals. On my library shelf here, I have Graphis Annuals going all the way back to the late '60s and early '70s.

**Albert Watson** www.albertwatson.net
*See his Graphis Master Portfolio on graphis.com.*

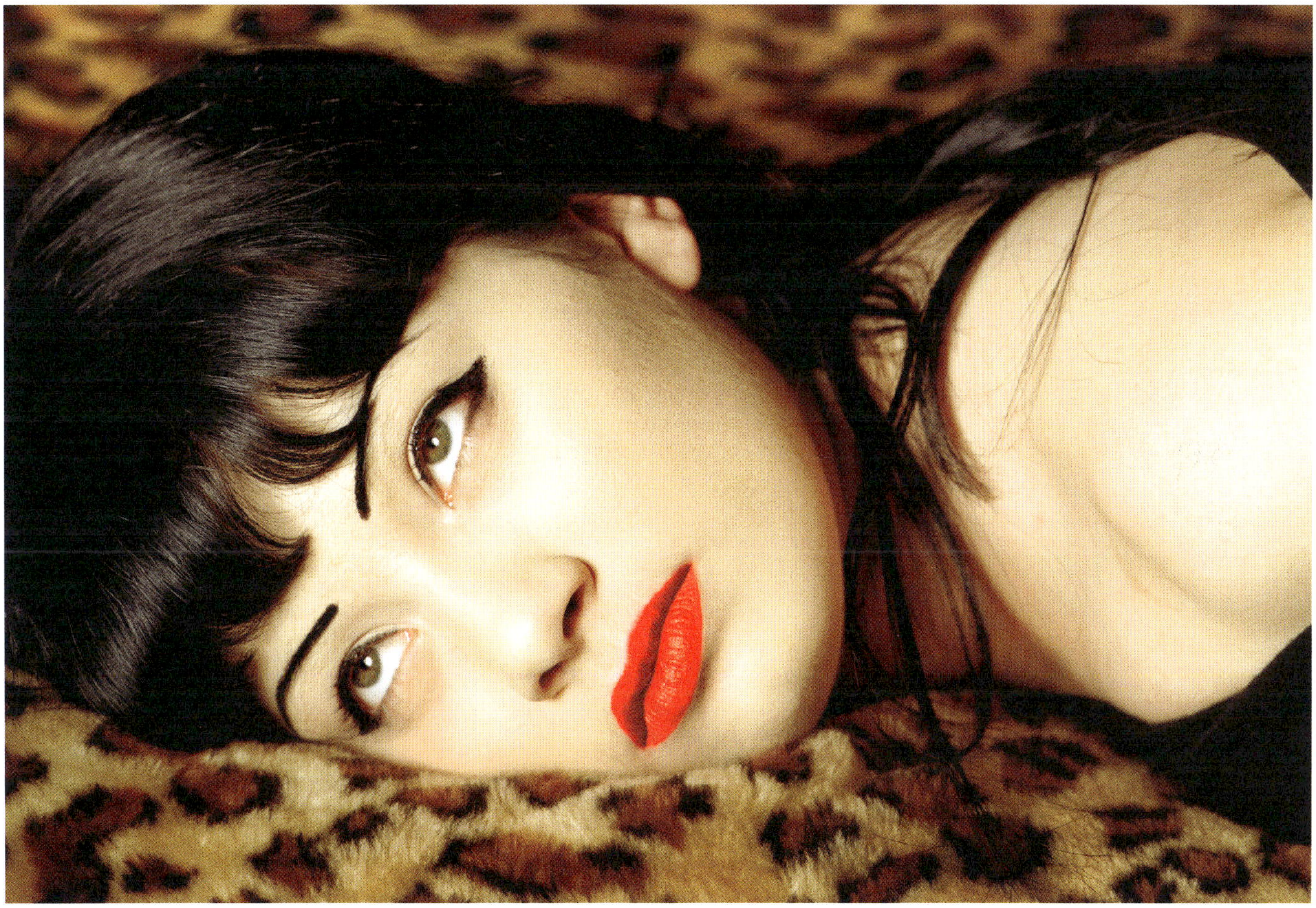

*Breaunna on Leopard Print Bedspread, Las Vegas Hilton, 2001*

# 50 YEARS AGO, I WAS HAPPY WHEN THERE WAS SOMETHING ON THE FILM WHEN IT CAME BACK THE NEXT DAY.

**Albert Watson,** *Fine Art, Commercial, and Fashion Photographer*

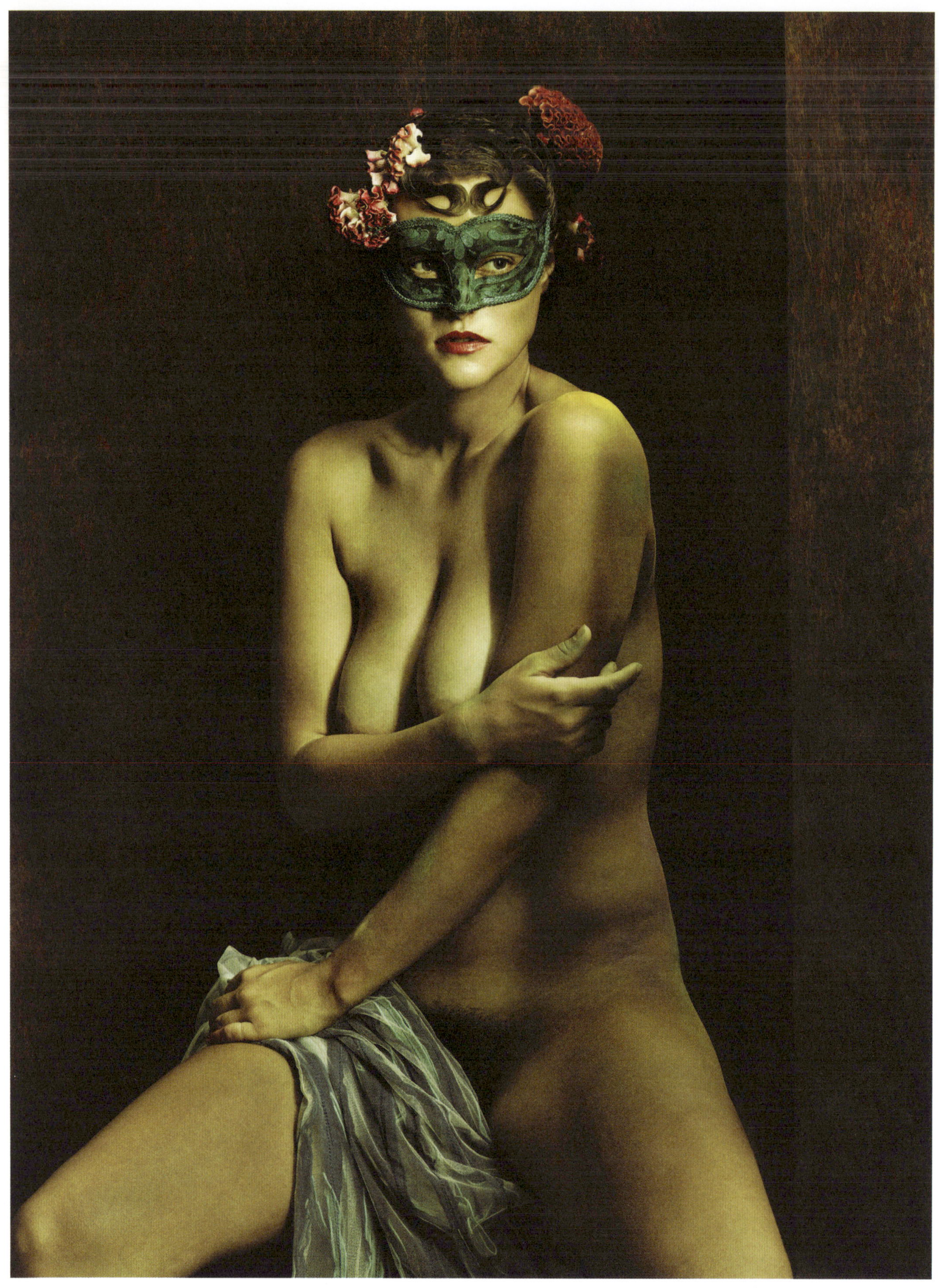

*Myla Dalbesio in Mask, 'Dreamscape' Series, New York City, 2017*

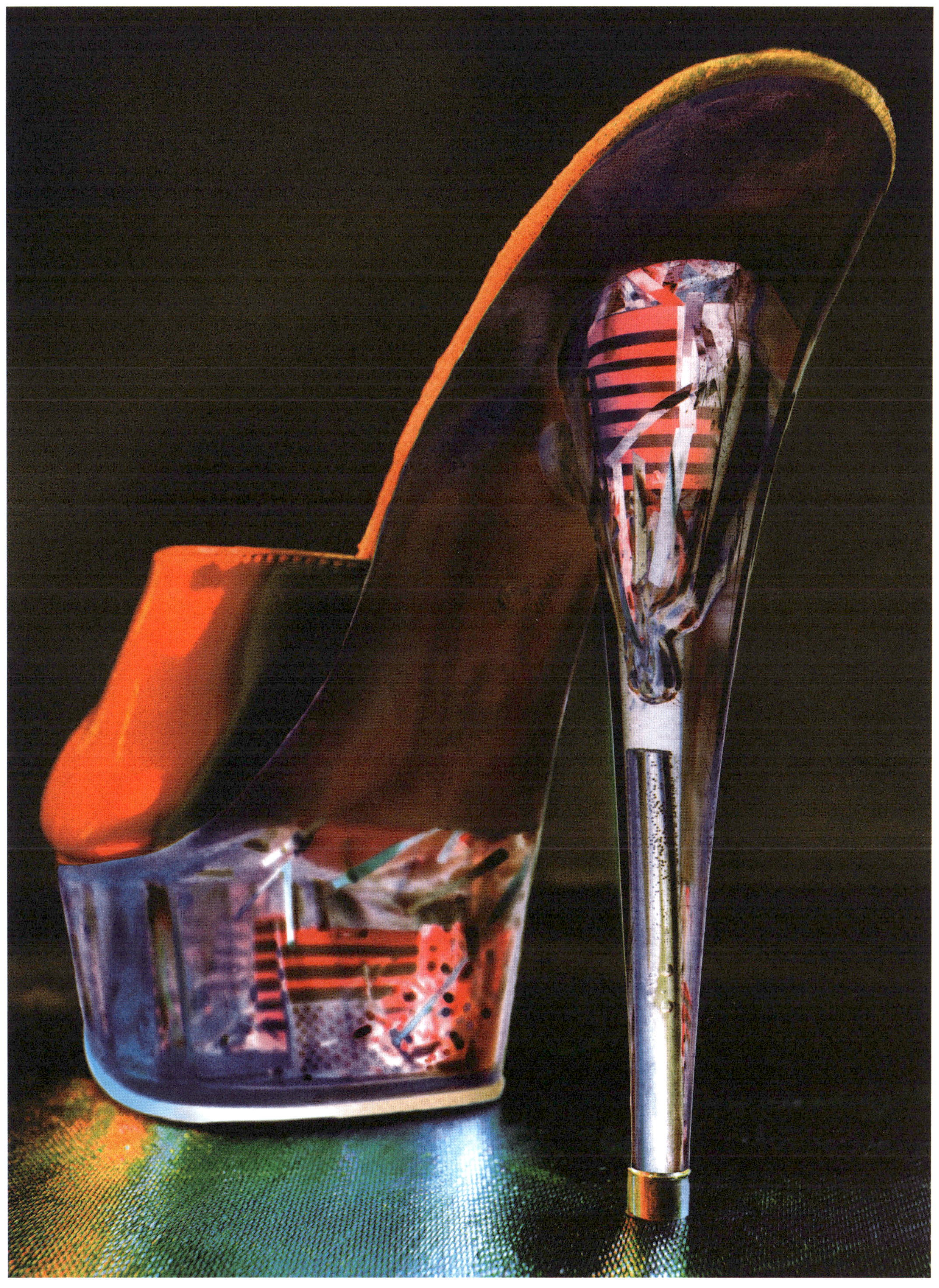

*Stripper Stiletto, Budget Suites, Las Vegas, 2000*

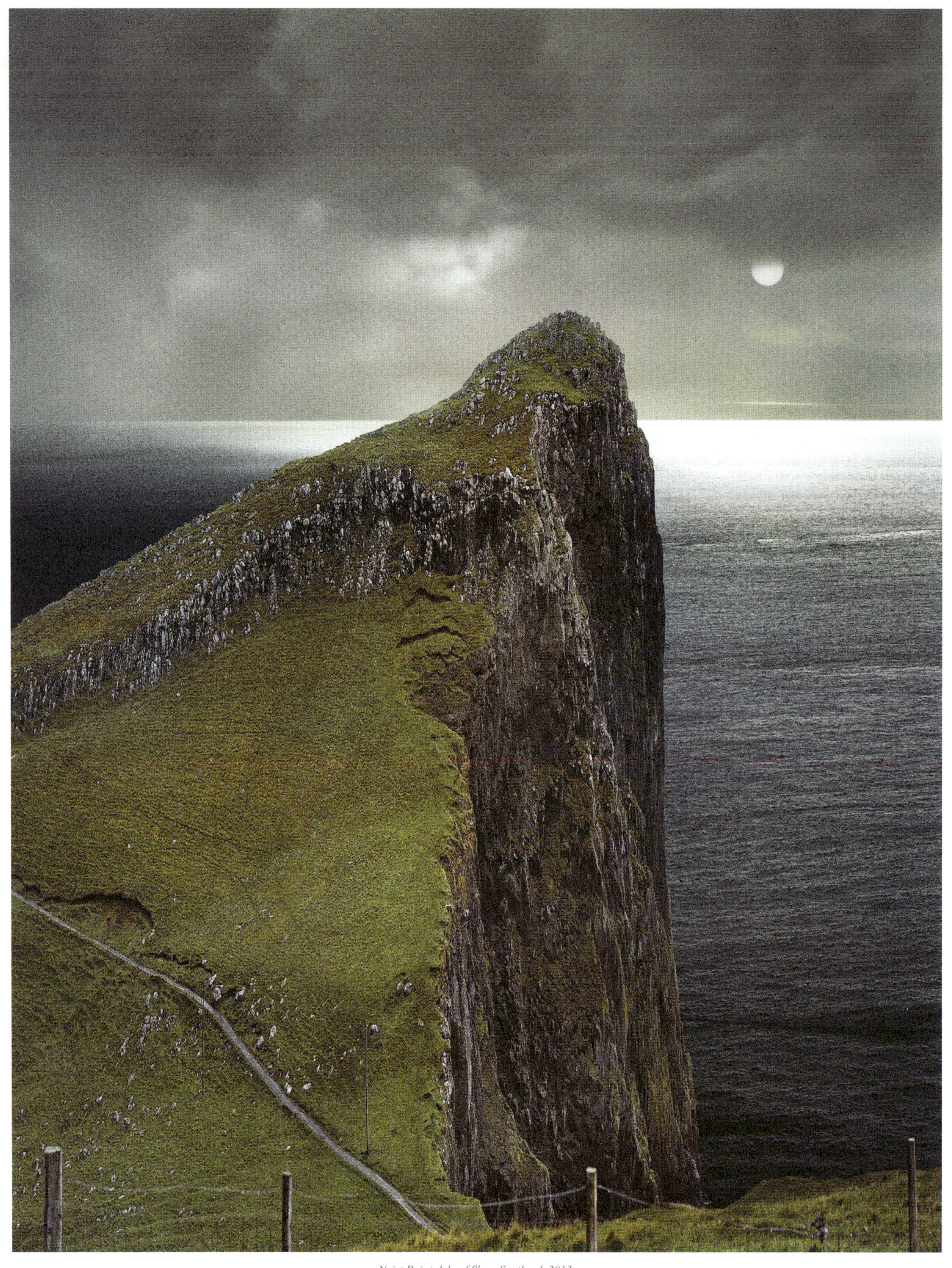

*Neist Point, Isle of Skye, Scotland, 2013*

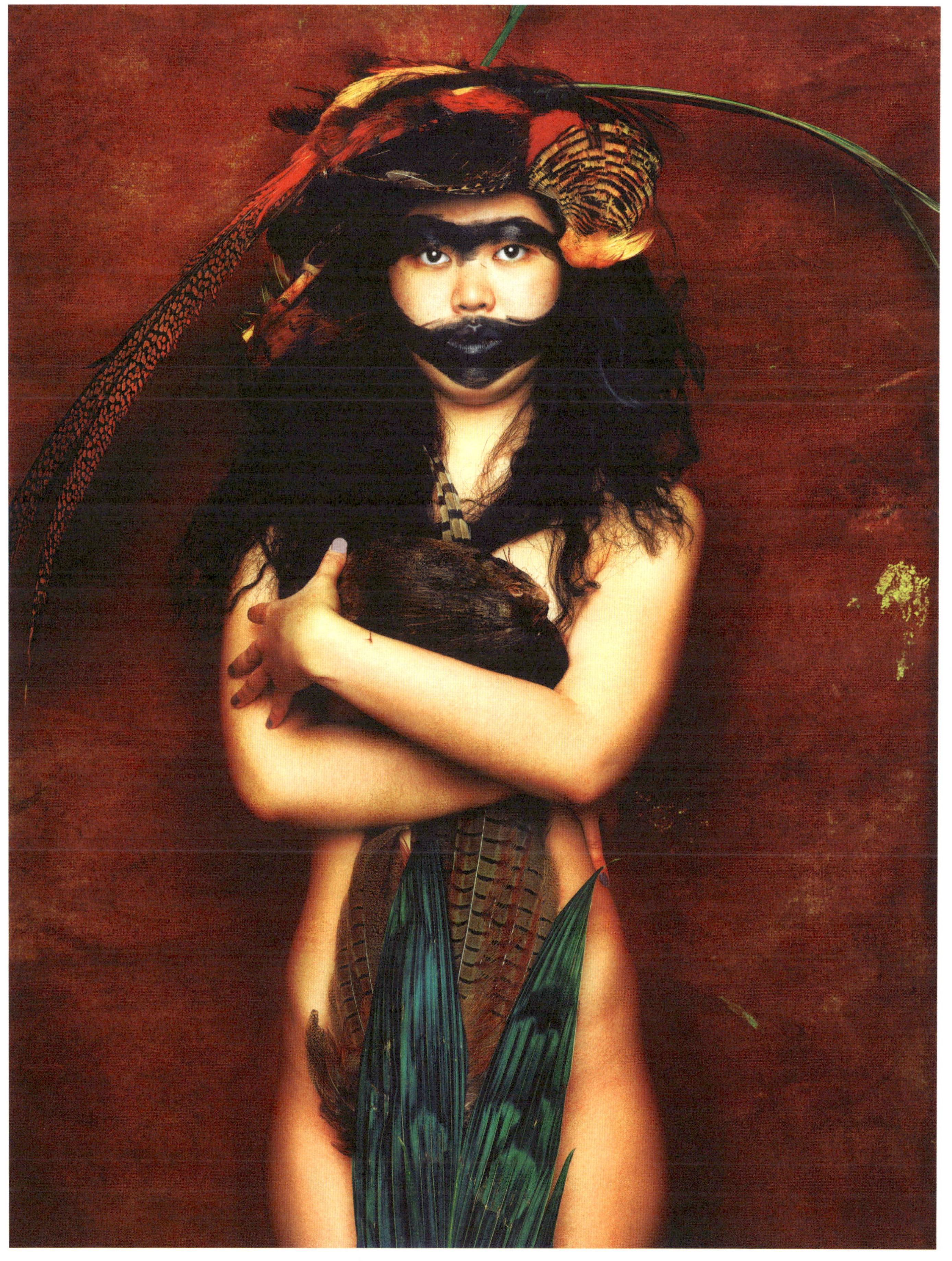

*Feather Woman, 'Lost Diary' Series, New York City, 1997*

GREGORY'S WORK EXPLODES COLOR, EXHUMES
PRECISION, AND EXHIBITS MASTERY IN COMPOSITION.
HIS CONCEPTUAL STORYTELLING IS LIGHTNING
FAST—THE VIEWER GETS IT RIGHT AWAY.
**Athena Azevedo,** *Photographer, Graphis Photography Master*

HE IS AN AMAZING STILL LIFE PHOTOGRAPHER. HIS
IMAGES ARE MODERN, FUN, SURPRISING, COLORFUL,
AND BEAUTIFULLY COMPOSED AND DESIGNED. WHAT
A TREAT TO REVIEW, STUDY, DELIGHT IN, AND EVEN
SAVOR HIS WORK. HE HAS A REMARKABLE EYE.
**Howard Schatz,** *Photographer, Graphis Photography Master*

HIS IMAGES ARE IMPACTFUL AND GRAPHIC AT FIRST
GLANCE, BUT WHAT SEPARATES AND ELEVATES HIS
VISION IS THAT HE ADDS A CONCEPT. HIS PICTURES
ENGAGE YOU AND ASK YOU TO RESPOND.
**Craig Cutler,** *Photographer, Graphis Photography Master*

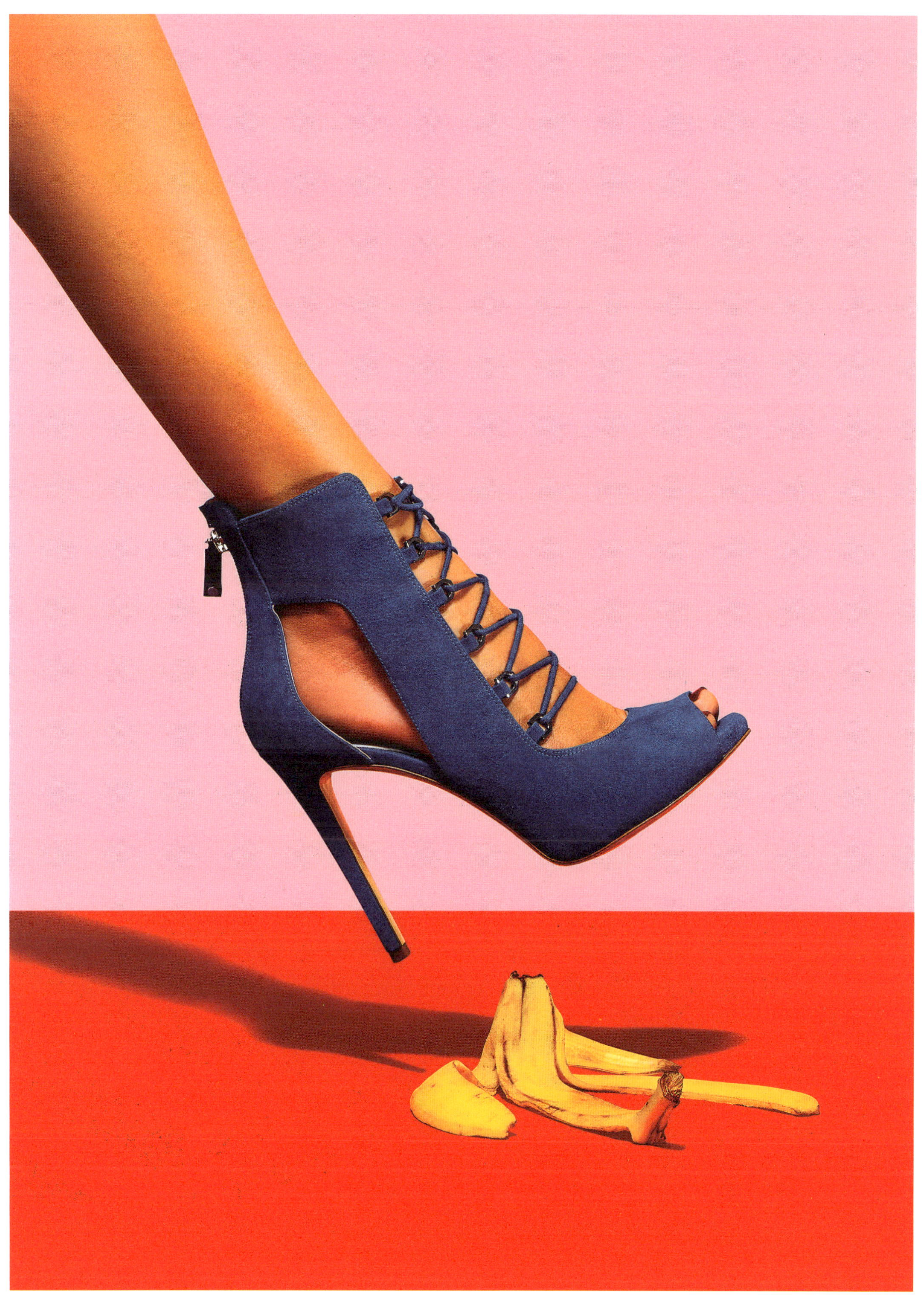

*WTF is Stress Doing to My Body; Client: Cosmopolitan*

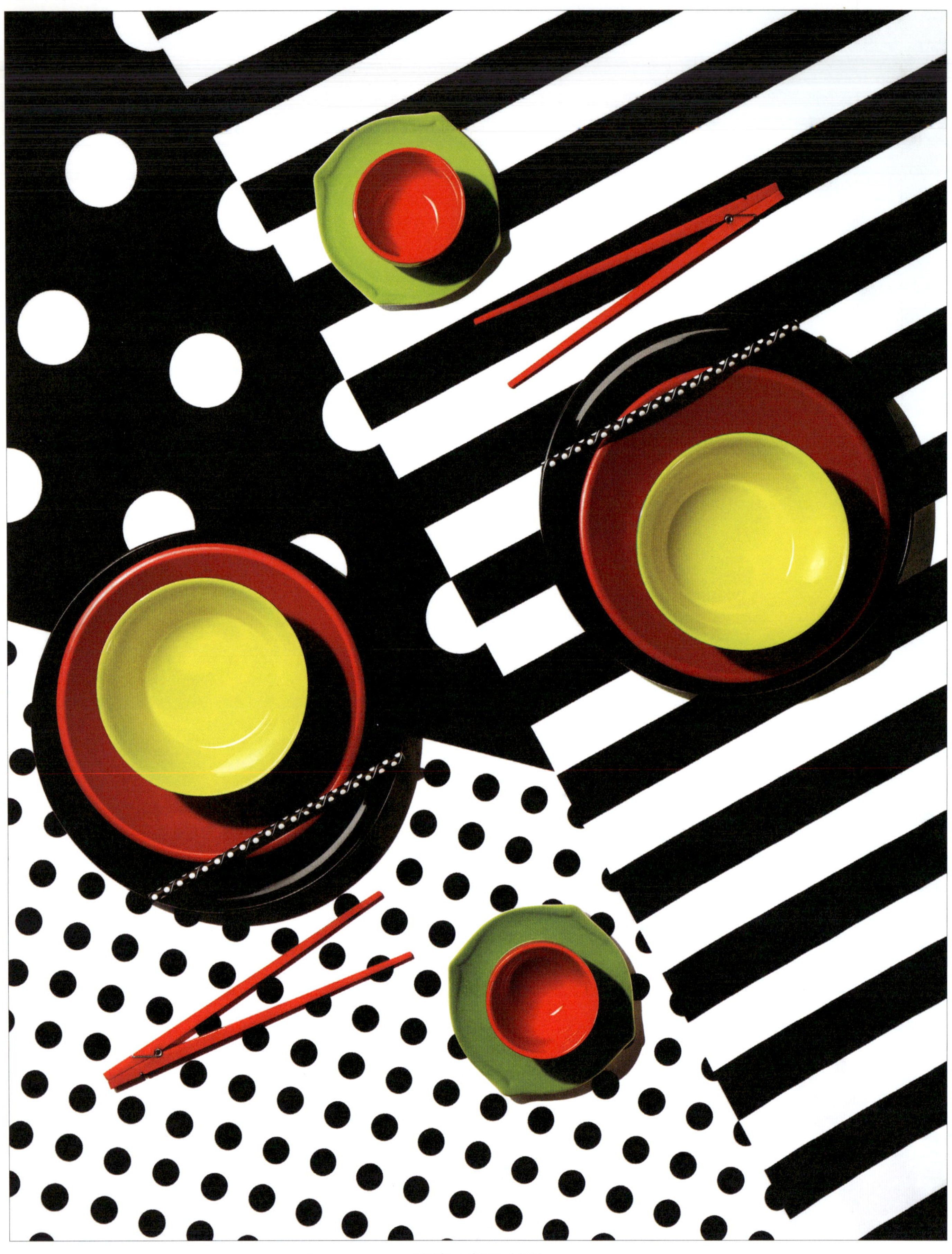

*"Circles and Lines,"* 2015

Smart and arresting with a deliberate thoughtfulness is how Gregory Reid's work initially hits you. Graphic and playful, the colors and the line work in his images vibrate with an intensity that creates an almost sculptural photograph. His work is so tactile and dimensional- a testament to his understanding of lighting and shape. I've known Gregory for more than a decade and he has worked harder than anyone I've known.  He is able to perfect and hone his craft with a deliberate care and understanding often lost in the modern digital version of the photographic medium. He has an eye for detail and a palette that's lush and indulgent. His images are like candy, decadent. The best working in our medium take the mundane object and the everyday and make it exceptional. Gregory Reid makes it look all too easy.

## WHEN YOUR AUDIENCE CAN RELATE TO WHAT YOU ARE MAKING, THAT'S SUCCESS TO ME.

**Gregory Reid,** *Still Life Photographer*

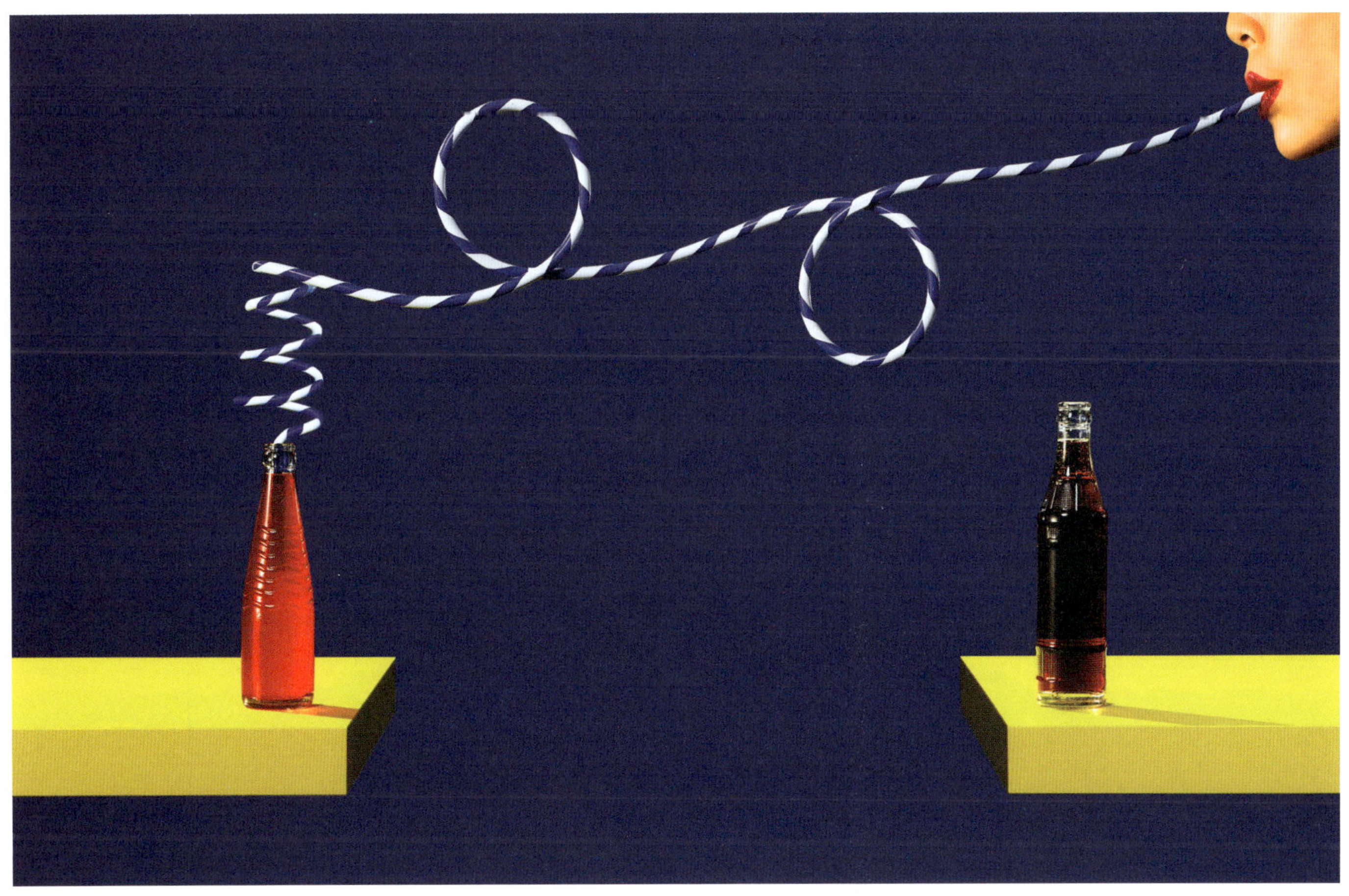

*2016*

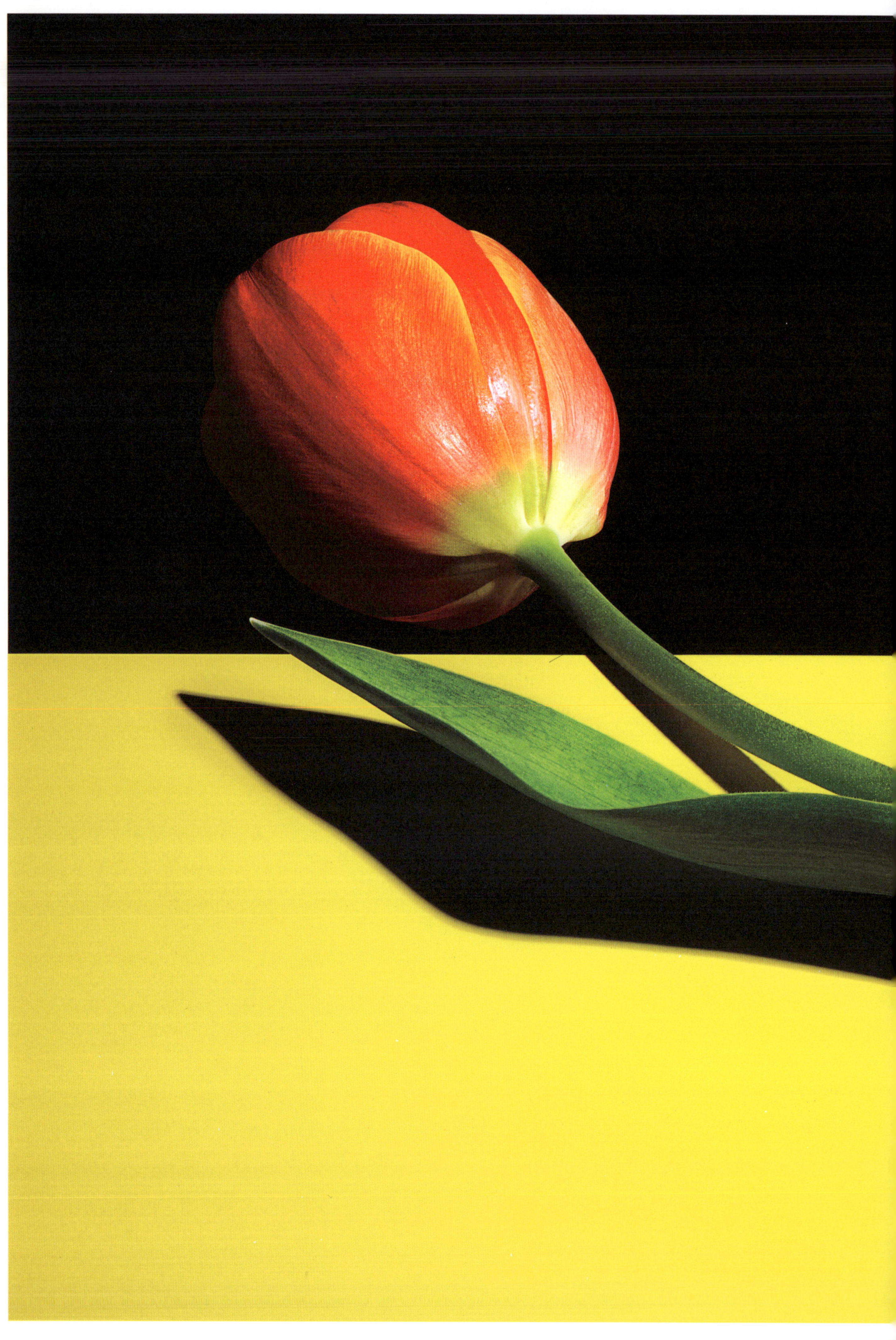

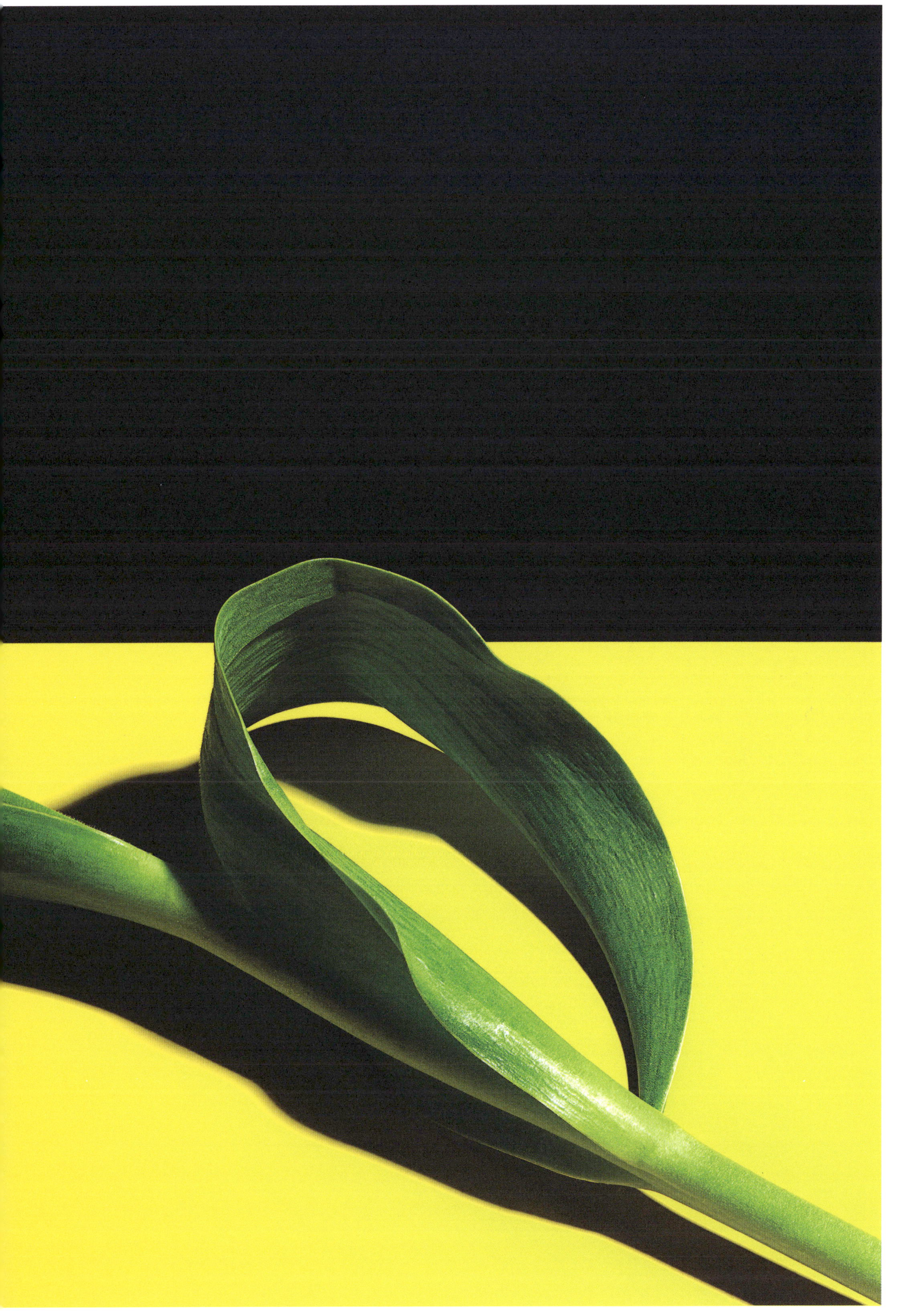

Floral

*What inspired or motivated you into your career?*
Growing up, films were a big influence on me and sparked my interest in visual storytelling. I originally went to college for Pre-Med and felt very uninspired and transferred to art school after the first year. I think that yearning to tell stories is what brought me back to art.

*What is your work philosophy?*
Always keep moving and creating personal work. Some of my favorite client work has come from a personal image I shot that inspired the creative direction of the project.

*What aspect of photography do you most enjoy?*
I enjoy the idea of creating a piece of art that can be viewed by many amongst multiple platforms.

*Who is or was your greatest mentor?*
While I was in college, I started interning for Dan Saelinger. I later went on to be his first assistant and studio manager. He has long since been a mentor and great friend to me.

*What is it about still life photography that is most inspiring to you?*
I enjoy how meditative it can be. The slow buildup to creating the image and then it all clicks.

*How would you describe your process?*
I tend to be methodical, usually going into a shoot with a gameplan. But I''m always open to improvisation as it arises.

*I see that you shoot accessories, cosmetics, food, tech, and more. What is your favorite genre to work in and why?*
One of my most favorite things about still life photography is the variation of genres that can be shot. I think that's what lures me to it, that every day can be completely different with a new problem to solve. But if I had to choose, I'd say accessories and conceptual work. I like that those genres generally tend to allow more creative exploration from my experience.

*Who were some of your greatest past influences?*
Jeff Wall, Taryn Simon, Larry Sultan, Bruce Nauman, and David Lynch.

*Who among your contemporaries today do you most admire?*
Grant Cornett and Maurizio Cattelan always make me smile.

*What are the most important ingredients you require from a client to do successful work?*
I'd say trust and the enthusiasm of collaboration. When it be comes a team effort, I feel that's where some of the strongest work is made.

*What is your greatest professional achievement?*
Growing up, my grandfather was a huge inspiration to me. When visiting, he always had a collection of magazines he'd have me read. Getting the opportunity to shoot for those same magazines later in life was an important personal achievement for me.

*What advice would you have for young photographers starting out today?*
Trust your vision and also don't rush the process. Interning and assisting are great ways to learn from people you admire at a personal level and also discover your own creative style.

*What interests do you have outside of your work?*
I'm a motorcycle enthusiast and recently started dabbling in neon bending. Both require a lot of concentration which wind up also feeling quite meditative. Similar to still life, I think that's why I'm drawn to them.

*Where do you seek inspiration?*
Typically, I find inspiration outside of photography. Sculptors and illustrators really inspire me. Music has also been a major influence for me as well.

*How do you define success?*
When your audience can relate to what you are making, that's success to me.

*What would be your dream assignment?*
Photographing all original members of The Cramps.

*Where do you see yourself in the future?*
Video and motion work have become another tool that photographers have been recently using to tell a story from their perspective. I'd like to see myself continue to explore that avenue as well.

**Gregory Reid Photo** www.gregoryreidphoto.com

# I THINK THAT YEARNING TO TELL STORIES IS WHAT BROUGHT ME BACK TO ART.

**Gregory Reid,** *Still Life Photographer*

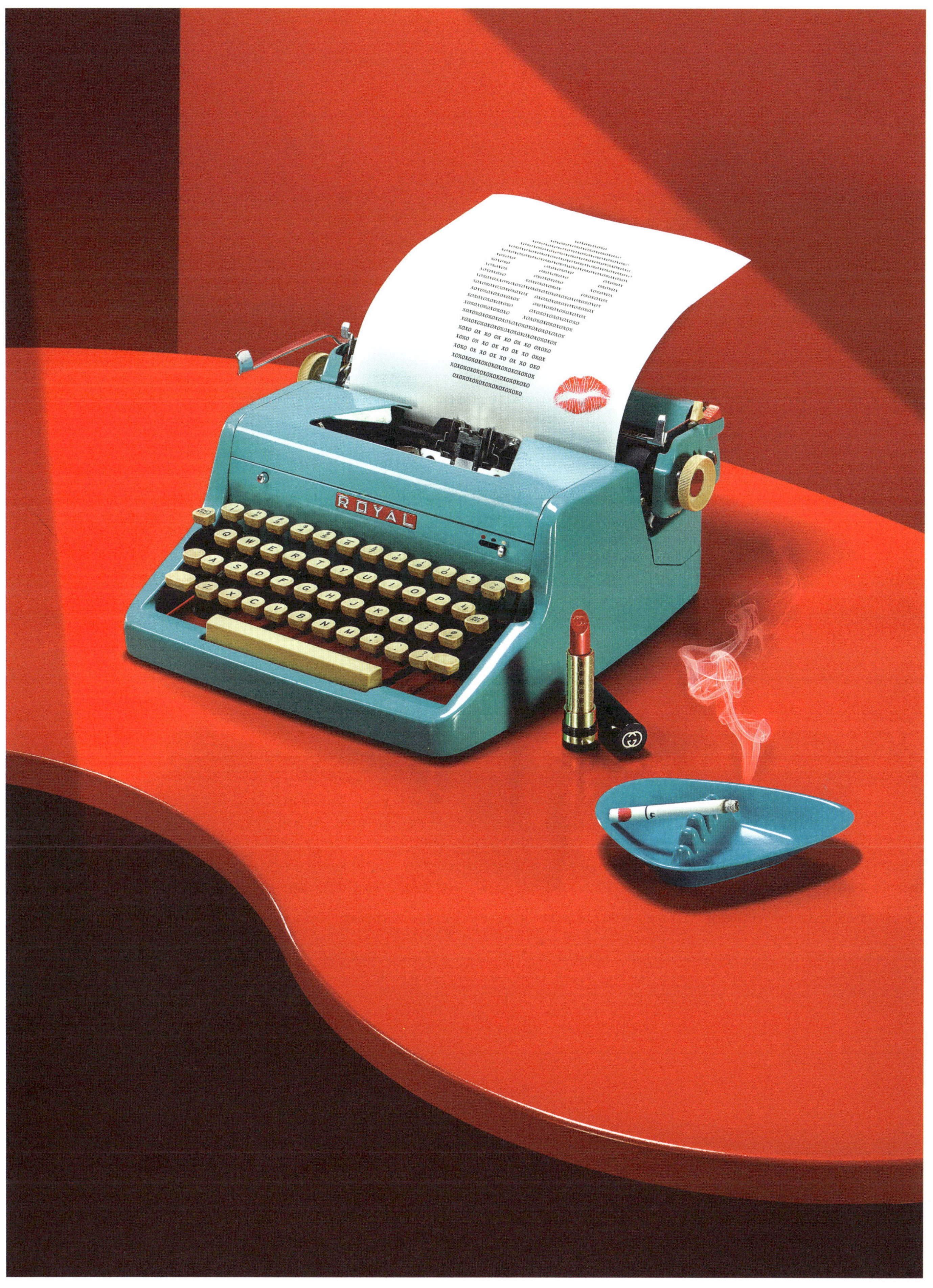

"Xoxo," 2016

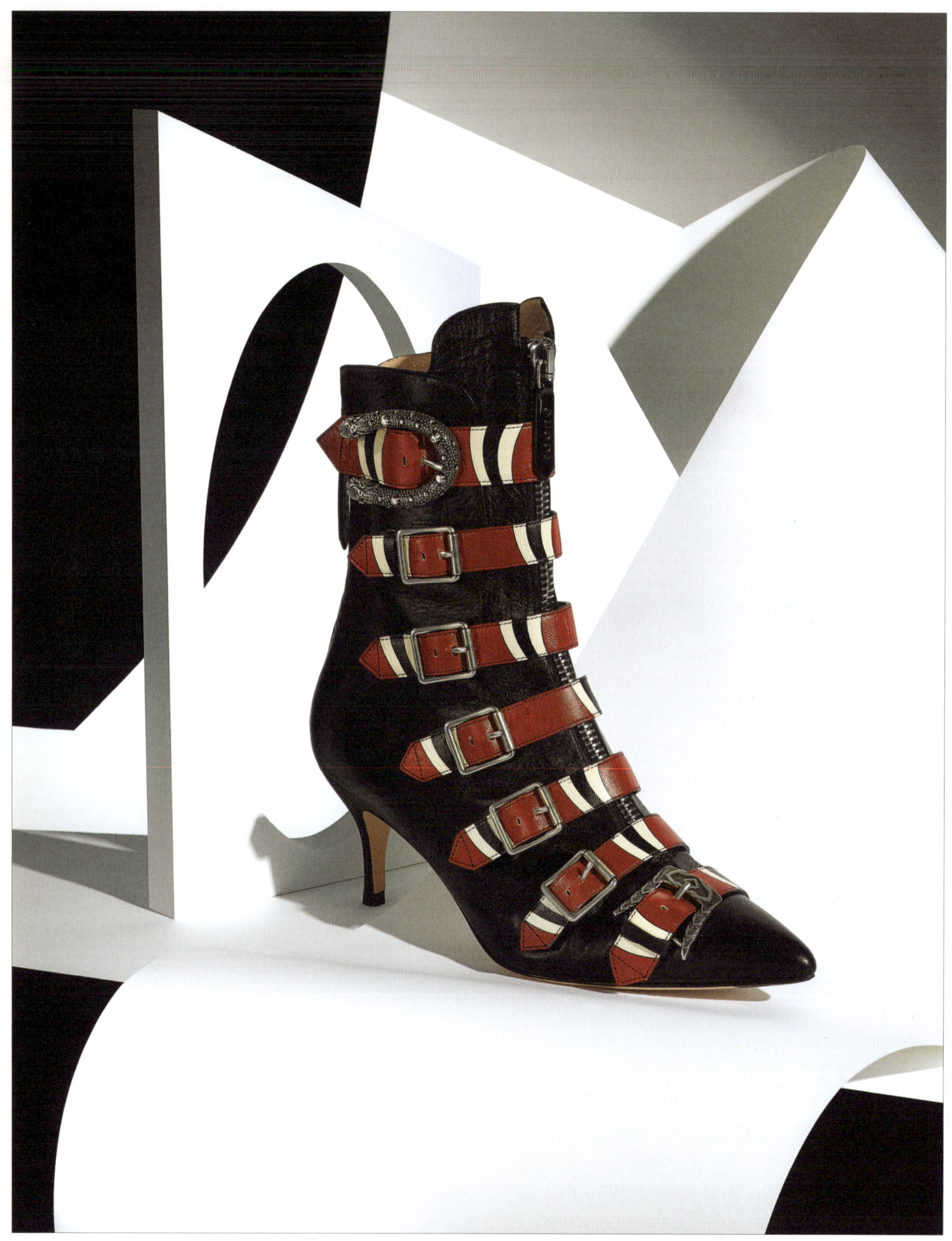

*W Magazine and Simons Malls, 2016*

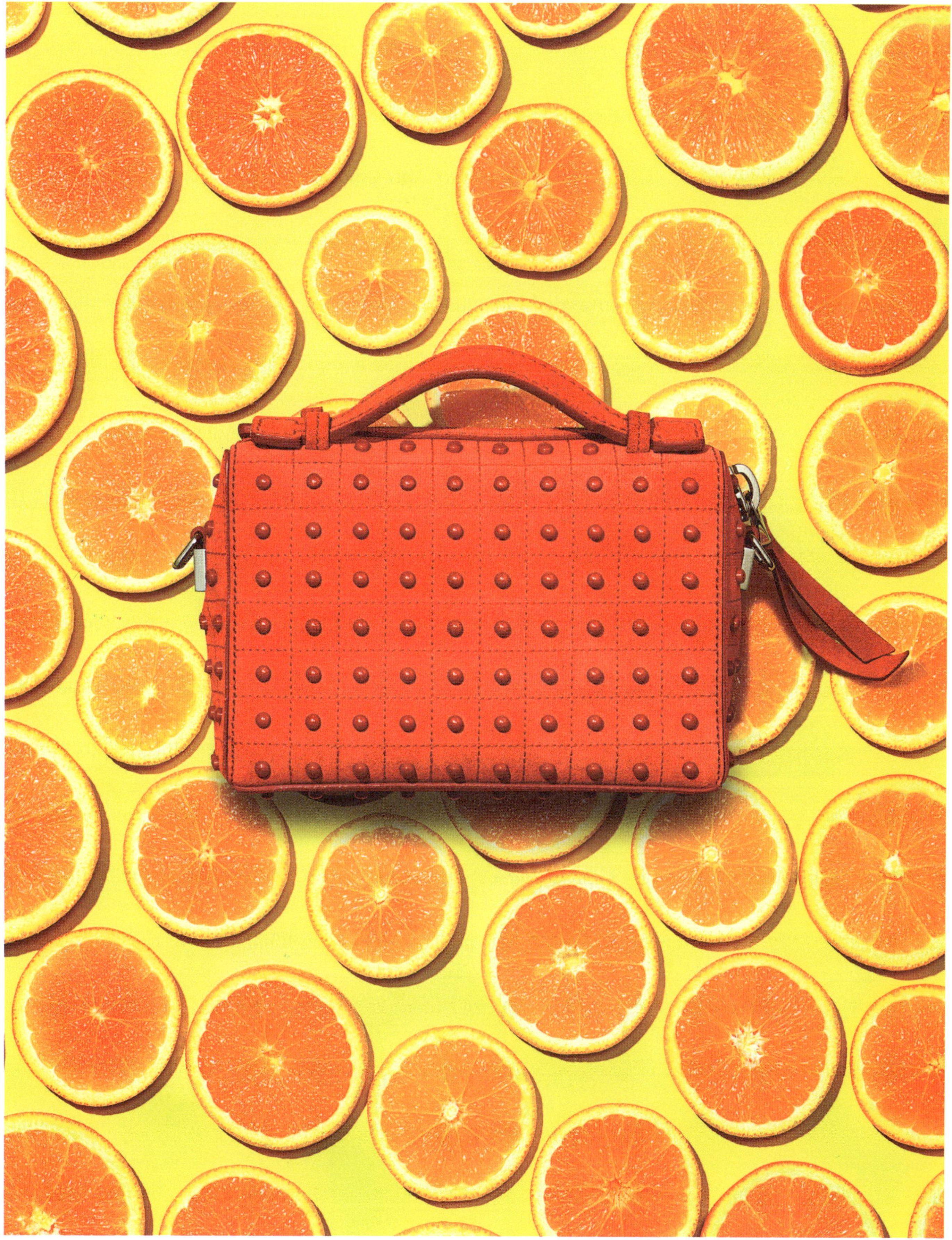

*Daily Front Row, 2017*

FRANK P. WARTENBERG HAS A WONDERFUL EYE FOR LIGHT AND THE PERFECT SETTING. HIS FOCUS CATCHES THE RIGHT DETAILS AND HE TRANSPORTS EMOTIONS IN A UNIQUE WAY BY TELLING THE WHOLE STORY.

**Karsten von Kuczkowski,** *CEO, DvonK Stylisten \ Berlin*

WORKING WITH FRANK IS ALWAYS INSPIRING. HIS TRUE INTEREST IN PEOPLE CREATES A SPECIAL ATMOSPHERE AND CONNECTION, WHICH CAN BE SEEN IN HIS PHOTOGRAPHS. INNOVATIVE SCENERIES GIVE HIS PHOTOGRAPHS A UNIQUE SIGNATURE.

**Franziska Lorenz,** *Fashion Designer*

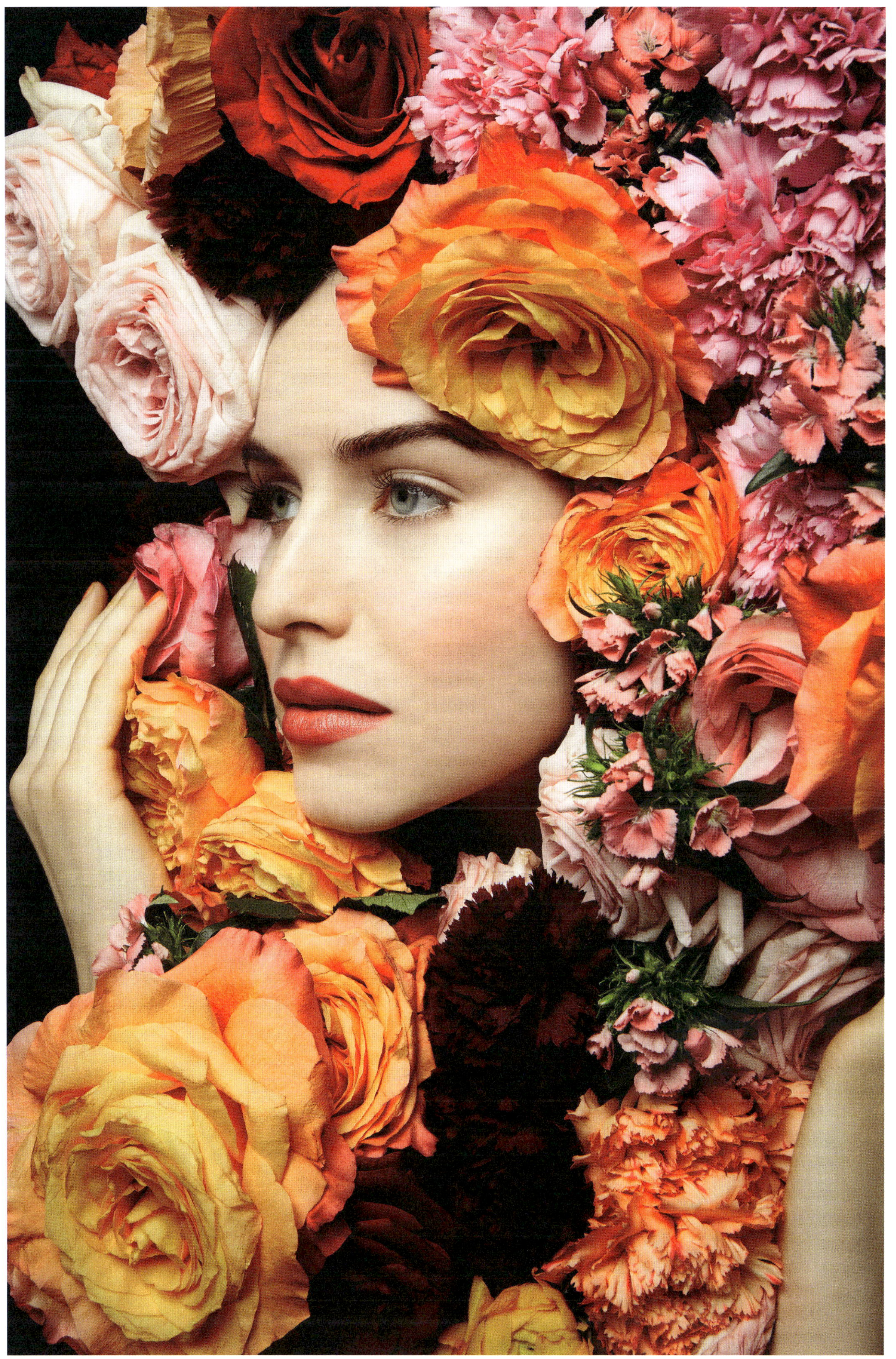

Cappelli - Flowerheads; Client: Picture Press

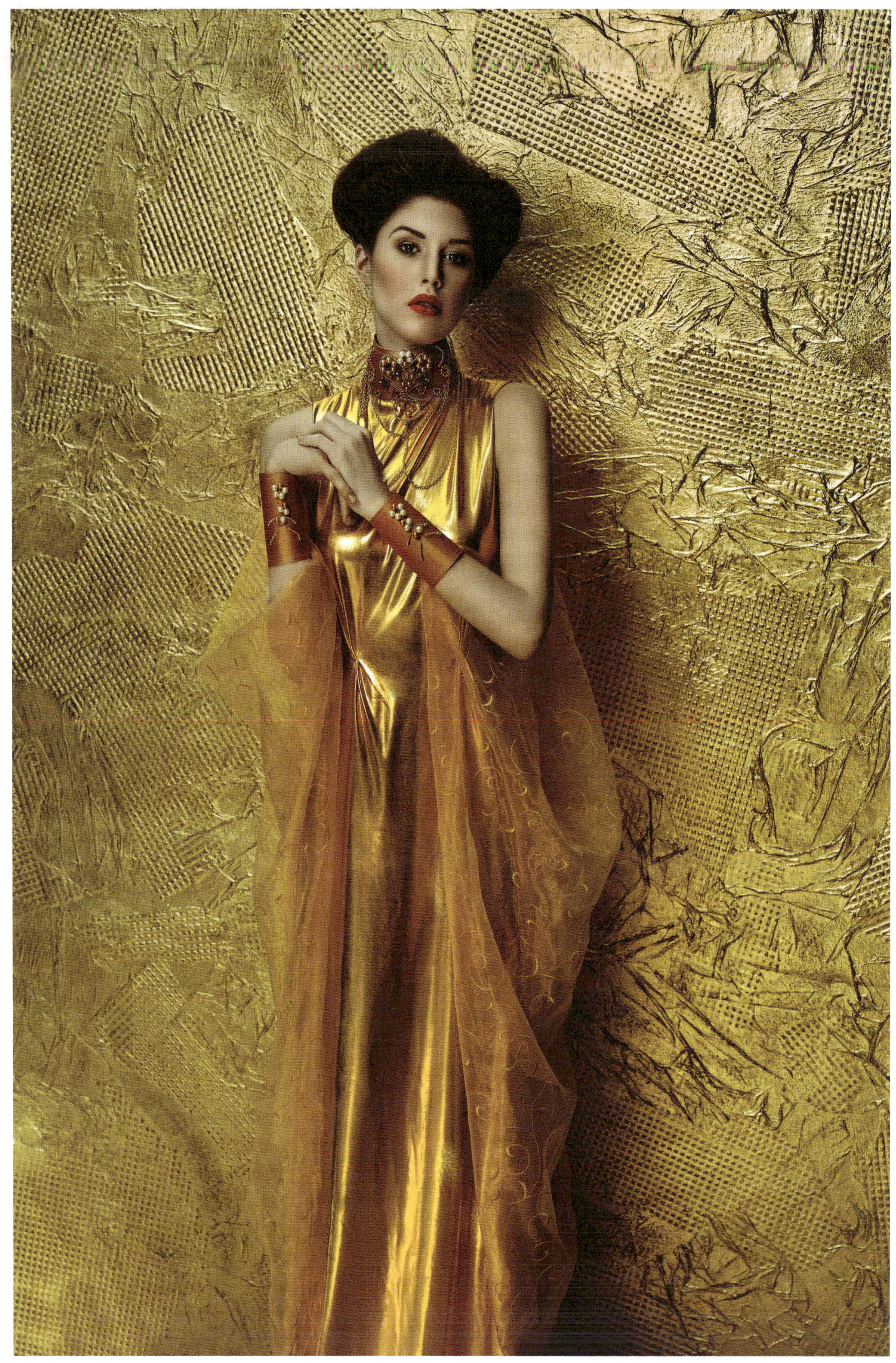

*Golden Adele*

Frank P. Wartenberg has been contributing his work to our agency for almost 25 years. His versatility is breathtaking. He is constantly orchestrating new scenarios and settings at the highest level. Whether shooting beauty, fashion, or lifestyle, everything converts into something special. His dense visual language creates outstanding art, which is often magical. Frank is highly empathic and good with people; this quality is reflected in all of his work.

PHOTOGRAPHY IS ALREADY A DAILY SATISFACTION TO ME. THE GREATEST SATISFACTION IS THAT I AM ABLE TO CREATE ARTWORK THAT IS INTERESTING FOR OTHER PEOPLE. **Frank P. Wartenberg,** *Portrait & Fashion Photographer*

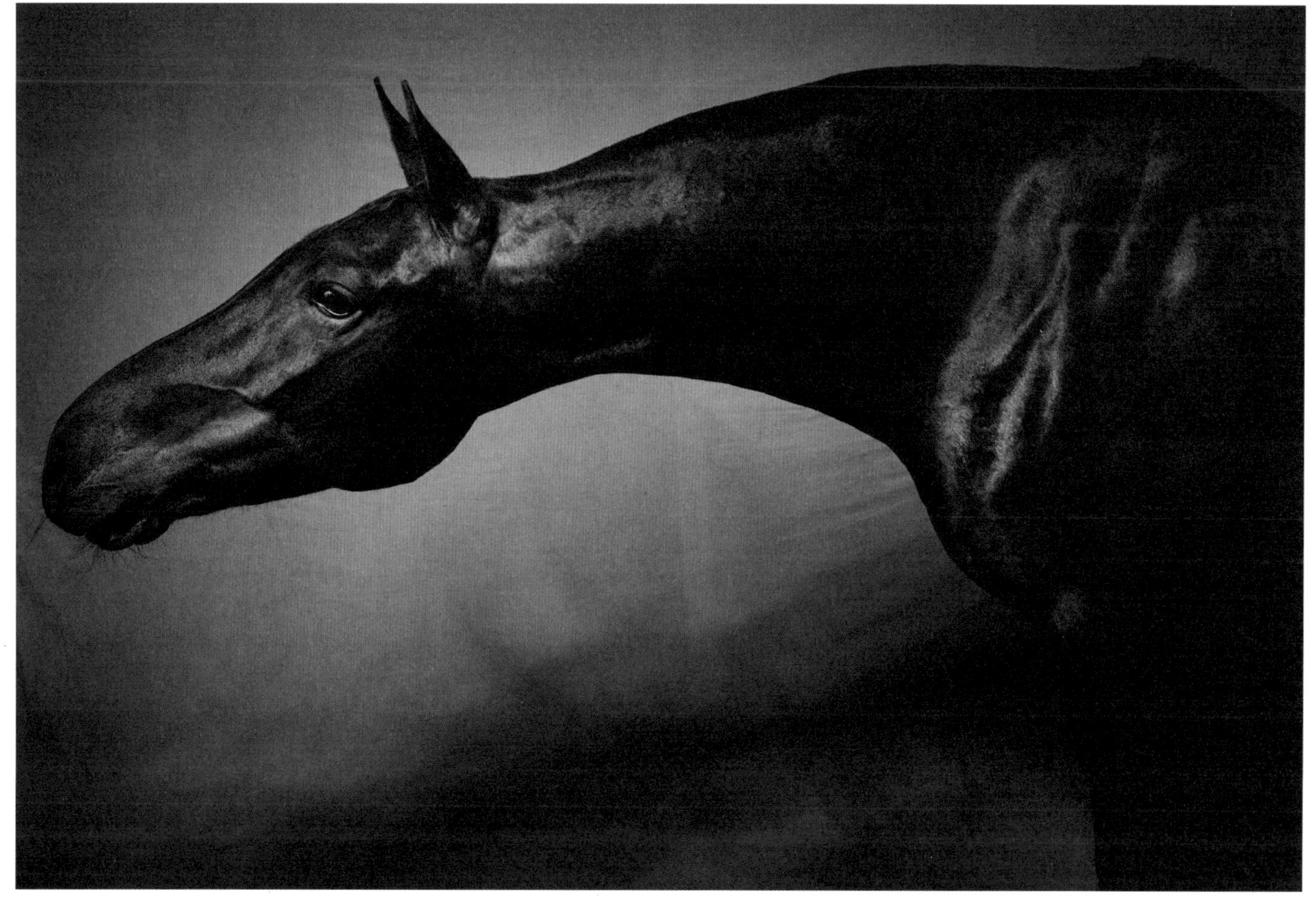

*Polo Book Project*

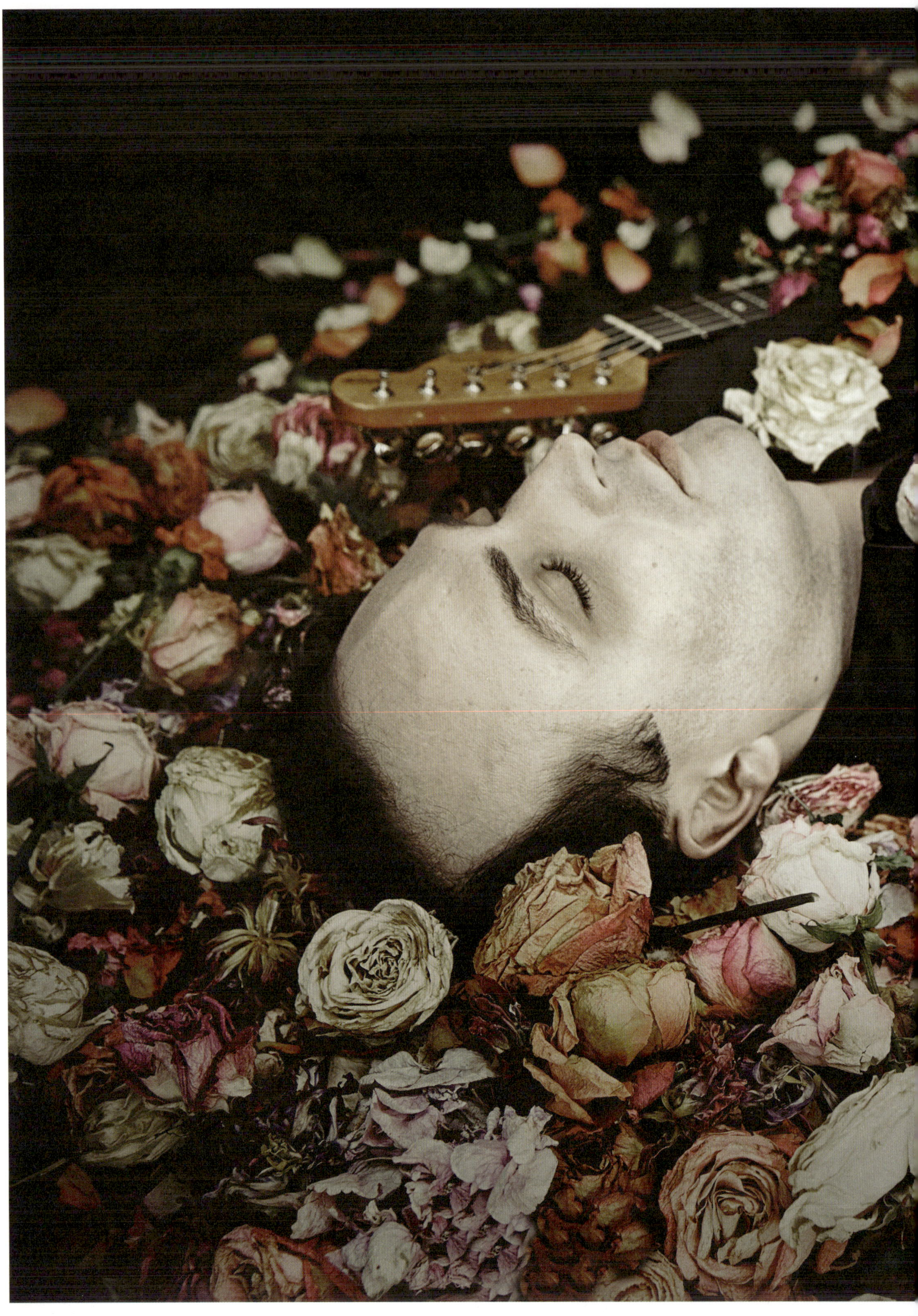

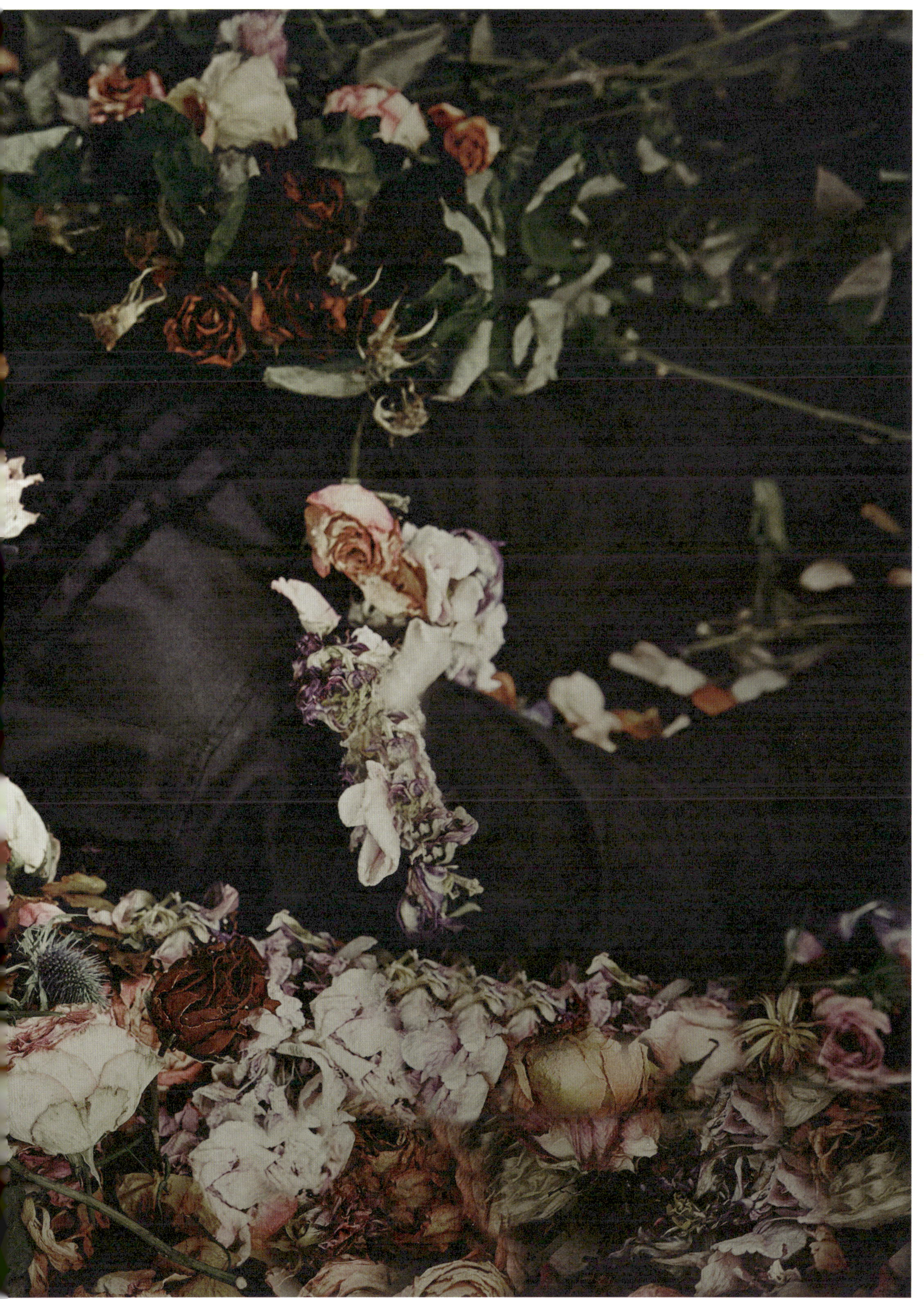

*Dead Phil - "Der Rest" Band Portrait; Client: Sonic Seducer Mag*

*What inspired or motivated you into your career?*
I always loved to take pictures. After school I wasn't brave enough to start photography right away. This was also because my family didn't encourage me to start something artistic. I studied law and after that, I finally had the courage to try photography. Over the years, my passion for photography never stopped.

*What is your work philosophy?*
You can do everything if you really want it. Be authentic.

*What aspect of photography do you most enjoy?*
I enjoy meeting people and getting in touch with different personalities and cultures. I love to travel.

*Who is or was your greatest mentor?*
My grandmother, my financial consultant/father figure, and for 30 years now, my wife.

*How would you describe your process?*
When I finally made the decision to start a career in photography, I gave maximum energy to that. I worked really hard and I always wanted to do my best. The funny thing is that working hard didn't feel like that. This is because I enjoy everything so much and have the chance to work together with my wife... it is always cool and relaxed.

*What is your most difficult challenge you've had to overcome?*
Handling different people, because in our industry there is so much individualism and everybody wants to live his individual personality. That's not always easy. Everybody expects from the photographer that he acts as the leader of the group. You need nerves of steel to do that under the pressure of the clients.

*What are some of your greatest past influences?*
·The change from analogue to digital photography.... I love, love, love to work with film. I can say that I am the master of it. I have a natural talent to feel the light and to work with the analogue process. Digital photography felt, at first, so boring to me. Today, I respect digital photography as well and I try to work in a different creative way to get my results. But before, it was challenging. I miss the demands of the analogue creative time.

*Who among your contemporaries today do you most admire?*
Peter Lindbergh.

*What are the most important ingredients you require from a client to do successful work?*
Communication is important. First, the client needs to communicate his ideas and aims and preferences. Then the client should relax and understand that now, it's my turn. I am the professional who is taking all of this in and who is fighting for the best results. Clients must trust.

*Who have been some of your favorite people or clients you have worked with?*
STERN magazine, NIKON, Peter Steiner, Wolfgang Behnken, and Franz Epping.

*What is your greatest professional achievement?*
To have a complete artistic work—so many pictures through the years and many classics that are, after 25 years, still great.

*What is the greatest satisfaction you get from your work?*
Photography is already a daily satisfaction to me. The greatest satisfaction is that I am able to create artwork that is interesting for other people.

*What part of your work do you find most demanding?*
Pre- and Post-production: finding the creative idea and picture selection.

*What advice would you have for young photographers starting out today?*
Take pictures, take pictures, take pictures.

*What interests do you have outside of your work?*
My family, music, film, tennis, and soccer.

*What do you value most?*
My family, health, and peace.

*Where do you seek inspiration?*
In my personal library and archive, by traveling, and by watching music videos.

*What would you change if you had to do it all over again?*
Not much—only to try not to be too stressed.

*What would be your dream assignment?*
To do a portrait shoot of Meryl Streep.

*Where do you see yourself in the future?*
I will always do photography and I will enjoy my family life. Maybe I will also teach a little bit.

**Frank Wartenberg** www.frank-wartenberg.com
*See his Graphis Master Portfolio on graphis.com.*

# OVER THE YEARS, MY PASSION FOR PHOTOGRAPHY HAS NEVER STOPPED.

**Frank P. Wartenberg,** *Portrait & Fashion Photographer*

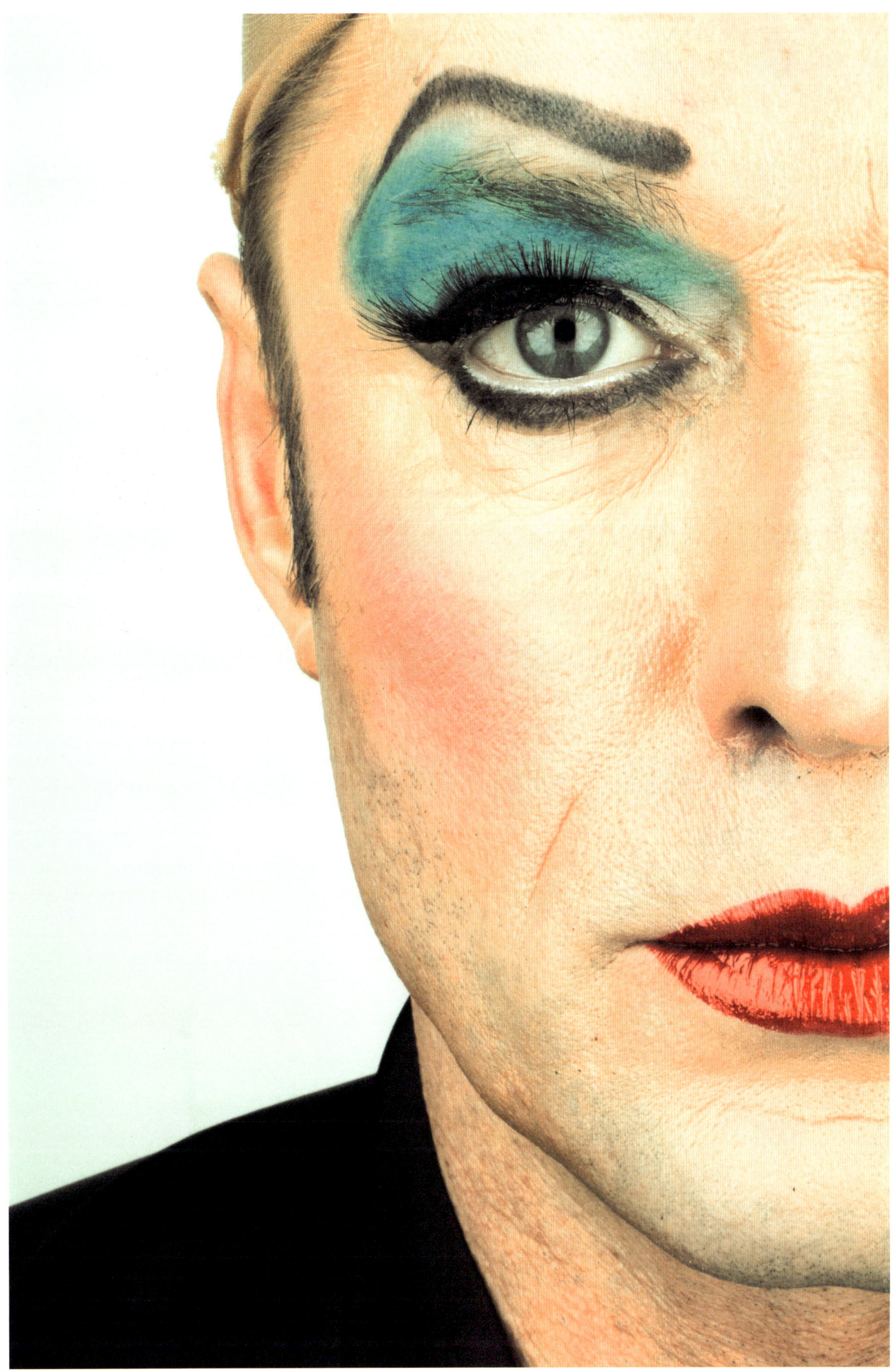

*Bruno; Client: Glampool Agency*

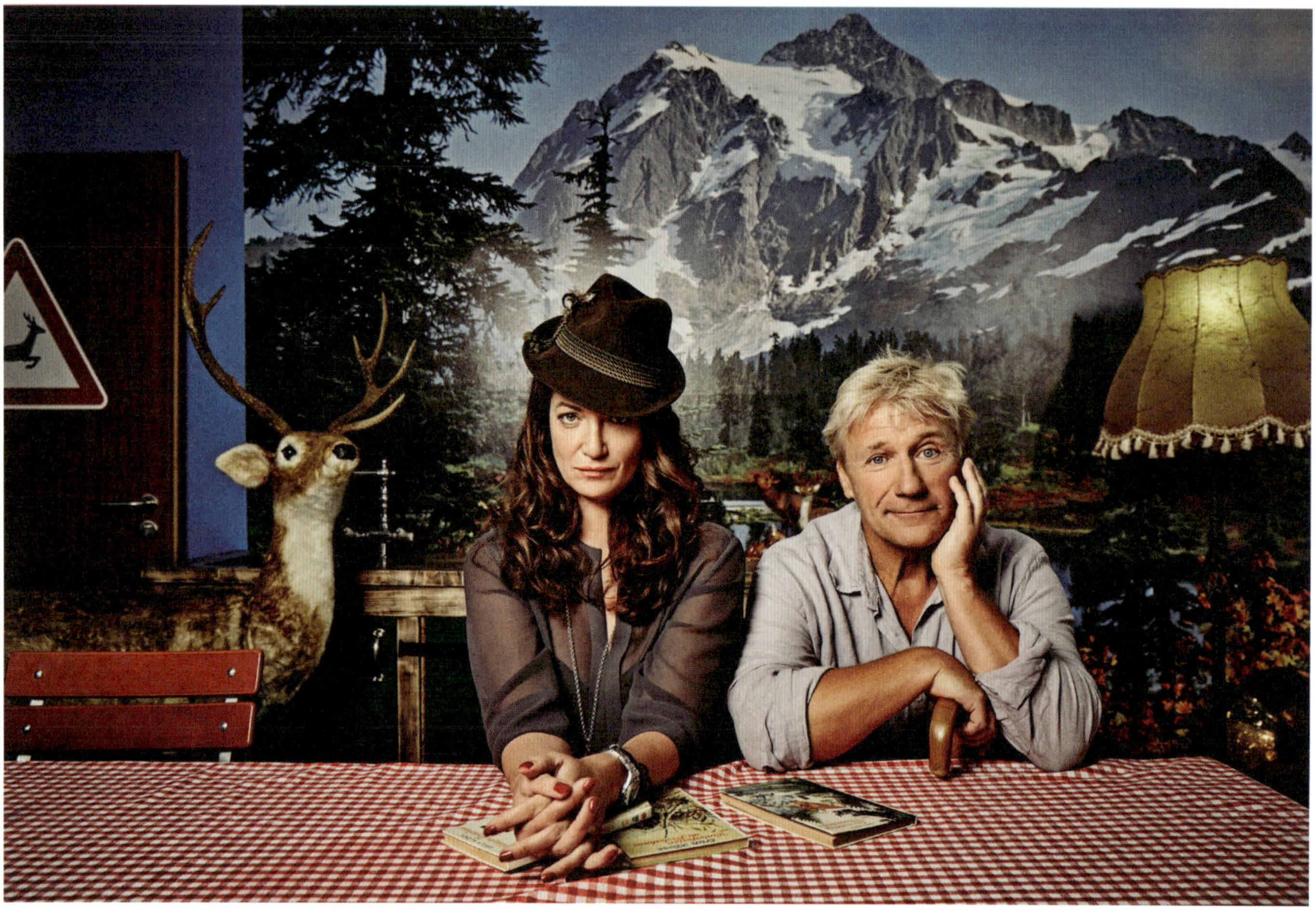

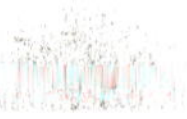

*Heimat; Client: Das Erste (ARD)*

EVERYBODY EXPECTS FROM THE PHOTOGRAPHER THAT HE ACTS AS THE LEADER OF THE GROUP. YOU NEED NERVES OF STEEL TO DO THAT UNDER THE PRESSURE OF THE CLIENTS.

**Frank P. Wartenberg,** *Portrait & Fashion Photographer*

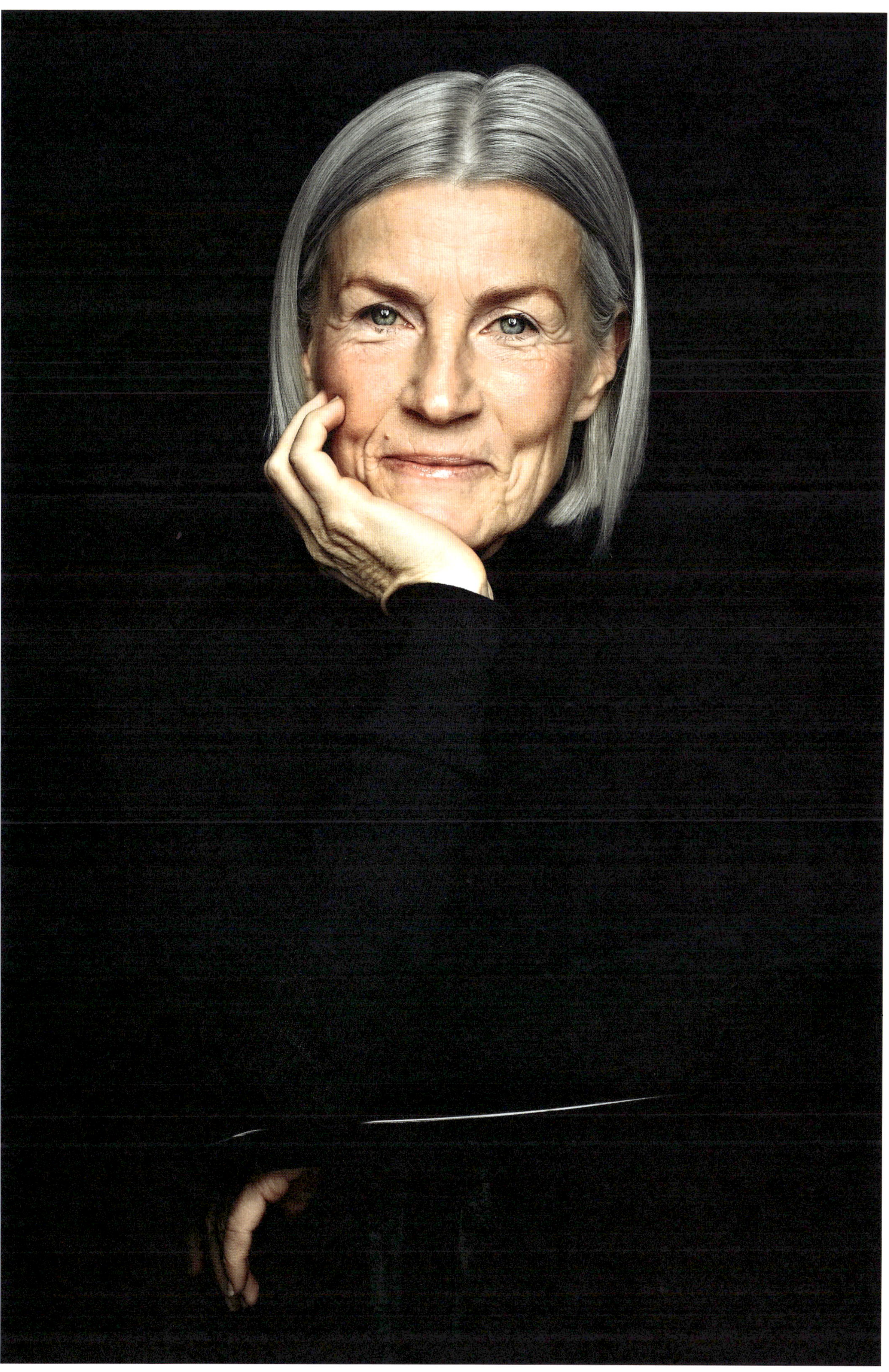

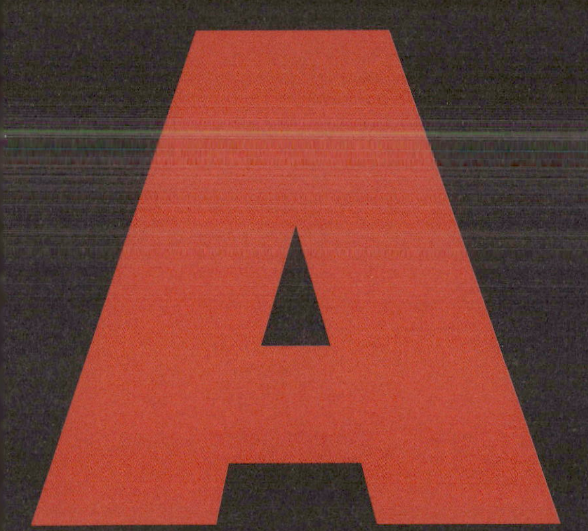

ART/ILLUSTRATION

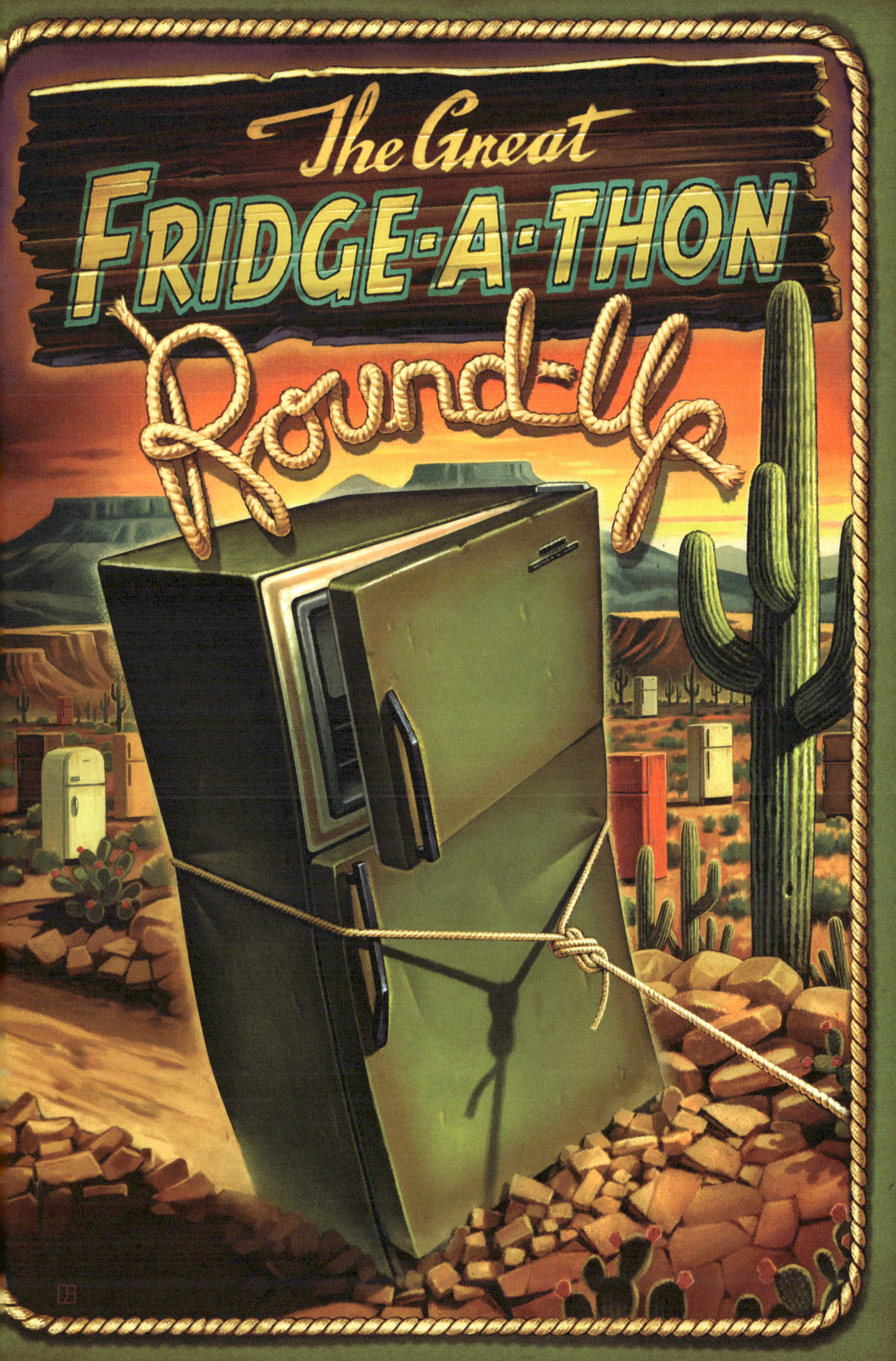

The Great
FRIDGE-A-THON
Round-Up

I HAVE WORKED WITH JEFF FOR 20 YEARS. HIS TALENT IS UNDENIABLE. EACH PROJECT ELICITS A CREATIVE APPROACH WITH MULTIPLE OPTIONS AND A REFLECTION OF MY DESIRED OUTCOME. HE TAKES A VISION FROM MY MIND AND MAKES IT A REALITY.

**Lisa Shaw-Ryan,** *Co-Founder of Chuck's Place, Chuckie Pies, and Casa Pequena Taqueria*

JEFF IS SO METICULOUS AND A PERFECTIONIST, THAT WE NICKNAMED HIM "THE ILLUSTRATOR."

OVER THE YEARS, JEFF AND HIS WIFE HAVE BECOME MORE THAN JUST A BRANDING COMPANY TO US, THEY ARE FAMILY, AND WE ARE BLESSED TO BE WORKING WITH THEM.

**Omar White,** *Co-Founder of American Soul Brothers*

HE IS AN AMAZING TALENT WHO BRINGS CONCEPTS TO LIFE THROUGH HIS WORK. HE EXCEEDED OUR EXPECTATIONS AT EVERY STAGE OF OUR COLLABORATIONS, FROM PRELIMINARY SKETCHES, TO COLOR STUDIES, AND THE FINAL ILLUSTRATIONS.

**John Krull,** *Principal, Creative Director, Shine United*

IT IS SUCH A PLEASURE TO WATCH HIM BRING OUR COLLECTION OF PHOTOS, COLORS, AND LOOSE IDEAS TO LIFE AS BEAUTIFUL AND ENGAGING ILLUSTRATIONS. EVEN AS FELLOW CREATIVES, WE FEEL LIKE WHAT HE DOES IS PURE MAGIC.

**Catherine Healy,** *Creative Director & Owner, Flint Design Co.*

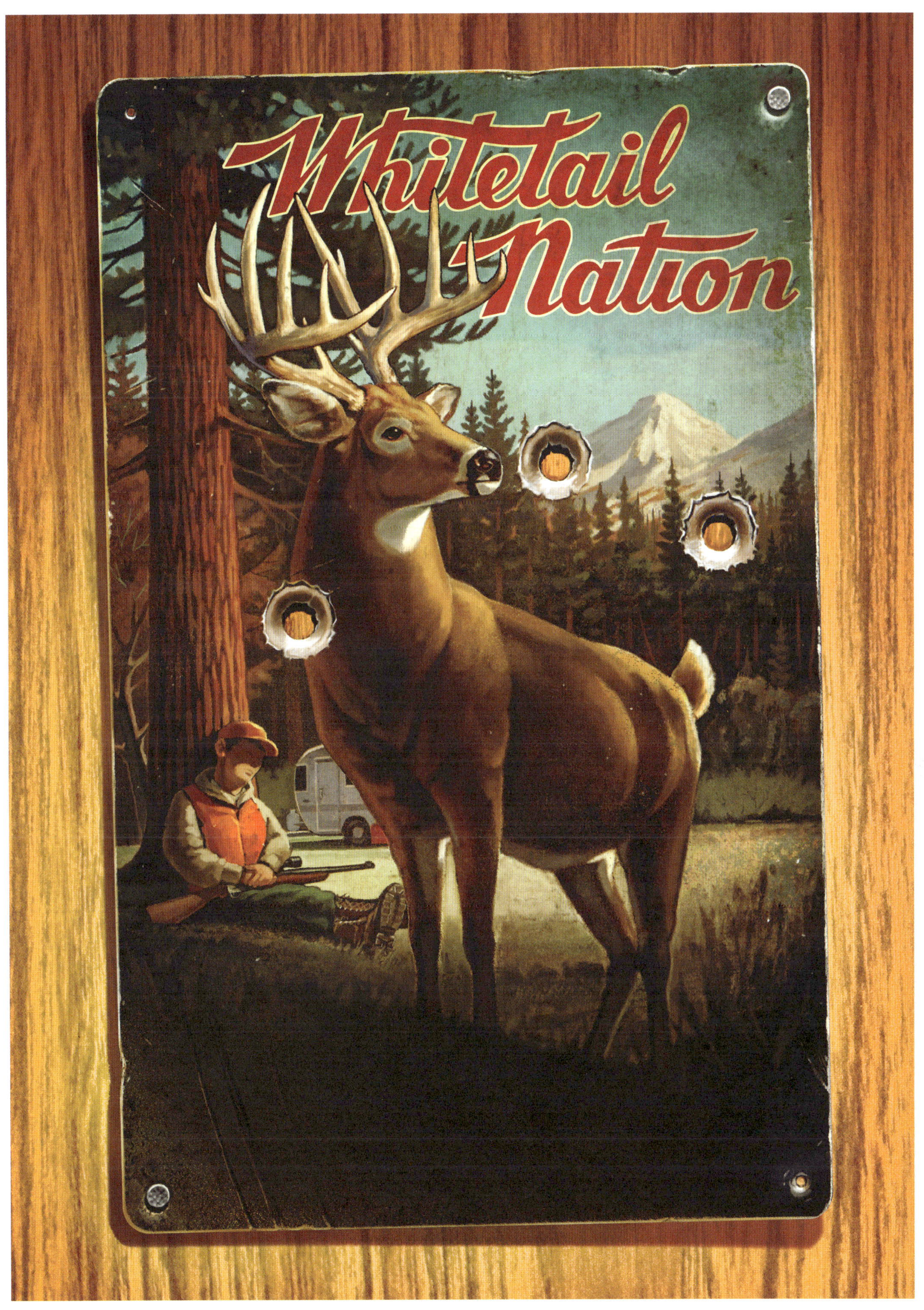

Whitetail Nation



(Page 91) Cramer-Krasselt; Art Director: Ben Bonnan; City of Phoenix; "The Great Fridge-a-thon Roundup"
(Above) Houghton Mifflin Harcourt; Art Director: Martha Kennedy; Book Cover

The Feral Cat Coalition of Oregon has worked with Jeff Foster for more than 20 years. Capturing his talent and skill in words is challenging. Seeing his work is the only way to understand and appreciate his incredible talent. He has provided his illustration talents, pro bono, for every one of our annual fundraising galas. We give him a new theme every year and he brings it to life. This is no small task as we use a play on words to create a one-of-a-kind event. Imagine "Catsablanca" with a Bogie-inspired cat and Ingrid and other characters as mice. He is masterful at creating a sense of time and place that is meaningful and inspiring with no detail missed. He creates a world that never existed before... he creates awe. It is an honor to know him and work with him.

# BE OPEN-MINDED, TRY SOMETHING A LITTLE DIFFERENT, COLLABORATE WITH EFFORT.

**Jeff Foster,** *Illustrator, Retro & Vintage Digital Artist*

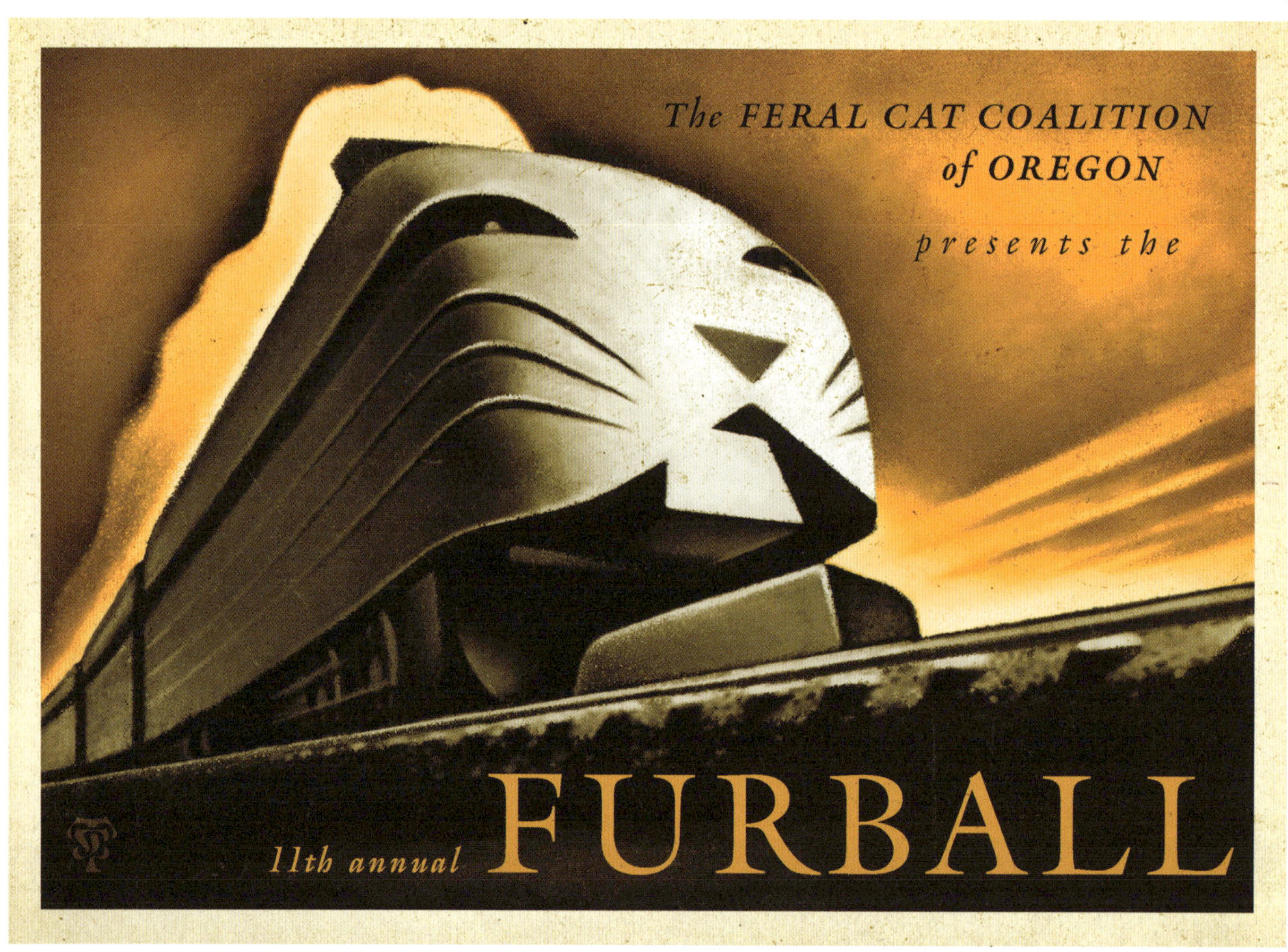


*Spot Design; Art Director: Etta Wilkins Foster; FCCO Furball invitation*

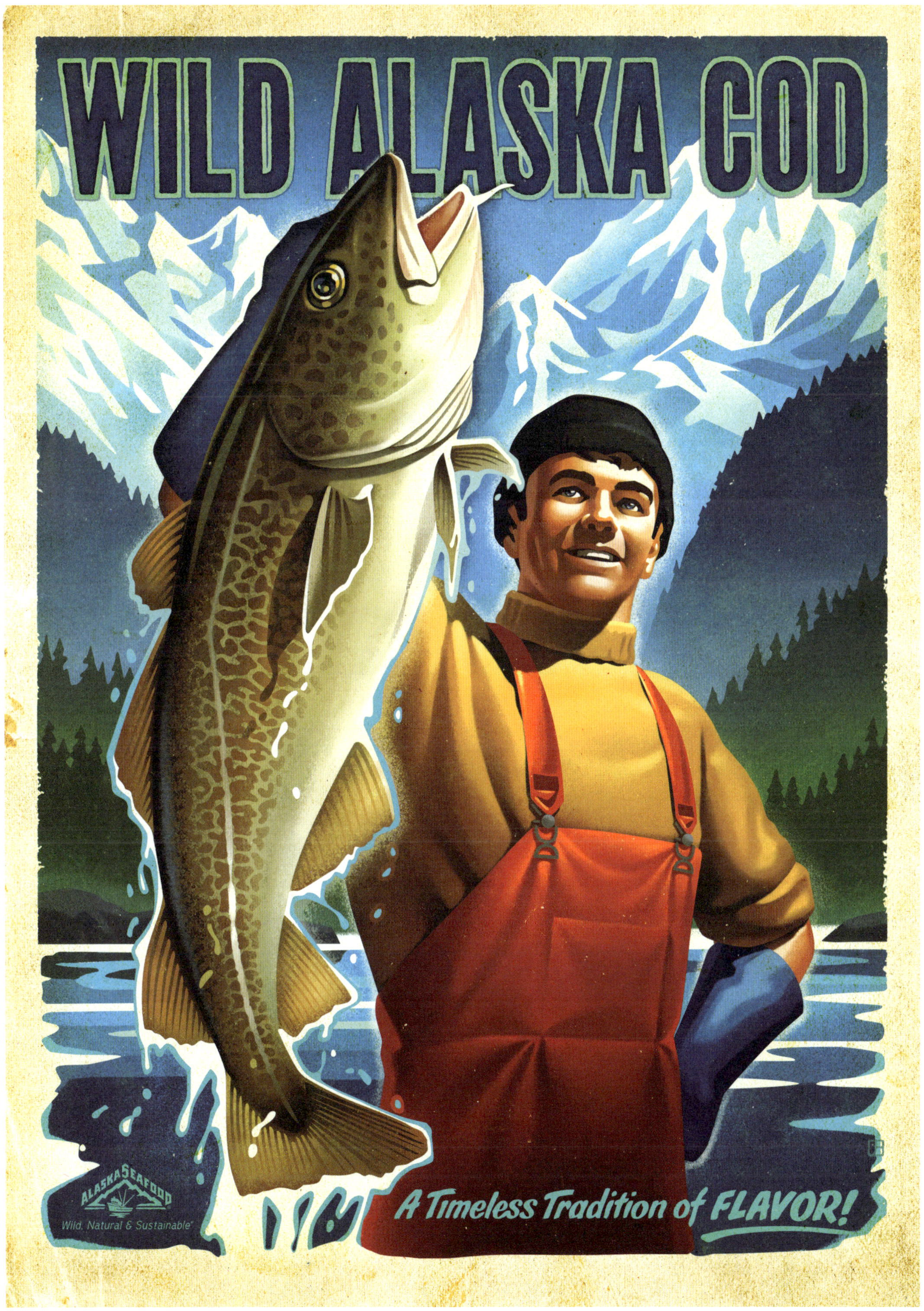


Schiedermayer & Associatesrtners; Art Director: Katie Reuter; Alaska Seafood Marketing Institute

*What inspired or motivated you into your career?*
I didn't even know this was a career until I went to art school.
I was pretty naive about the graphics world. I was naive about
everything. I grew up on a wheat farm near Joplin, Montana.
Lots of big skies. The world was pretty small. K-12 schooling
was all in one building. One grocery store. One bar.

Both my parents are deaf. My mother encouraged me to
draw when I was little. I spent hours in my dad's office constantly drawing on paper and a black chalkboard. I think I
might have white chalk lung disease. I should have asked for
colored chalk. My imagination was very active, which is a motivator. My greatest motivator was my high school art teacher.
I'm sure I wouldn't be here if it wasn't for him.

During my first job at BP&N and Wieden + Kennedy in the
80's is where I got my inspiration.

*What is your work philosophy?*
Be open-minded, try something a little different, collaborate
with effort. And for crying out loud, don't write emails when
you're upset.

*Who is or was your greatest mentor?*
It was my high school art teacher, Jay Oliver Gordon, who just
passed away a few months ago. The Mentor Gods were generous with me. I got the best. Mr. Gordon made me realize I had
a passion and motivation, and gave me the courage to pack my
paint brushes. He wanted me to go to Los Angeles to attend
ArtCenter College of Design, but my parents didn't have the
money. The cheapest option was to head to Portland, Oregon,
to attend Pacific Northwest College of Art (PNCA). Thanks
to Mr. Gordon, I packed my Chevy LUV pickup (with a leaky
topper), and headed west.

*What is it about Illustration that you are most passionate about?*
The creation and collaboration aspect. I get a kick when everything is turning out right, and everyone is happy with the
final result.

*What has been your most memorable project?*
A series of 3 posters for the Wisconsin Milk Marketing Board.
Also, I've always been fond of the RedWood Creek illustrations.

*What is the difference for you between working on illustrations
versus working on packaging design?*
In my world, none. My work is all commercial, so I don't see
the difference.

*What is your most difficult challenge you've had to overcome?*
I've been fortunate over the years, but every once in a while
budgets are the most difficult.

*Who among your contemporaries today do you most admire?*
Such a loaded question, I don't even know where to begin.

*What would be your dream assignment?*
To ride in a yellow submarine.

*Who have been some of your favorite people or clients you
have worked with?*
The people at Flint Design, Portland, Oregon. Fantastic people!

*What are the most important ingredients you require from a
client to do successful work?*
A solid direction, a good working brief, and good sense of humor.
Or, if they send me a good bottle of whiskey, that never hurts.

*What is your greatest professional achievement?*
To still be working.

*What is the greatest satisfaction you get from your work?*
To see it in public, on the web, on packages. To say, "I did
that." Or, maybe it's that check in the mail. Seriously, I love to
hear that my work has been well received. It means a lot.

*What part of your work do you find most demanding?*
The long hours. Often I do it to myself. The management of
time is a mystery to me.

*What professional goals do you still have for yourself?*
Keep myself healthy and to ride that yellow submarine.

*What advice would you have for students starting out today?*
Continue your education in the graphics world: advertising,
design studios, corporate in-house, pro bono, etc. Keep moving, keep working on your skills, don't get stuck in one place.
If you're fortunate enough like me to land a job at a well recognized place, like Wieden + Kennedy, you got lucky. I know
it's not that way for most young artists. The best advice is to
be patient, don't give up.

*What interests do you have outside of your work?*
Being with my best friend of 30 years, Etta. Playing cribbage,
seeing movies and fantastic TV programming, hanging out
with my daughters. Quantum and Astrophysics also interest
me. If I could, I would go back to school. The only problem is
I suck at math. Also, I have an interest in getting a new key-
board concept developed.

*What do you value most?*
This planet. It's all we have.

*What would you change if you had to do it all over again?*
Buy all the tech stock. Retire at 25. Get my PhD in Astrophysics. Grow old and realize I should have married that art
school hotty, adopt two crazy kids from Kazakhstan, and get
paid to do art.

*Where do you seek inspiration?*
Anywhere I can get it. Movies, books, poking around on the
web. Mostly family and friends. I'm always on the prowl for
interesting and innovative illustrations.

*How do you define success?*
A beating heart.

*Where do you see yourself in the future?*
Plotting my next escape.

**Jeff Foster** www.jefffoster.com
*See his Graphis Master Portfolio on graphis.com.*

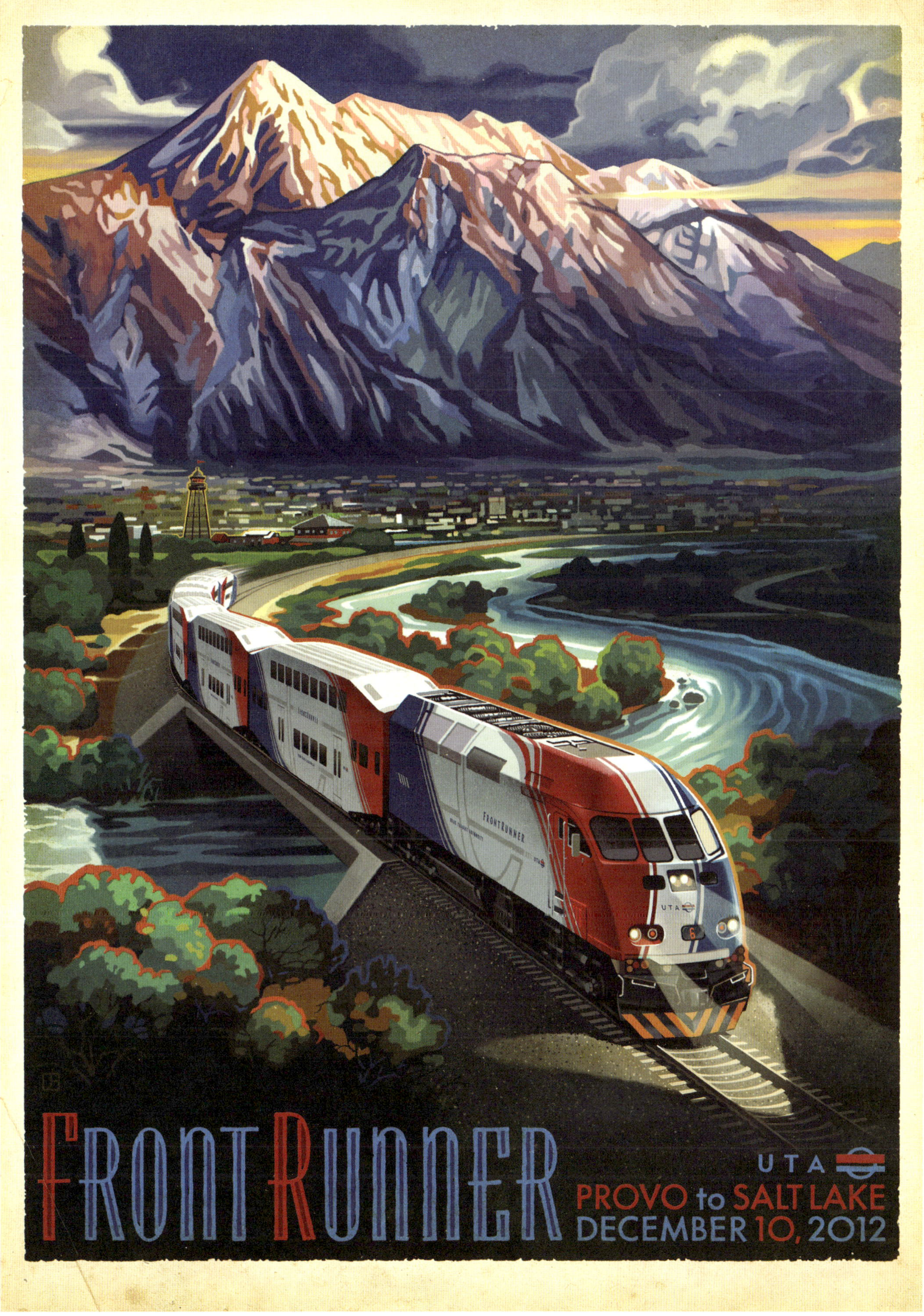


R&R Partners; Art Director: Patrick Buller; Utah Transit Athority; Provo to Salt Lake promo poster

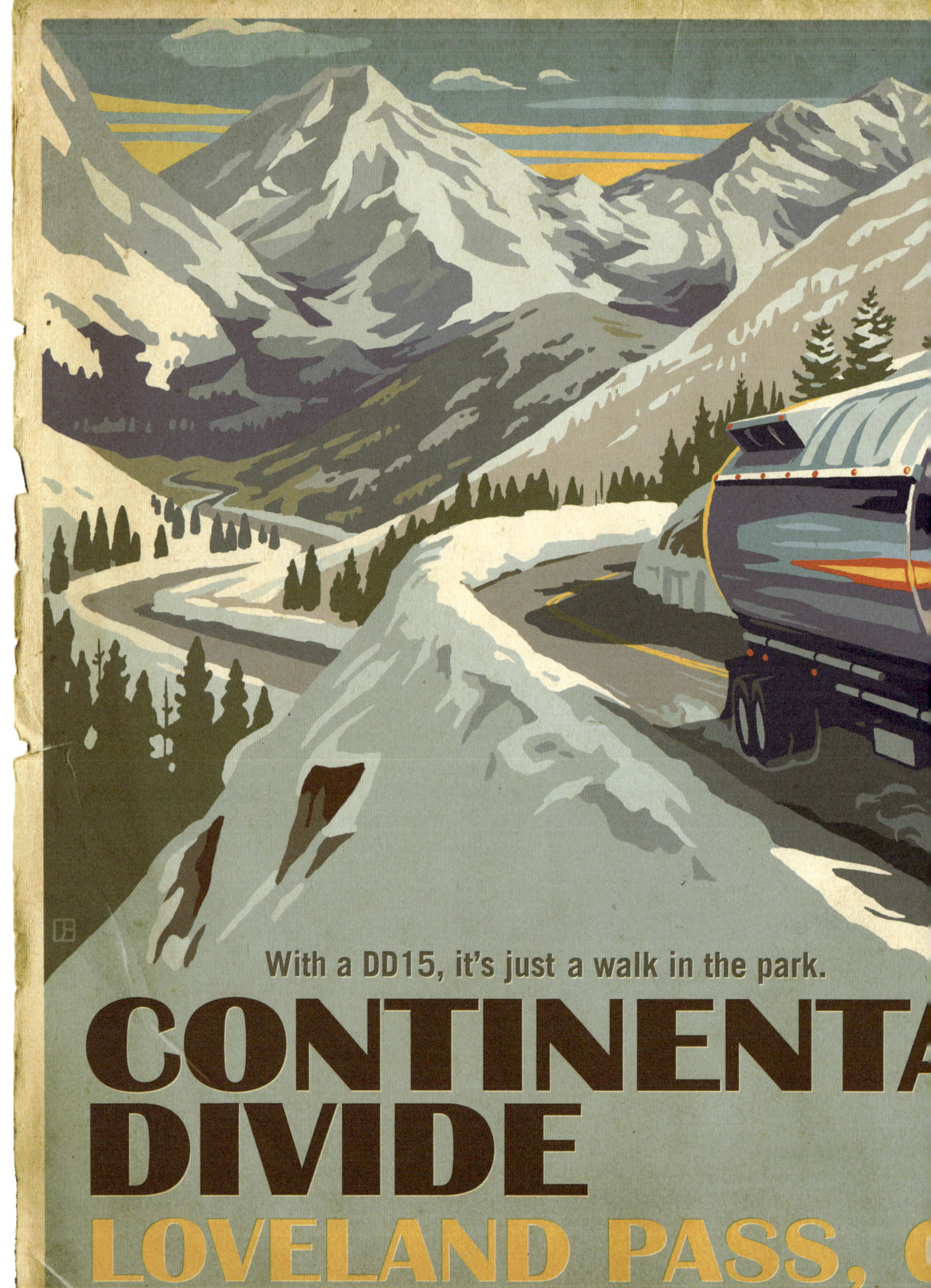
With a DD15, it's just a walk in the park.
CONTINENTAL
DIVIDE
LOVELAND PASS, C

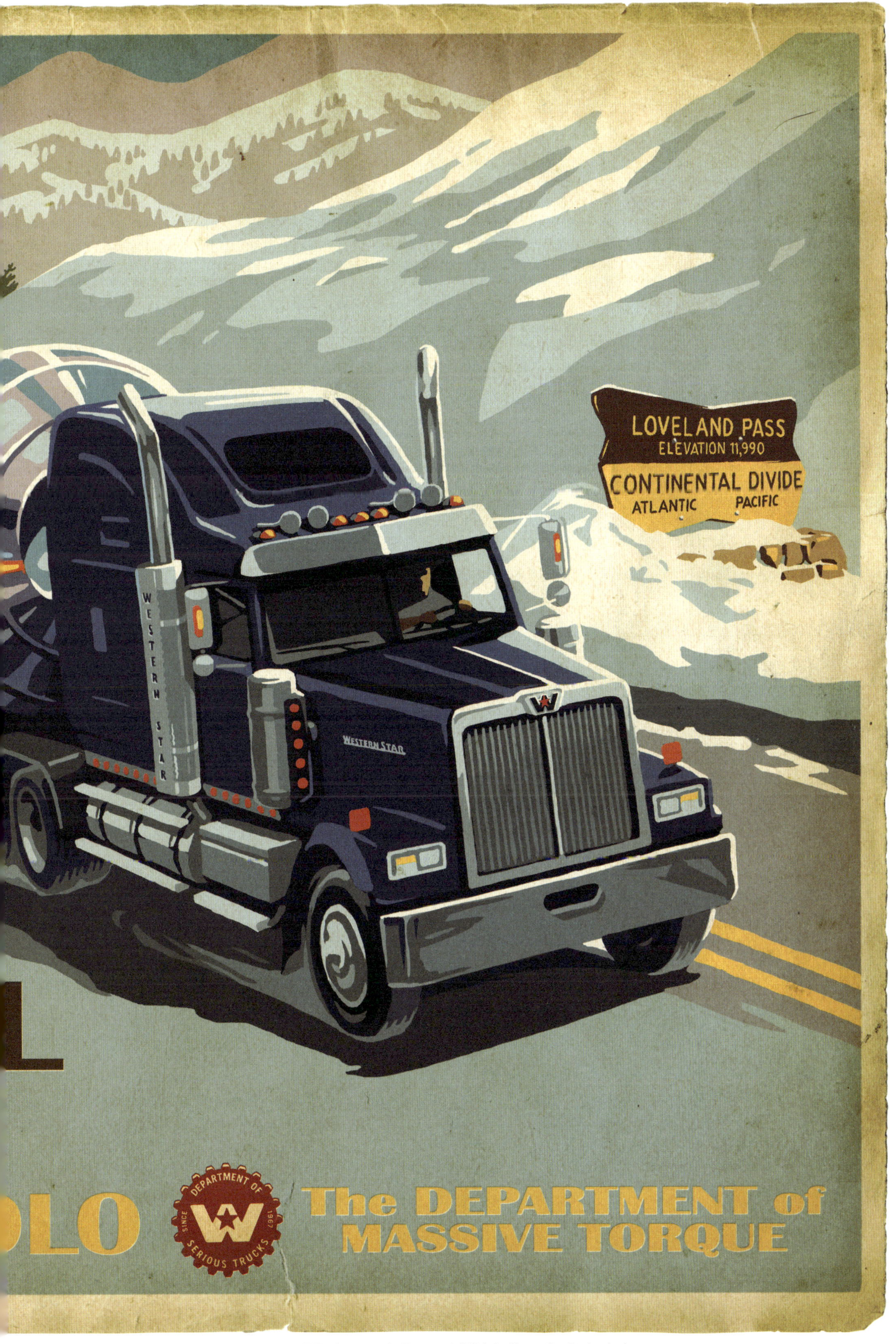


*CMD advertising: Art Director: Jeff Nichols: Western Star Truck calendar*

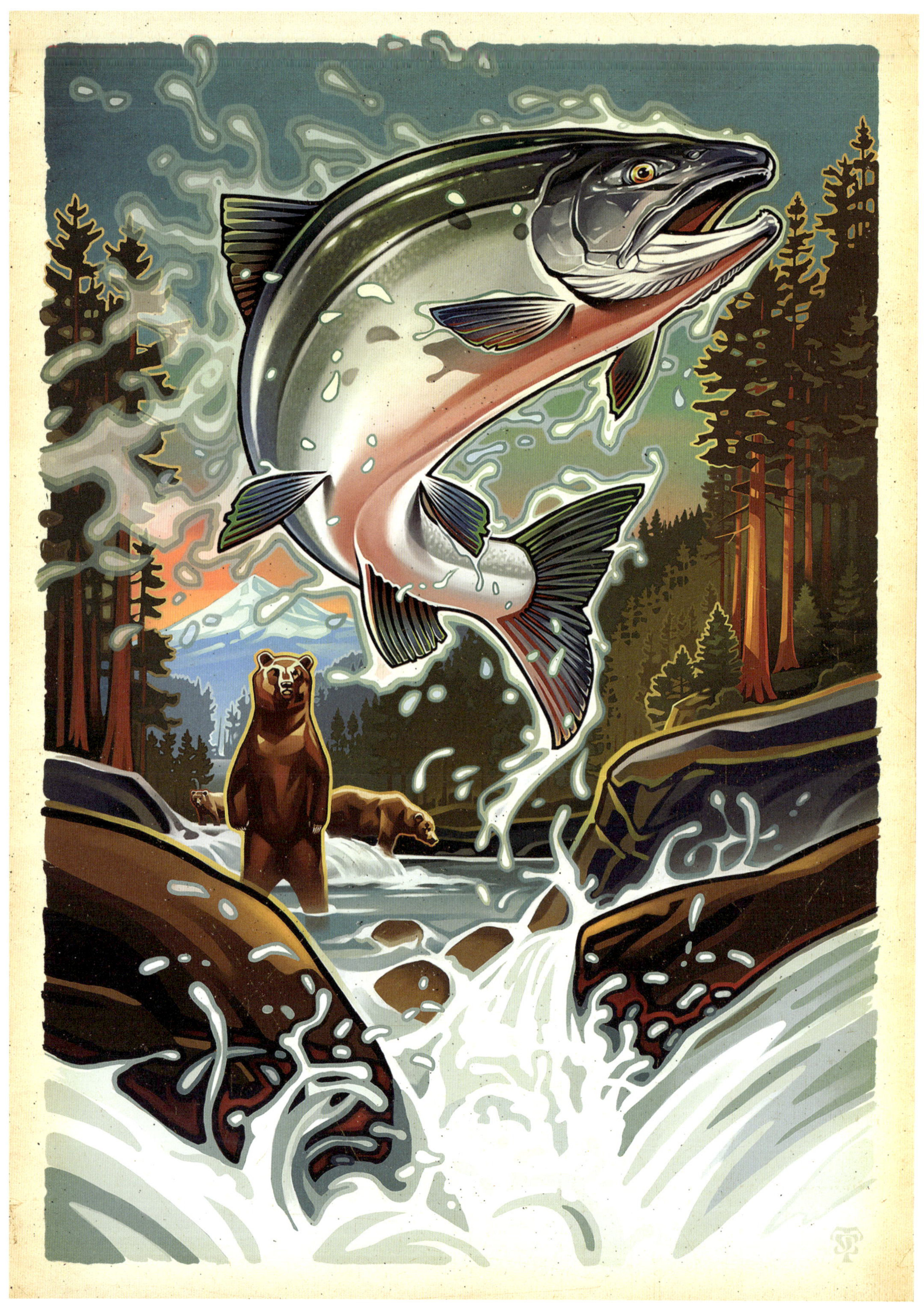

*Self Promotion; Art Director: Jeff Foster*

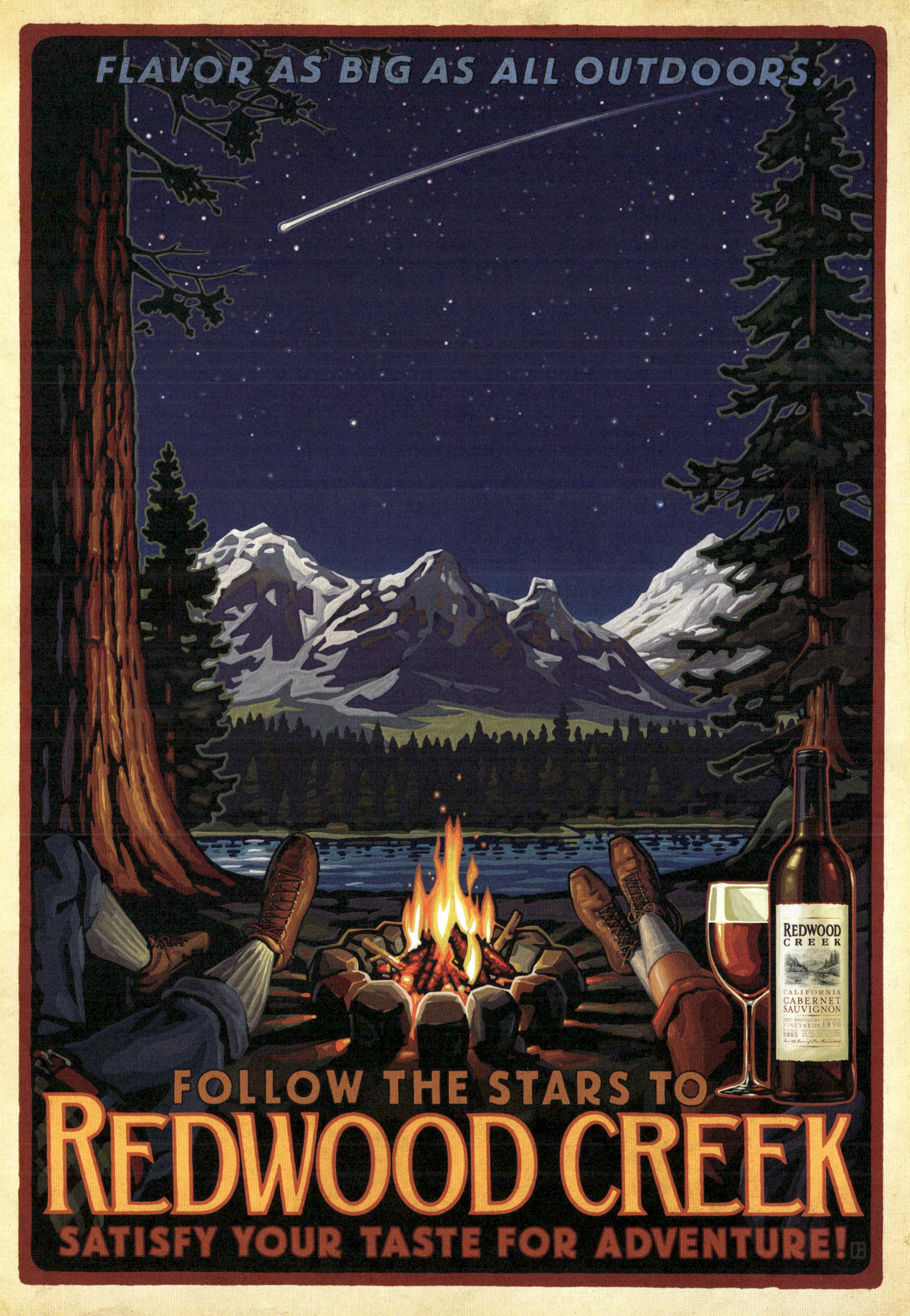


*BBDO West; Art Director: Reece Hoverkamp; Redwood Creek Wines*

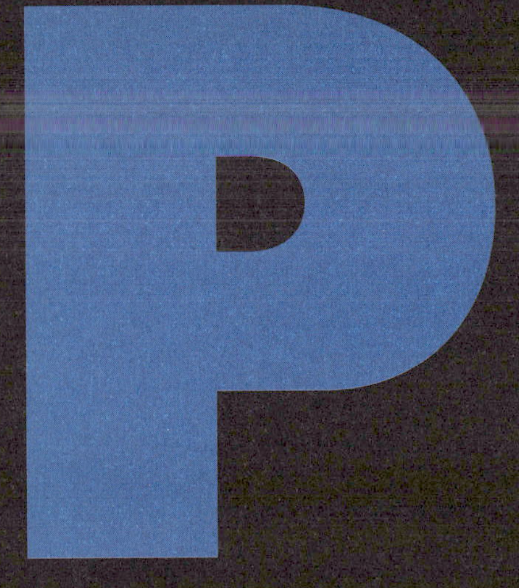

**PRODUCT & INDUSTRIAL DESIGN**

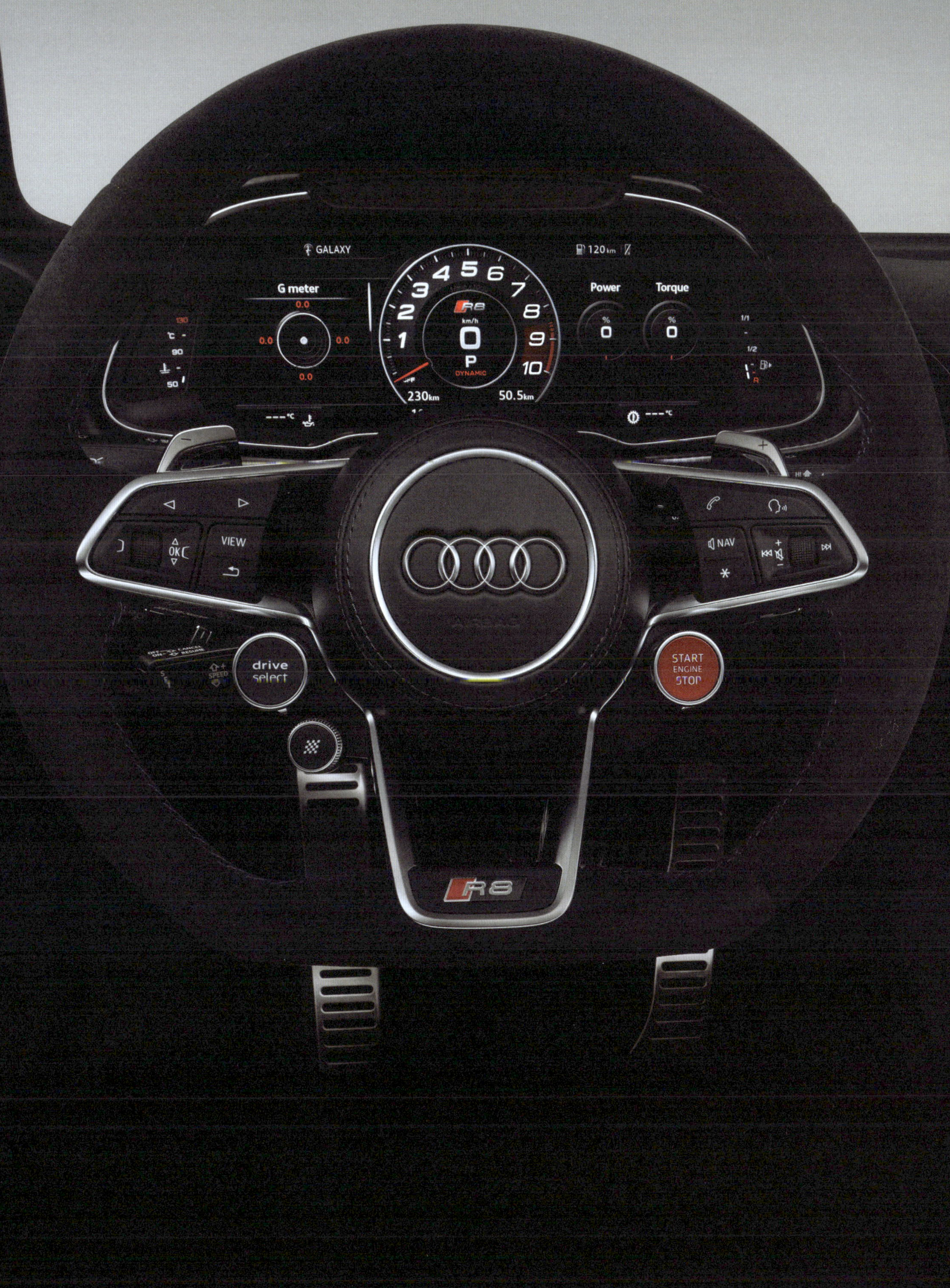

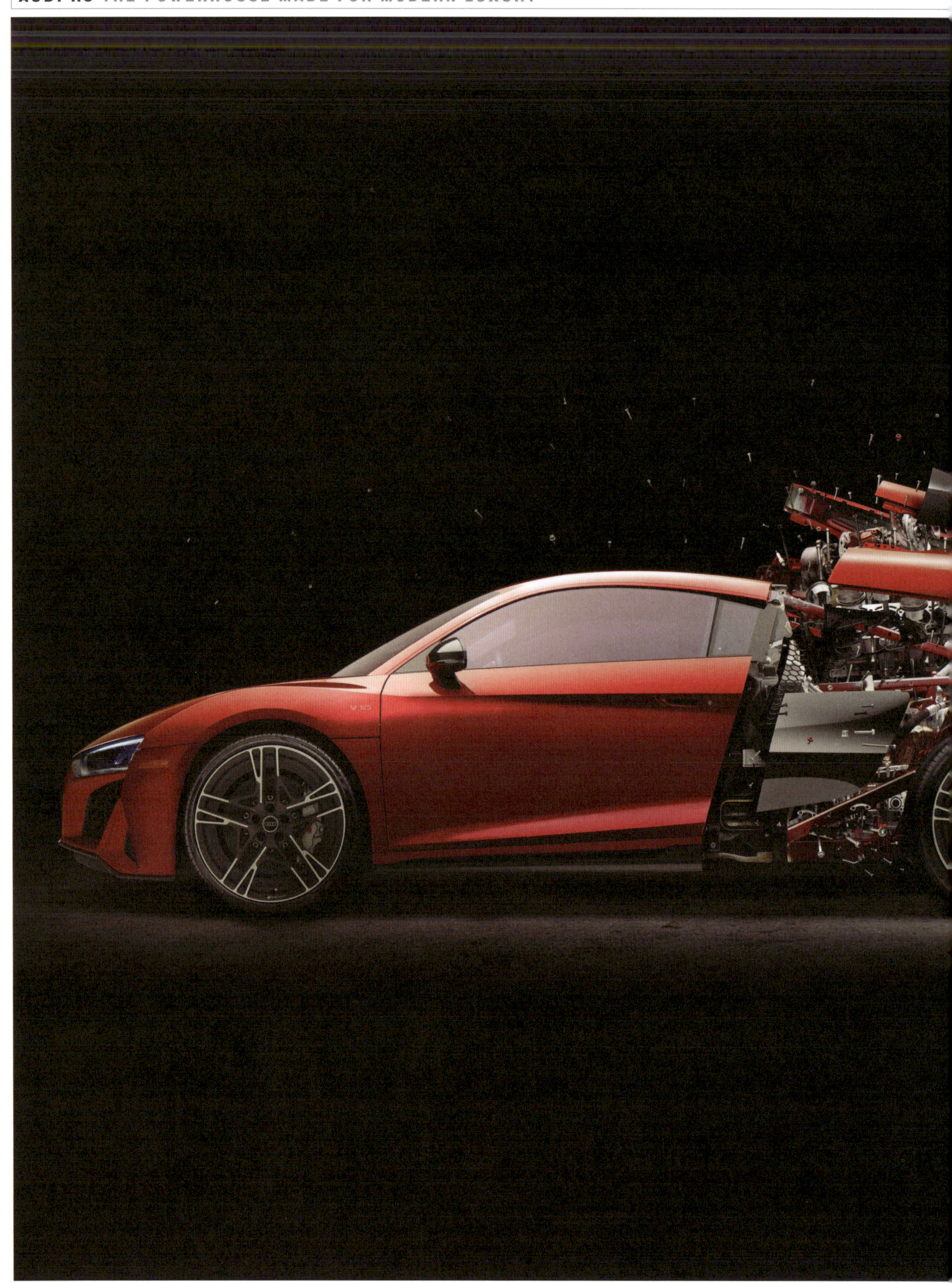

MOTORSPORTS ARE PART OF OUR DNA. WITH
LMS GT3, NO OTHER AUTOMOBILE IS AS CLOSE

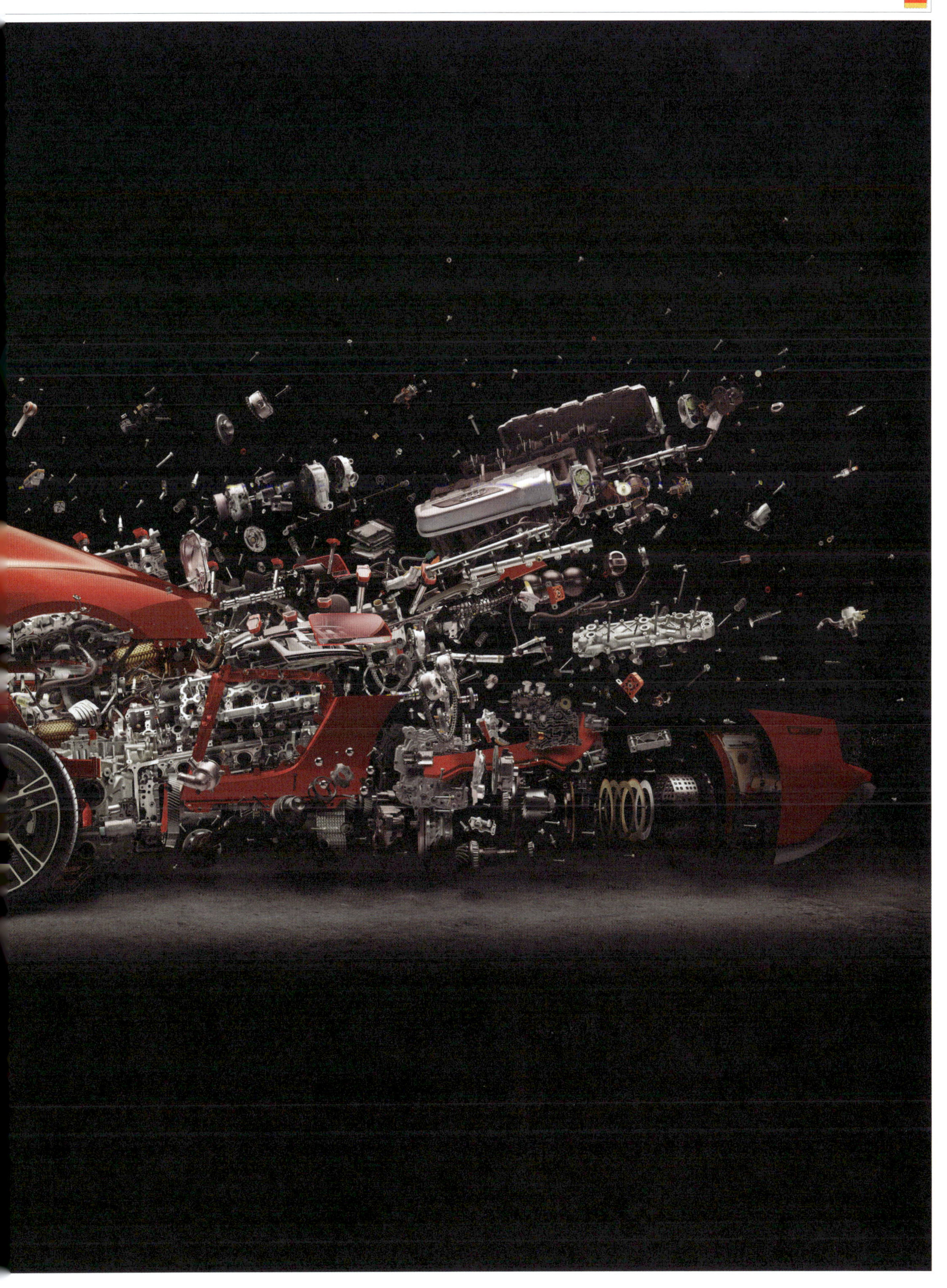



AROUND 50 PERCENT SHARED PARTS WITH THE R8
TO MOTOR RACING AS THE R8. **Oliver Hoffmann,** *Managing Director of Audi Sport GmbH*

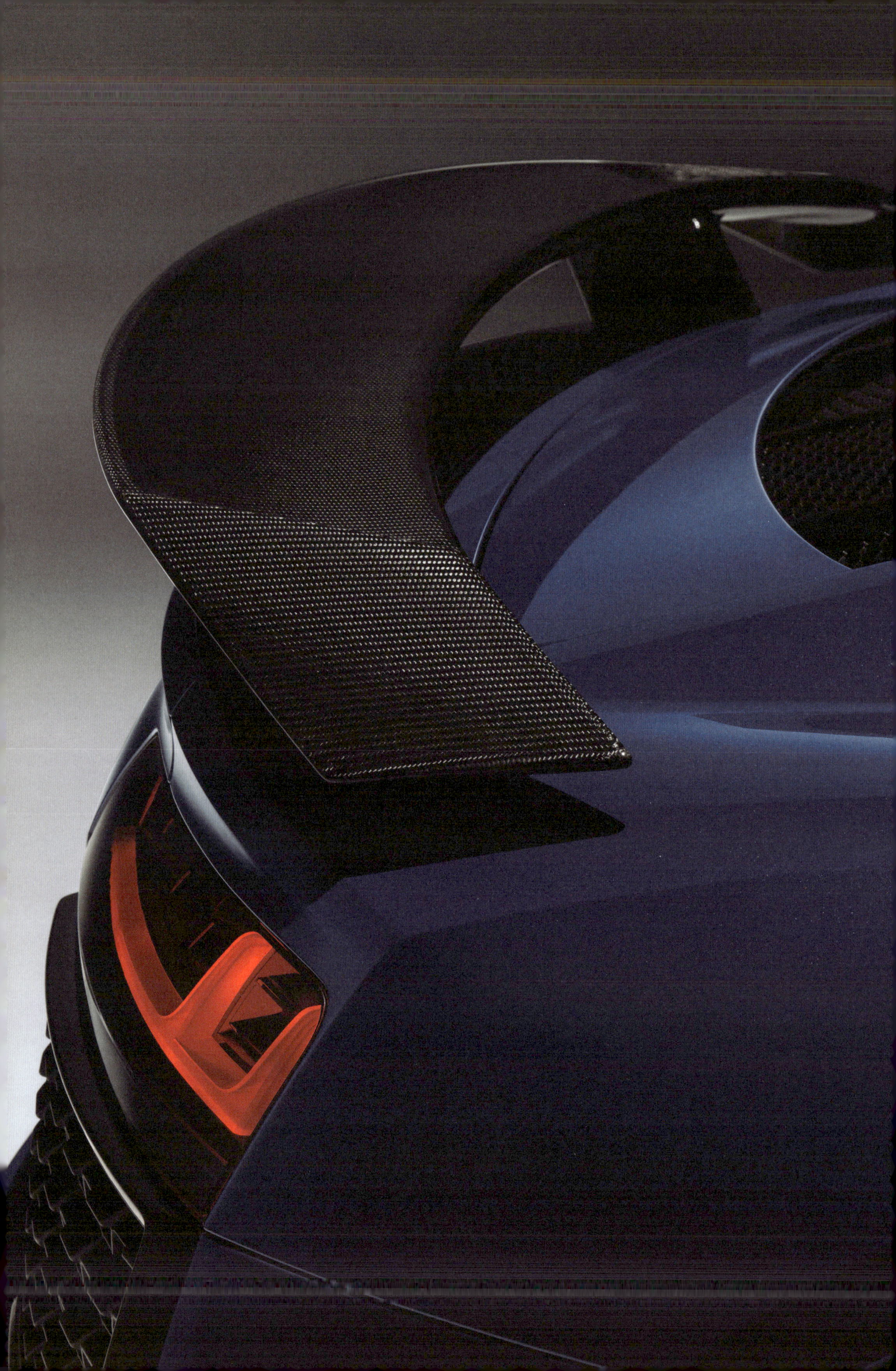

The Audi R8 is more powerful and faster than ever before. As a leader in the world of sports cars, the high-performance R8 sports car is designed for maximum dynamics in all technical areas. ▪ For the new models, modifications have been made to the suspension, which provide increased precision and response. With optional dynamic steering and electromechanical power steering, the response is more direct and precise throughout the entire speed range. This ensures optimum steering with continuous and excellent road contact for every driving situation.

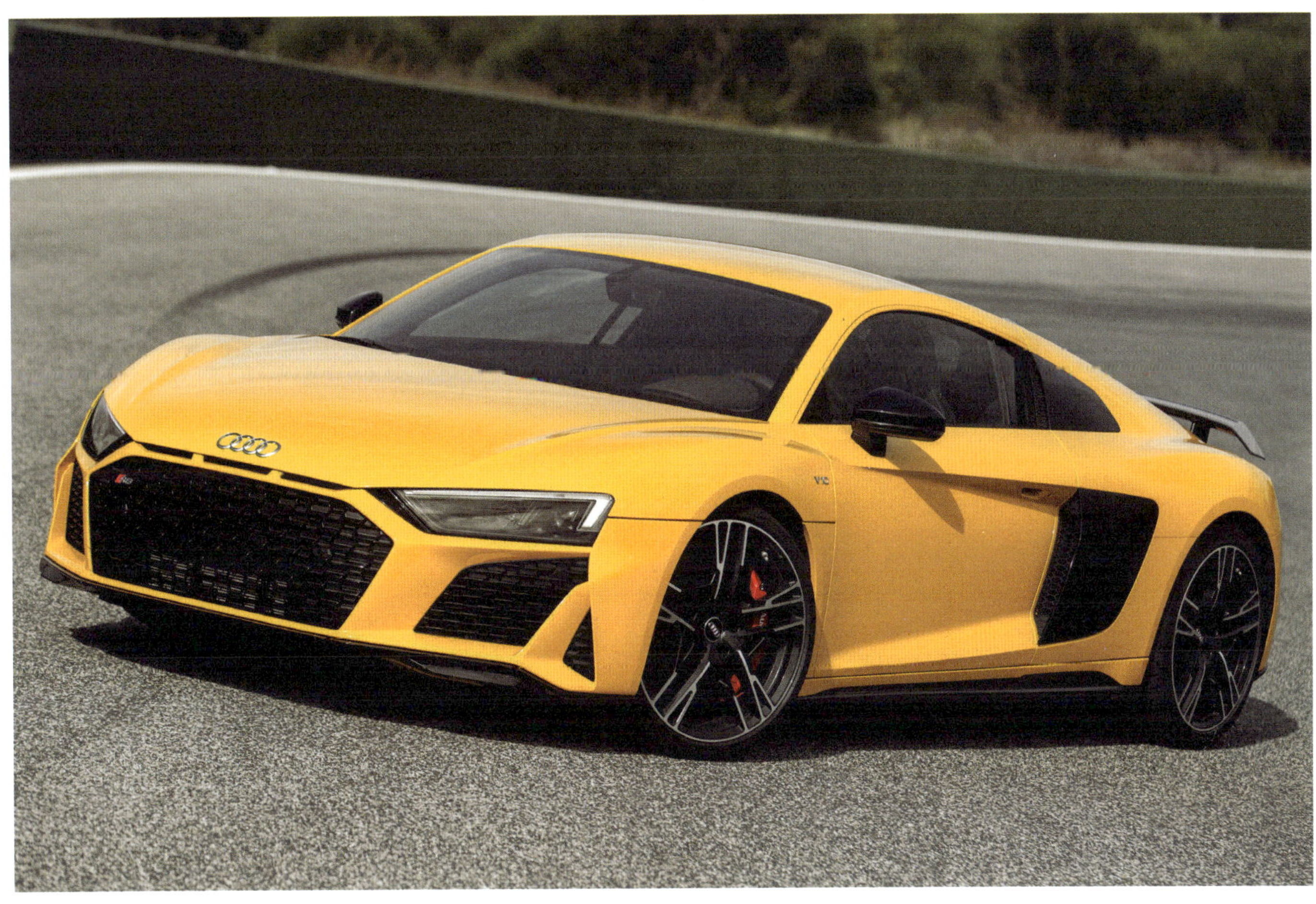

*AUDI AG*

All variants of the Audi R8 are equipped with
a quattro drive powertrain and 7-speed S tronic transmission.
The following specifications are for the U.S. models.

**Audi R8 V10 quattro**
**Horsepower (SAE):** 602
**Torque (lb-ft):** 413 (560Nm)
**Acceleration 0-60 mph (sec):** 3.2
**Top speed (mph):** 205

**Audi R8 V10 performance quattro**
**Horsepower (SAE):** 602
**Torque (lb-ft):** 413 (560Nm)
**Acceleration 0-60 mph (sec):** 3.3
**Top speed (mph):** 204

Featuring dimmed headlights and adjoining design elements, the R8 continues to maintain a sharp look. Reminiscent of the Audi Sport quattro, the new Audi R8 combines the sport elements of its predecessor and modern elements meant for the dynamic driver.

Individuality is a signature characteristic of the Audi R8. Its paint range includes eleven colors, including the new metallic colors Kemora gray and Ascari blue.

The R8 Coupé/Spyder V10 will become the R8 Coupé/Spyder V10 quattro models. The Audi R8 Coupé/Spyder V10 plus will change to the Audi R8 Coupé/Spyder V10 performance quattro, serving as an analogy to the most powerful RS models from Audi Sport.

The new R8 models arrived at dealerships in Germany and other European countries within the first quarter of 2019, with the upgrade of the classic model. Customizable inside and out, the Audi exclusive range offers customers the opportunity to change their car with the highest standards of quality in mind.

The base R8 with a V-10 tuned to make 562 hp and 406 lb-ft of torque will cost $169,000 for the Coupé and $182,100 for the Spyder. For the 602-hp R8 V10 Performance, the price will be $195,500 for the Coupé and $208,100 for the Spyder.

In honor of the V-10-powered R8's 10th anniversary, Audi has also created a limited edition R8 V10 Decennium. Audi revealed that it would only build 222 examples for this model, which will be available in the U.S from a limited global production. The 2020 Audi R8 V10 Decennium will cost $214,995.

**Design features:** The new Audi R8 is equipped with factory-installed 19-inch wheels. 20-inch fully milled wheels in five-V dynamic design with new summer and sport tires, which convey even more precise handling, are available as an option. For the standard-fit steel disks, Audi offers red as opposed to black painted calipers as an option. The calipers for the ceramic brakes generally come with a gray or red finish. The stabilizer at the front axle is optionally made from carbon fiber-reinforced polymer (CFRP) and aluminum, which cuts weight at the front axle by around two kilograms (4.4 lb).

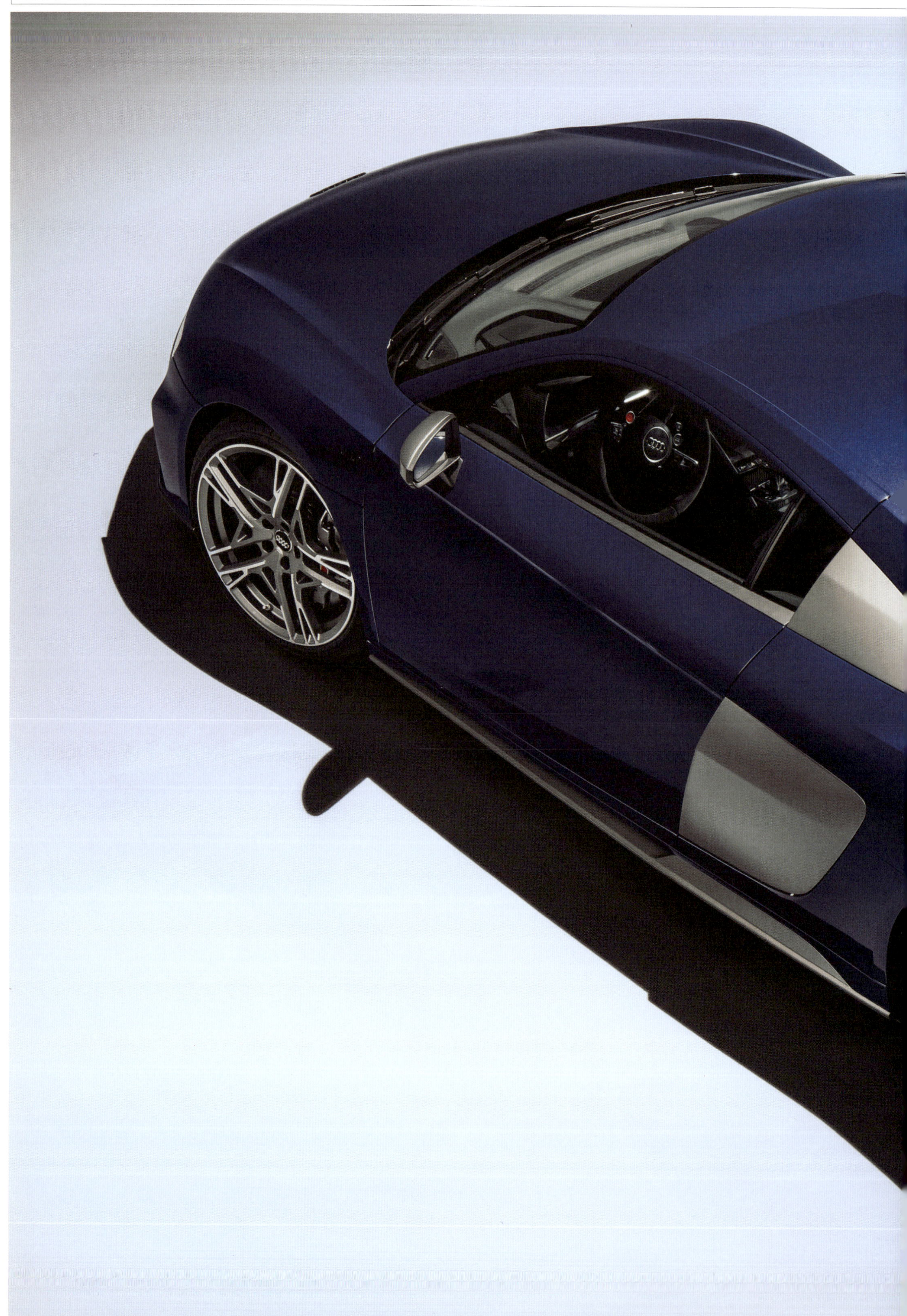

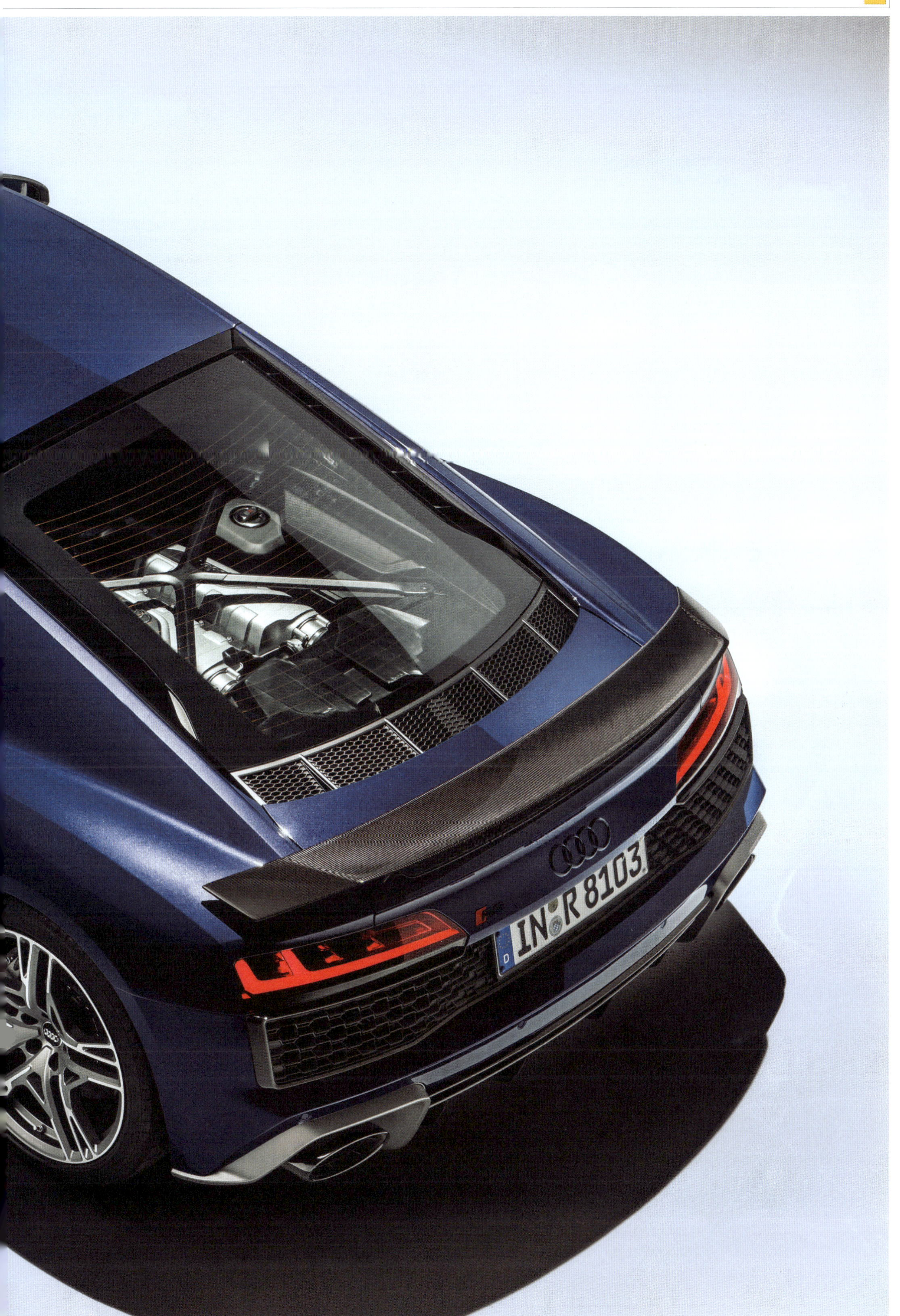


IN R 8103

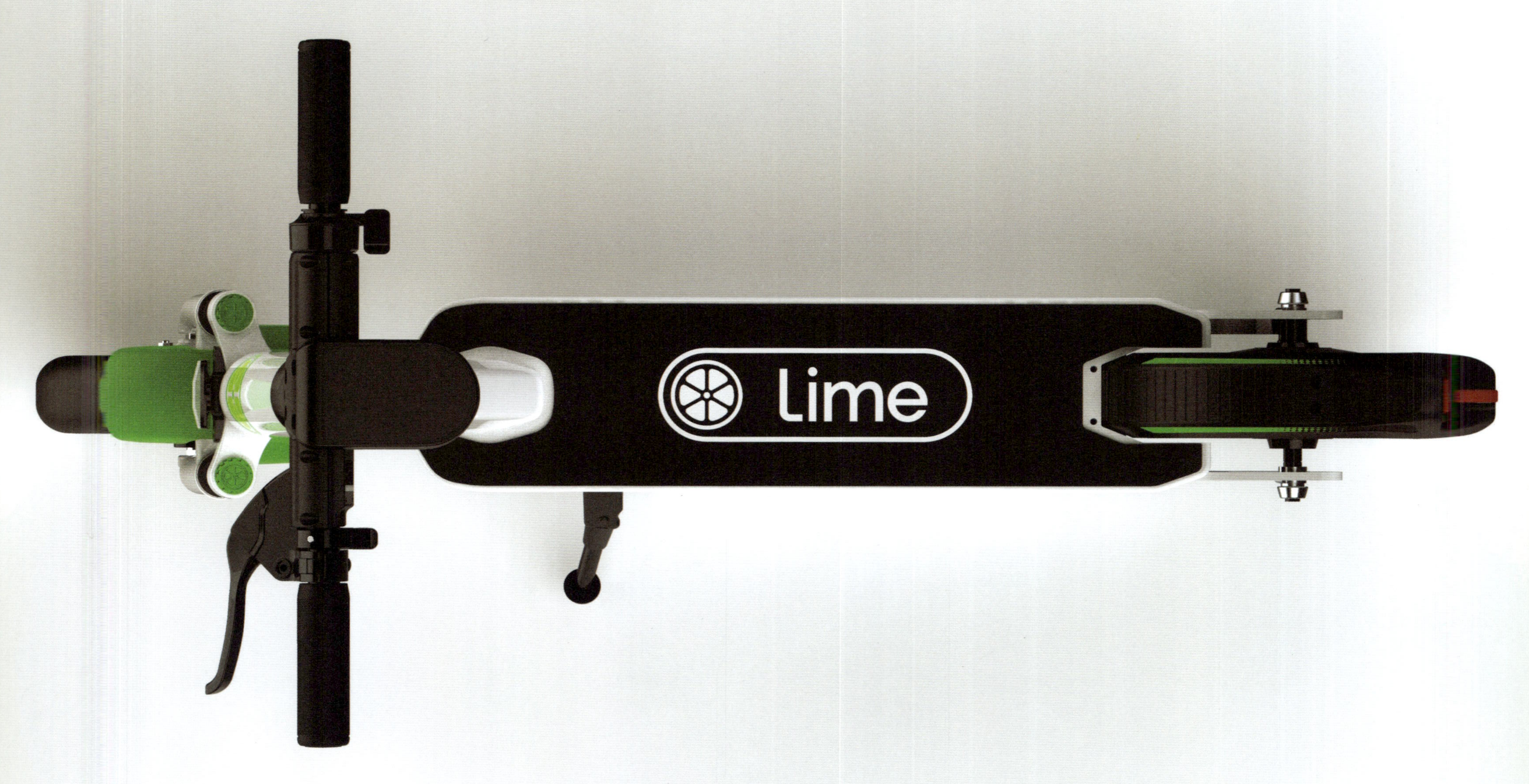

Lime

# LAUNCHED IN OVER 100 CITIES, LIME IS PROUDLY WORKING WITH OUR CITY, UNIVERSITY AND COMMUNITY PARTNERS TO ENABLE SMART MICRO MOBILITY AROUND THE WORLD. **Lime**

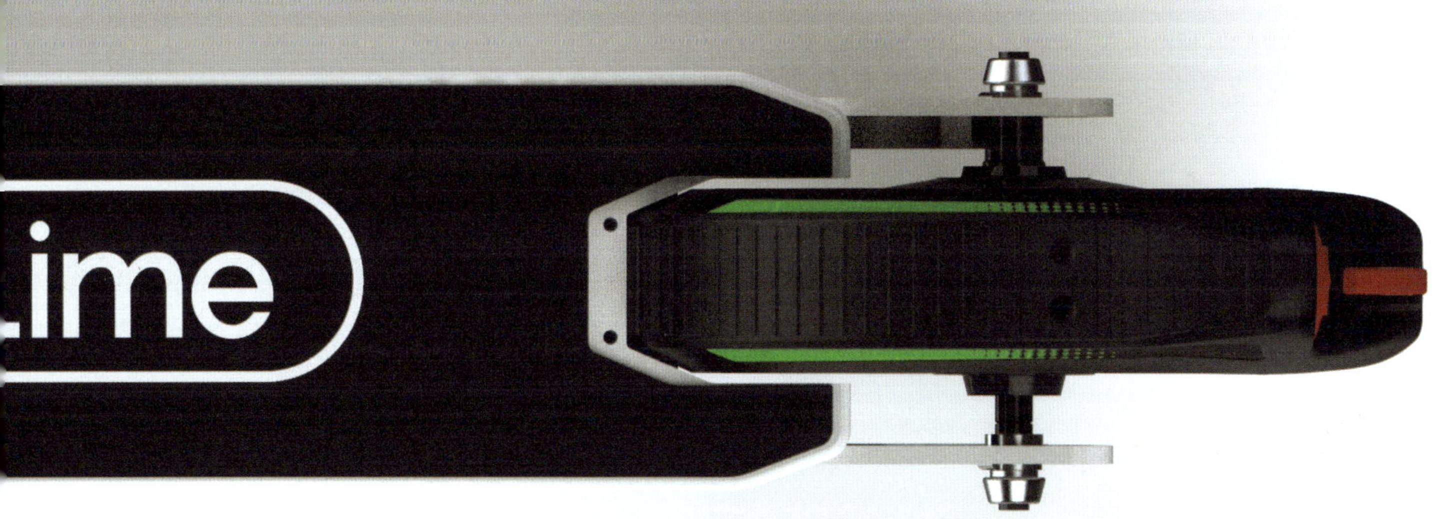

*The Lime-S Generation 3*

Based in the U.S., Lime offers an affordable and eco-friendly solution for commuters who are looking for an easy way out when public transportation is slowing you down. In 2018, the company released the newest model of their electric scooter, titled "The Lime-S Generation 3." Many of its improvements focus on increasing ride comfort.

While the previous scooters featured 8" wheels, the newest model has 10" wheels. The larger wheels roll over bumps, curbs, and potholes more easily, which results in a much smoother ride. The new electric scooter features built-in suspension. The Lime-S Generation 3 scooter includes multi-modal braking, with electrical, drum, and foot brakes. It is designed to be more rigid and withstand any environmental harm. The aluminum frame is considered to be significantly more substantial than previous models. Additionally, there are no external wires or cables.

The battery for this model features a 20% capacity bump, which is meant to increase the scooter's range to 30 miles/48 kilometers. The display screen has also been upgraded to show speed, battery status, and other important data. Checking your battery status can be a hassle, but Lime has made the features of the new model more accessible for riders. With the display's battery indicator, riders can determine a scooter's battery level from as far as a block away with the new LED status indicator lights.

The Lime-S electric scooters are also monitored remotely by local staff along with an independent team of 'Lime Juicers.' If a scooter is running low on power, Juicers will come pick it up, charge the battery, and redeploy the scooter into the community.

In order to follow speed regulations, the Lime scooter has a speed limit of about 14.8 mph, with most cities maintaining a speed limit of 15 mph.

The Lime scooter costs $1 to unlock, plus a small fee per minute. In most cities, the small fee is 15 cents a minute. You will be charged when you relock the scooter.

As modern technology and advancements in transportation continue, Lime understands that our mobile devices are the key to everything. By accessing the Lime app on your phone, you can find the nearest Lime scooters in your area anytime. Ride safely and avoid the traffic in your city.

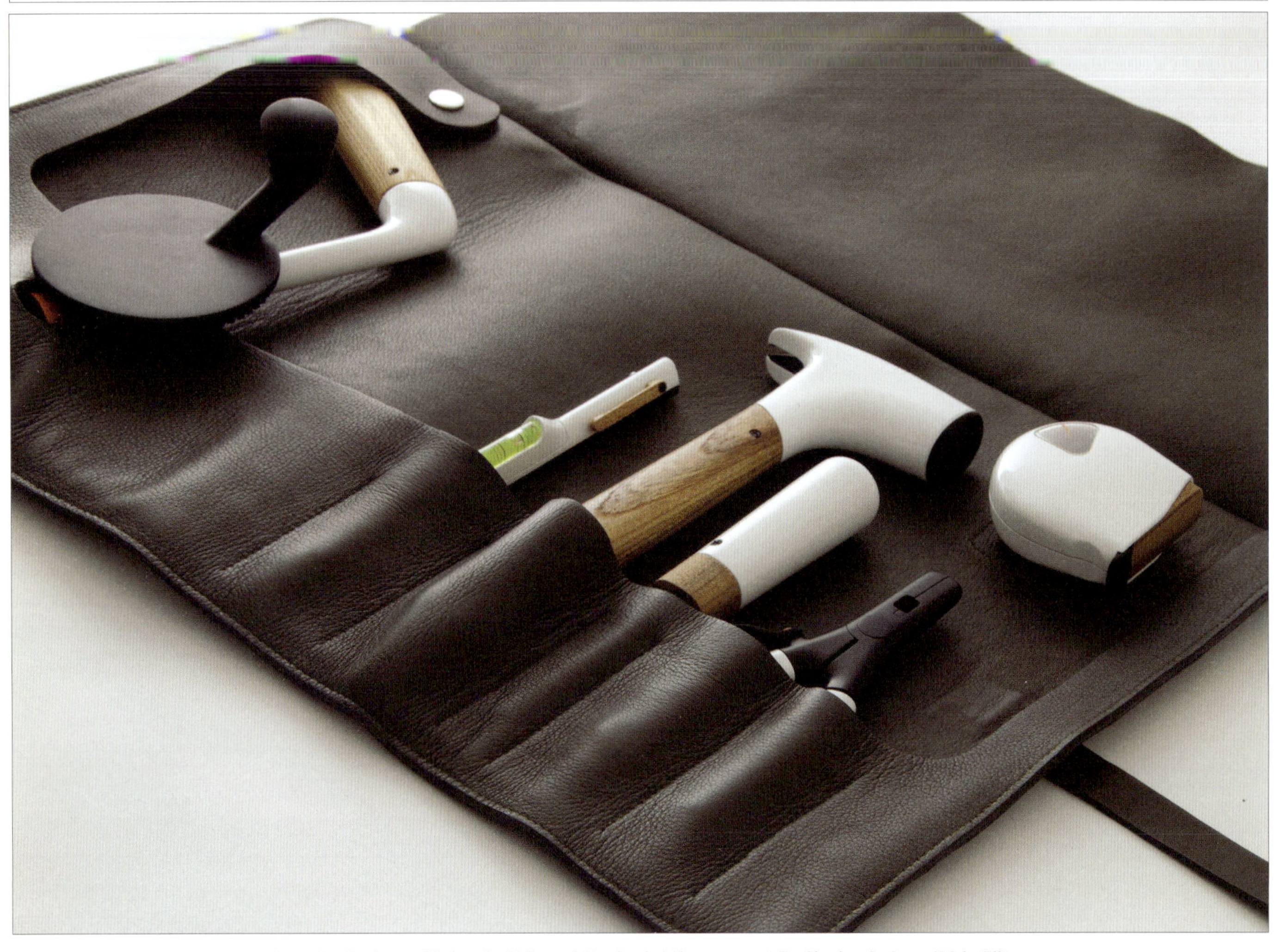

*(Above) Tej Chauhan and Fiskars for Wallpaper* Handmade / (Opposite page) Tej Chauhan for Lexus X John Elliott*

Based in London, Tej Chauhan is an award-winning industrial designer. Chauhan's visual approach to design is strongly held by the belief that every object has the potential to evoke joy, whether it's through form, color, and texture. Regardless of brand position or production budget, the product should resonate with an audience first and foremost. Inspired by everyday interactions and experience, Chauhan's team of multidisciplinary creatives understand how an emotional connection can be a powerful tool in today's market.

The latest project from Tej Chauhan is an unexpected collaboration, fusing together the automotive industry with streetwear. Inspired by the design of the Nike Air Force 1's, luxury car manufacturer Lexus developed the idea for an exclusive car tire with an artistic spin on the sneaker. Tasked by Lexus and advertising agency TeamOne, Chauhan created a set of tires for Lexus' first crossover vehicle, the 2019 UX. The resulting product "Sole of the UX" was formed as a collaboration between Chauhan, Lexus, and Los Angeles streetwear and athleisure designer John Elliot.

For the concept, Chauhan envisioned the product as the 'footwear' of the car, taking design elements from Elliot's NikeLab Air Force 1 sneaker. The tire includes the classic white on white, high platform of the sneaker to give it dimension and distinct space between each curve of the tire. Chauhan's team developed the textures and patterns for the tires, and worked closely with their prototyping partner 3D Systems Benelux to construct them.

The Nike Tyre encapsulates the signature, sleek, and modern design of the sneaker, distinguishing it as a class of its own in the Nike collection. With the 'swoosh' logo across the sides, the tire becomes an extension of the Nike brand while maintaining a sense of individuality.

The set of 18-inch Lexus UX wheels were revealed at 2019's New York Fashion Week in early February. Although they are not being sold to the general public, the tire will make appearances at various fashion shows throughout the year. "The "Sole of the UX" is a one-of-a-kind creation, drawing from urban style. Fashion-forward and innovative products await for the future of the automotive industry.

**Features:**

- The tire's tread designs include rubber imprints of the Nike logo, and swirls and waves in multiple textures and patterns.
- The tire's metal air valve is intended to evoke the metal lace tip that Elliot designed for the sneaker.
- The Lexus logo is included in the center of the wheel
- Metallic black spokes
- The internal structure was created using a CNC (Computer numerical control) machine
- Exterior elements formed using a mix of 3D printing and handcrafted materials
- Specialized rubber paints
- Specially sourced premium tumbled leather
- Each tire consisted of 60 parts
- The tire carries the full weight of the Lexus UX

With a flashback to the past, Tej Chauhan has also delved into the creation of imaginative utensils. As a collaboration with Finnish brand Fiskars, the collection of six hand tools consists of simple and elaborate design elements, which explores the dichotomy of the old and the new. The 2013 Wallpaper* Handmade collaboration is featured above.

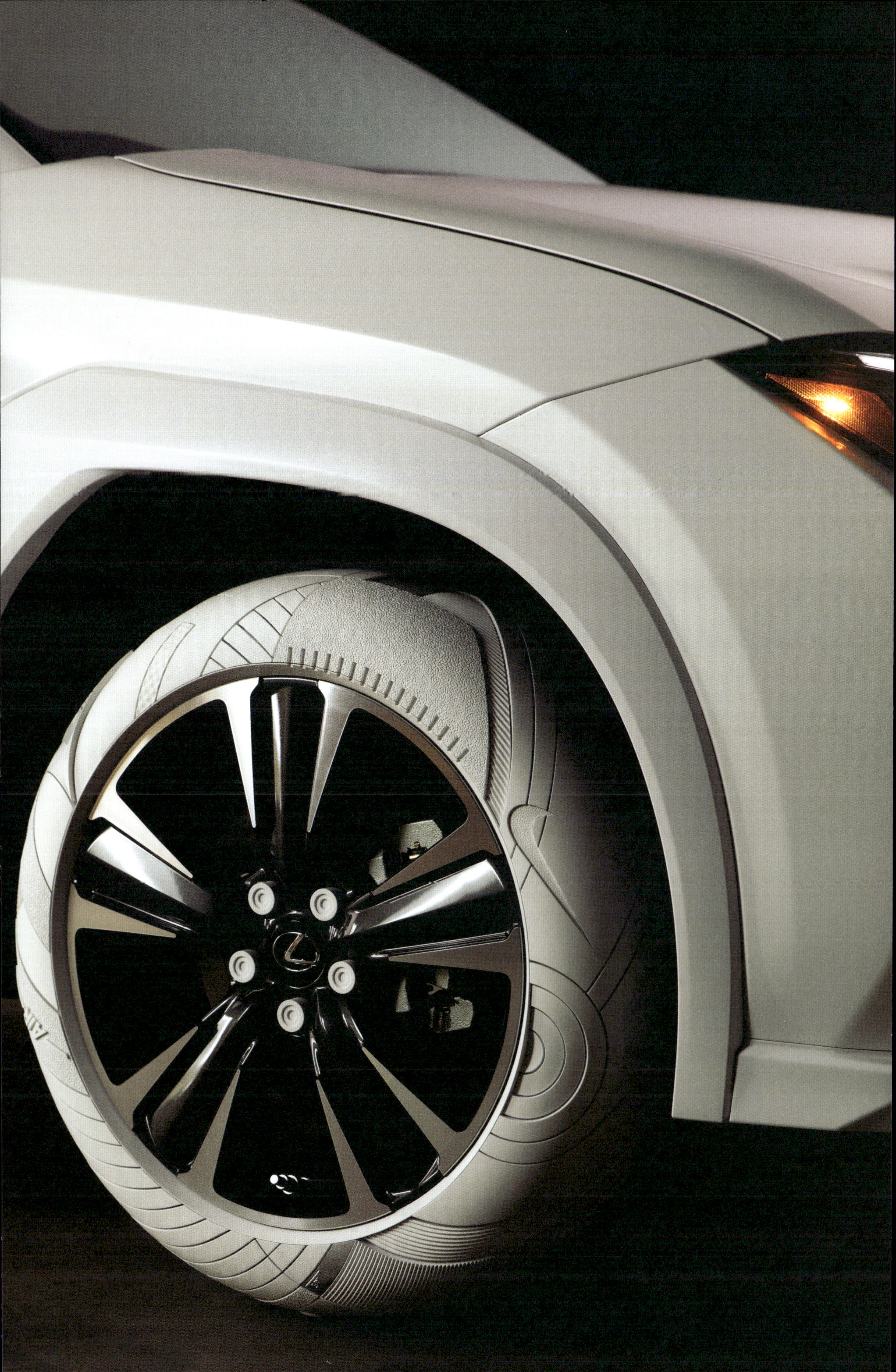

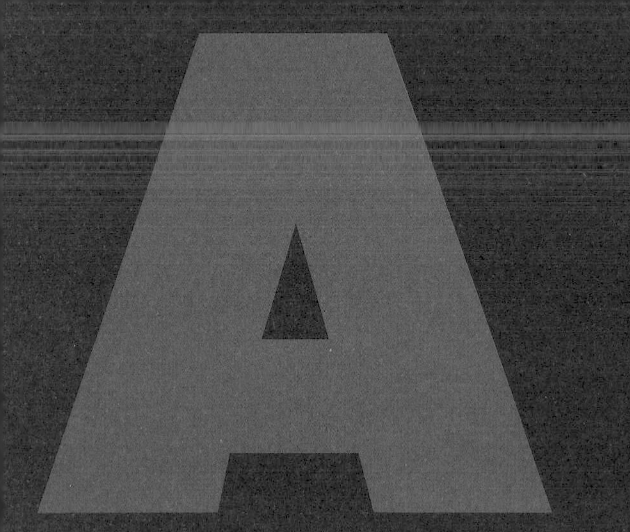

**ARCHITECTURE & EXHIBITS**

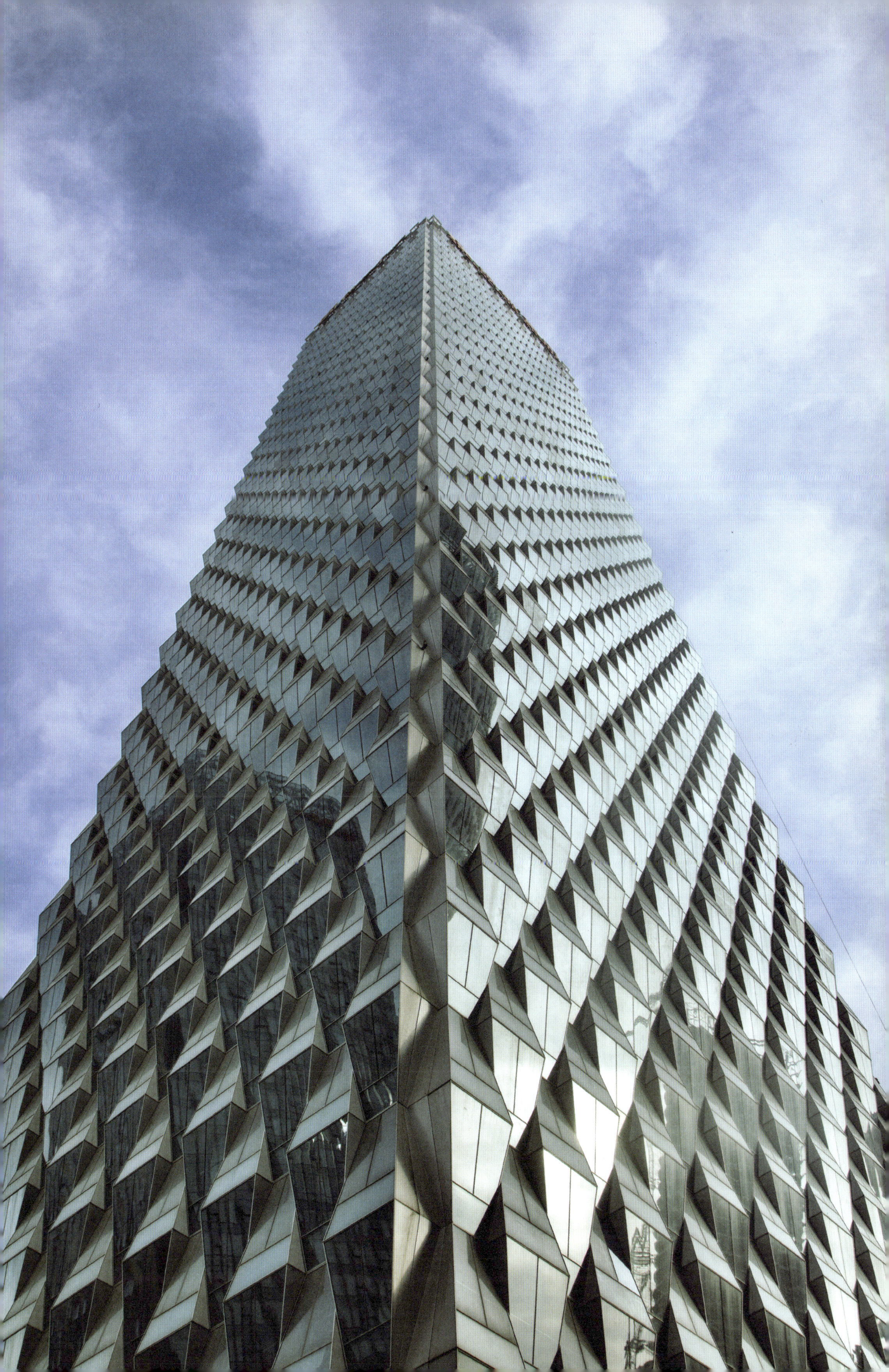

Architecture 2030 is a non-profit, non-partisan, and independent organization established in 2002, focused on creating solutions for the climate change crisis. Architecture 2030 pursues two primary objectives: to achieve a dramatic reduction in the energy consumption and greenhouse gas (GHG) emissions of the built environment; and to advance the development of sustainable, resilient, equitable, and carbon-neutral buildings and communities.

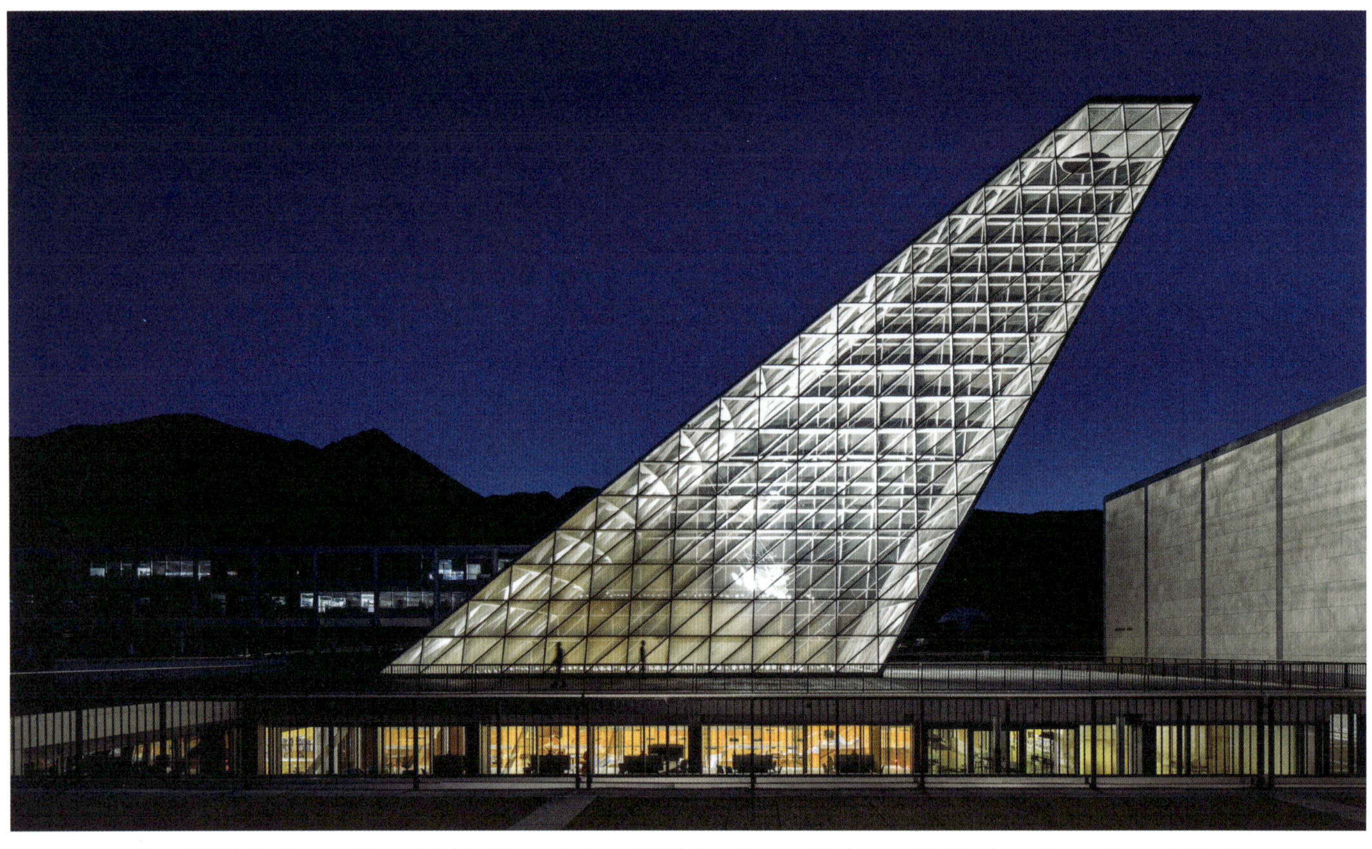

*(Page 115) "Beijing Greenland Center;" Architect, Interior Designer, MEP Engineer, Structural Engineer, and Civil Engineer: Skidmore, Owings & Merrill; Image courtesy SOM / © LV Hengzhong / (Above) "U.S. Air Force Academy – Center for Character & Leadership Development;" Architect, Interior Designer, Structural Engineer, MEP Engineer, and Civil Engineer: Skidmore, Owings & Merrill; Image courtesy SOM / © Magda Biernat*

Architecture 2030 initiated the 2030 Challenge in 2006, which led to the zero emissions movement in the global building sector. The challenge has been adopted by architectural design firms, states, cities, counties, the American Institute of Architects (AIA), International Union of Architects, US Conference of Mayors, and the China Accord.

To support the 2030 Challenge, the American Institute of Architects created the 2030 Commitment Program, which aims to transform the practice of architecture to respond to the climate crisis in a way that is holistic, firm-wide, project-based, and data-driven. Over 400 A/E/P firms have joined the 2030 Commitment Program since 2010. Two firms committed to the challenge are ZGF and Skidmore, Owings & Merrill LLP (SOM).

ZGF is a sustainable architecture and interior design firm with several offices across the U.S. and Canada. ZGF has garnered more than 1,000 design awards, including the American Institute of Architects' highest honor, the Architecture Firm Award. The featured project from ZGF is the Central Energy Facility at Stanford University in California. Part of the Stanford Energy System Innovation (SESI) Initiative, the new energy system replaces a 100% fossil fuel based combined cogeneration plant with grid-sourced electricity and a first-of-its-kind heat recovery system. It has yielded substantial results for the entire campus: greenhouse gas emissions decreased by 68%, fossil fuel use reduced by 65%, and water use reduced by 18%. Designed by ZGF, in partnership with Affiliated Engineers, the facility integrates into the surrounding campus, with sustainability at the forefront. The Central Energy Facility embodies the latest technological advances and ecodistrict planning solutions. The award-winning project presents the future of sustainable architecture and what can be achieved to combat climate change.

Founded in 1936, SOM has become one of the largest and most influential architecture, interior design, engineering, and urban planning firms in the world. With more than 10,000 projects in over 50 countries, SOM is committed to design excellence, innovation, and sustainability. In support of the 2030 Challenge, SOM has developed various projects including the Beijing Greenland Center, the Poly International Plaza, the Denver Union Station, and the U.S Air Force Academy, Center for Character & Leadership Development. With nearly 2,000 awards, SOM is the only practice to have won the Architecture Firm Award from the American Institute of Architects twice. To confront the climate change crisis, SOM aims to pursue sustainability with a holistic approach. By redefining the standards of sustainable design, SOM is committed to being a leader within the industry.

Take a look around every city environment, and ask yourselves whether we are doing enough to combat climate change. The 2030 Challenge aims to transform the architecture industry, one building at a time. By 2030, let's make a difference, as architects, engineers, designers, and planners, join together to make a difference.

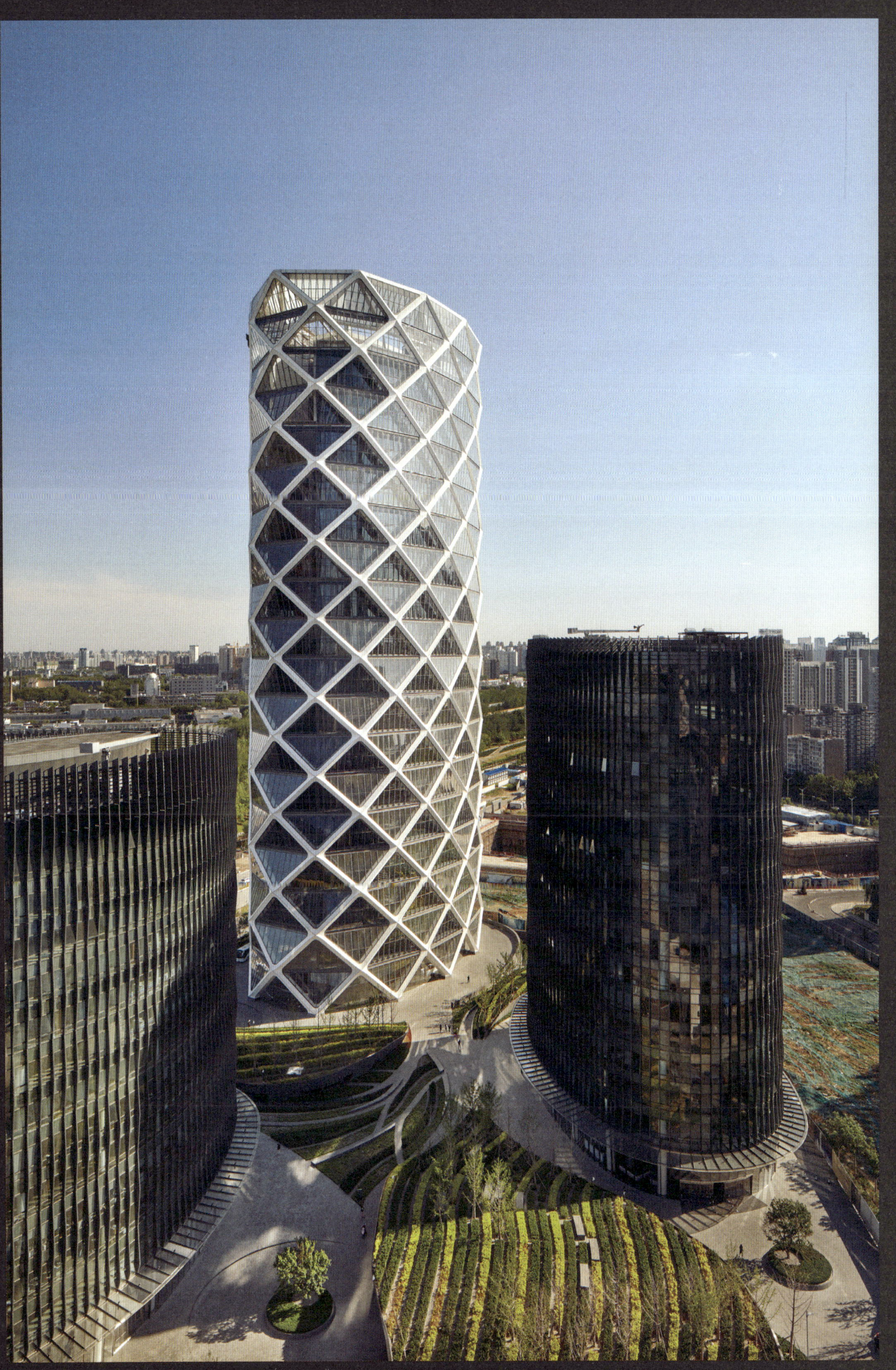



*"Poly International Plaza;" Architect, Interior Designer, Structural Engineer, and Civil Engineer: Skidmore, Owings & Merrill; Image courtesy SOM / © Bruce Damonte*

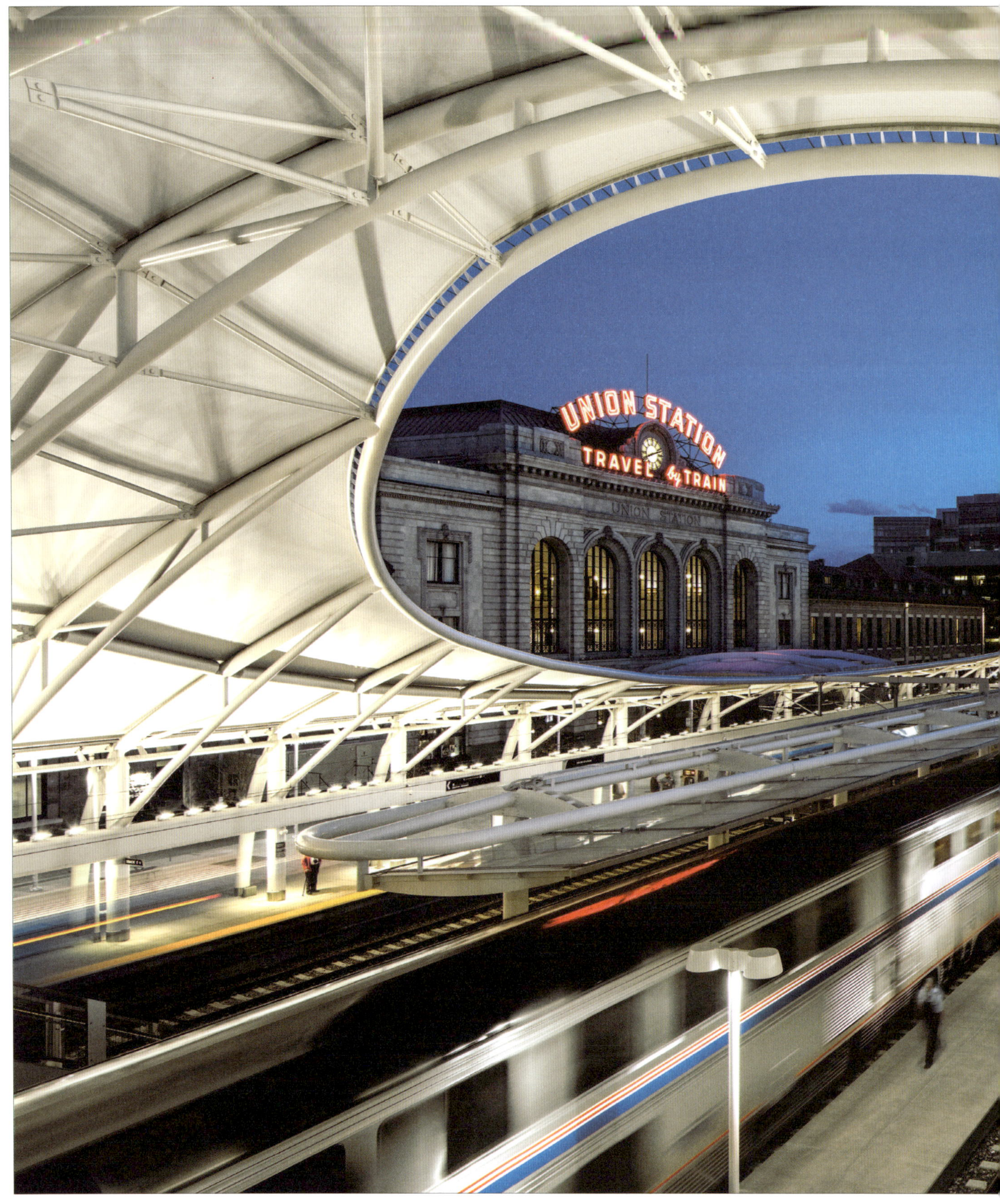


WHEN A DESIGN TEAM TAKES ON A PROJECT WITH A CLEAR VISION AND A HOLISTIC APPROACH, IT HAS THE POTENTIAL TO CREATE THE MOST MEANINGFUL, INNOVATIVE, AND ENDURING ARCHITECTURE OF OUR TIME. **SOM architect Mina Hasman**

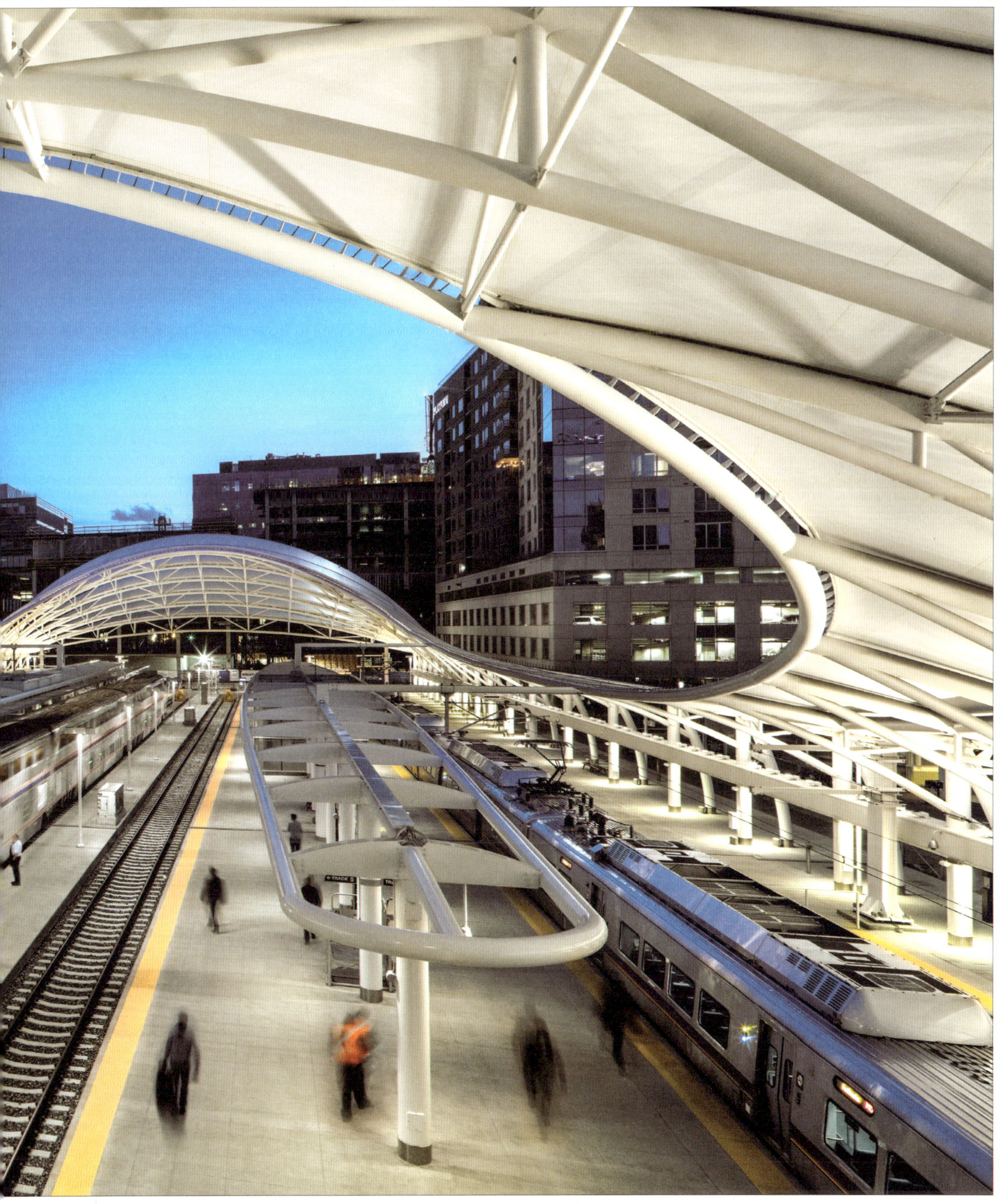

*"Denver Union Station;" Architect & Designer of the project's master plan: Skidmore, Owings & Merrill; Image courtesy SOM / © Magda Biernat*

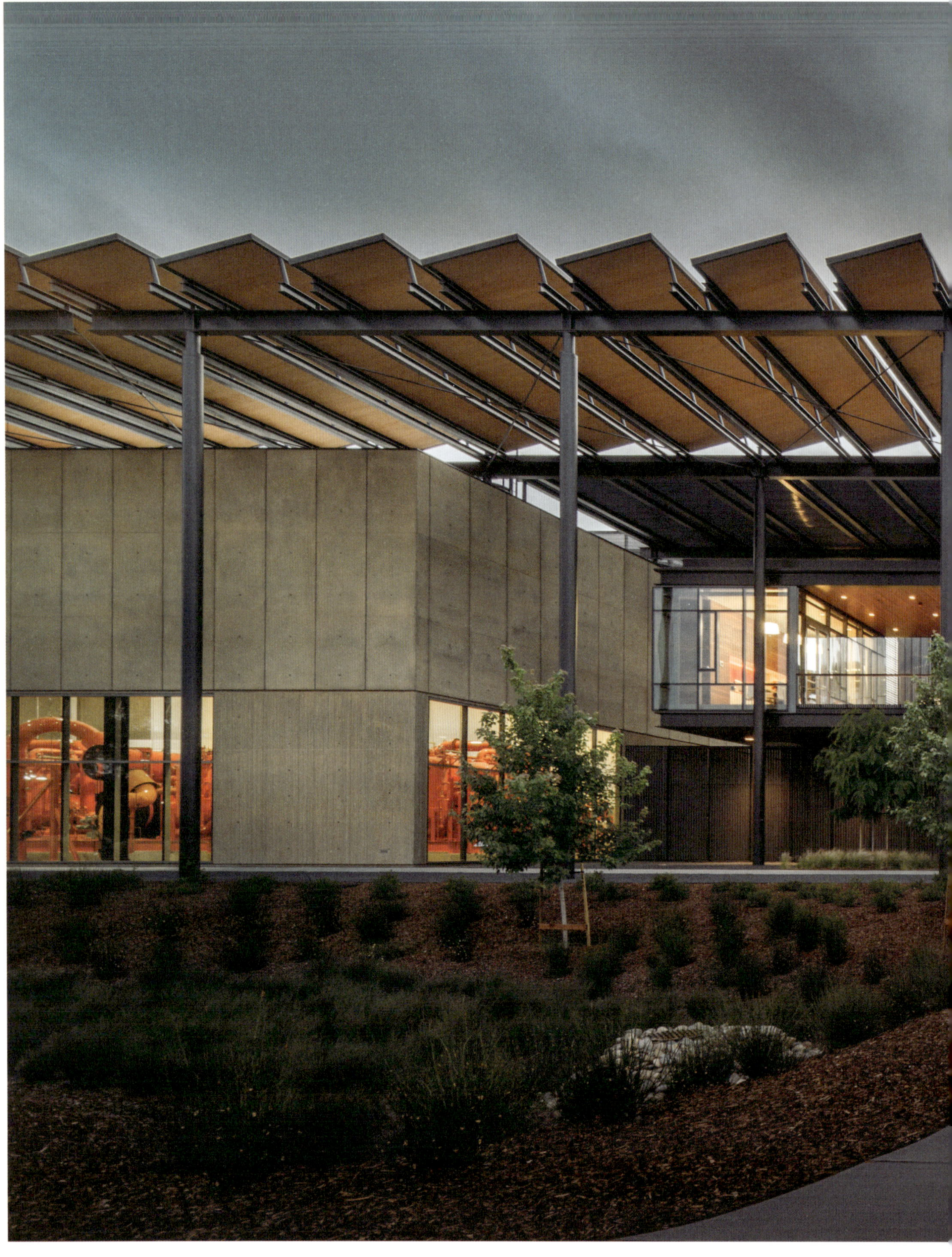

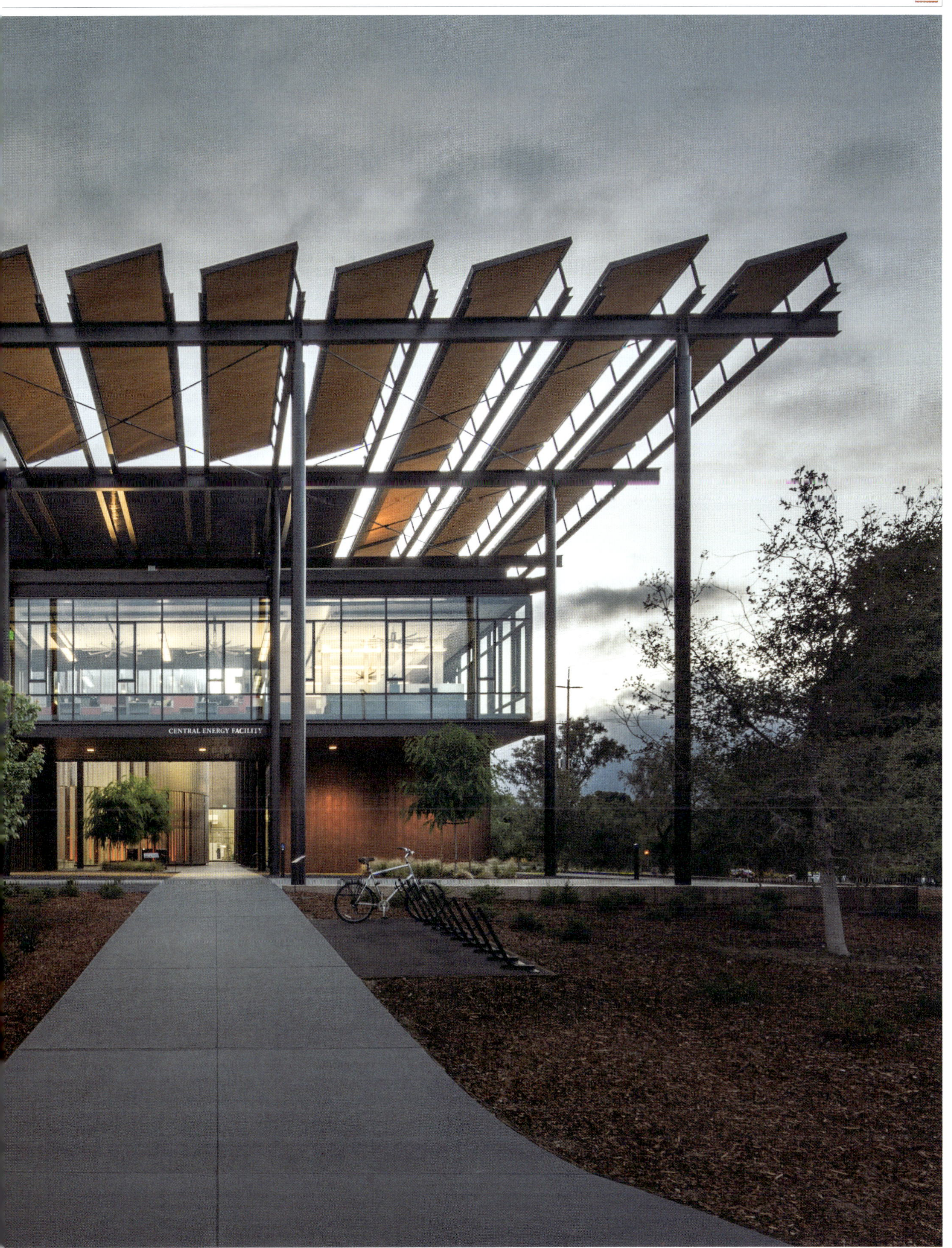

*Exterior at evening; Photographer: Matthew Anderson*

Based in Melbourne, Matt Gibson Architecture + Design has rapidly become one of Australia's best architectural and interior design studios within the past decade. MGA+D has garnered awards over several categories including residential, corporate, and retail from the Design Institute of Australia and the Australian Institute of Architects. In 2009, MGA+D won the World Award for Retail Design in Dubai by the International Federation of Interior Designers. They have also won the Inaugural Award for Australia's Best Emerging Practice from the Design Institute of Australia.

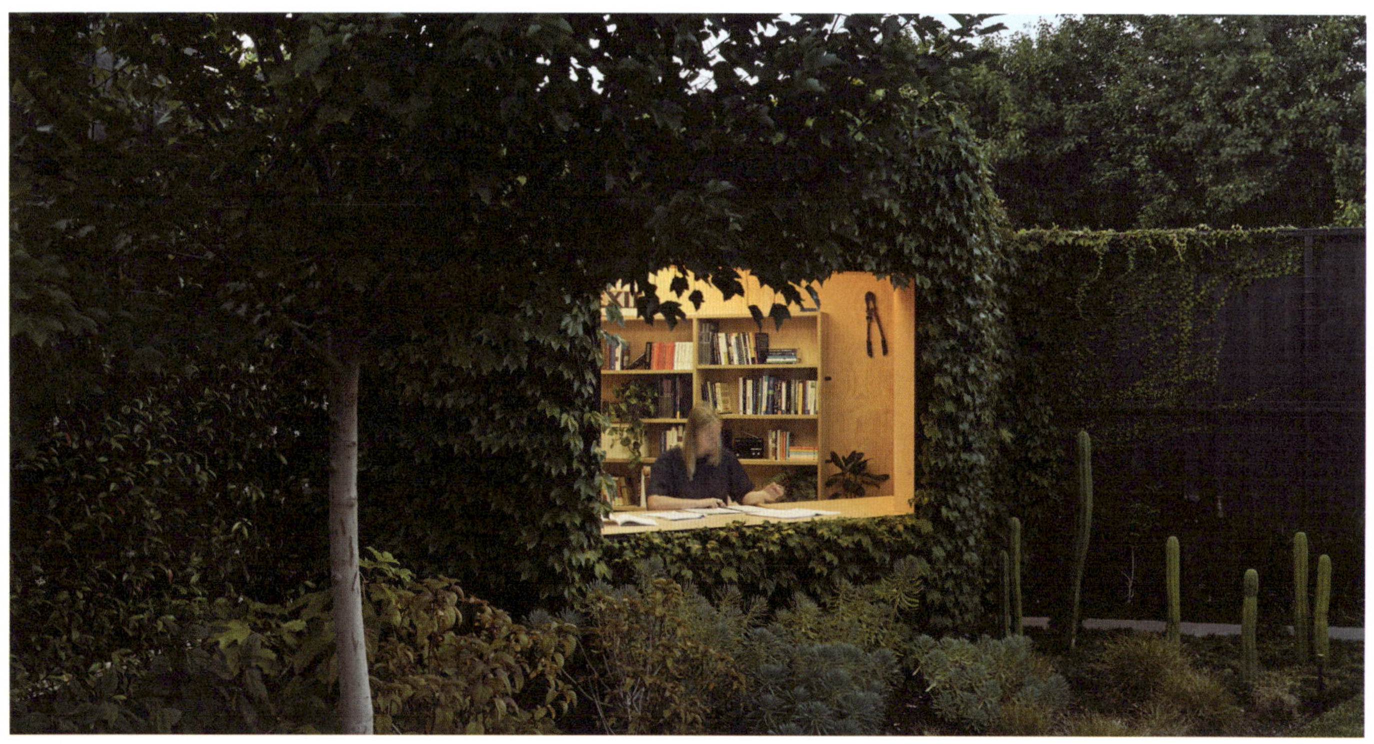

*"Writer's Shed;" Photos by Shannon McGrath; Architecture and Interior Design by Matt Gibson Architecture + Design; Matt Gibson (Principal Architect); Wei-an Lim (Design Architect); Cassie Southon (Project Architect); Landscape Architecture by Ben Scott Garden Design; Date: 2017*

MGA+D creates spaces that address the primal experiential nature in people, through basic attractions to light, material, and patterns of movement. With close attention to detail, scale, surface, and the exploration of old patterns, they aim to innovate and promote the collaboration of the human experience with nature.

Their latest project includes the Writer's Shed, an isolated workspace for the dedicated writer, searching for a place to find their creativity. The outbuilding is located in the rarely used back corner of the block, camouflaged by a garden of Boston Ivy. Hidden within the leafy residential suburb in Melbourne's Southeast, the modern shed exists as a part of the ever-growing landscape.

The creative space is 10 square meters and was sized to fall into a Class 10a structure, which allowed for economical building and planning methods. It is considered to be a rather simple, low-tech, modestly-priced and modestly-constructed solution.

There is a generous and simple interior that awaits inside the shed. As you work, you can look out to the serene view of the garden, from the desk or mirrored doorway. While the shed becomes united with the surrounding nature, you can break free from an overstimulating and populated environment.

With this project, MGA+D aims to provide an architectural space that helps people find balance in their work life. As we continue to adapt to changes in the environment and technology, MGA+D strives to explore ways to help those who opt for various locations outside of the standard and often rigid workspace.

The Writer's Shed is an intimate environment that is both modest and modern in its design.

MASQUERADING ITSELF AMONGST THE GARDEN LANDSCAPE AND BOUNDARY FENCES, THE SHED IS ONE WITH THE LANDSCAPE—A LIVING PART OF THE GARDEN RATHER THAN AN IMPOSITION ON IT.

**Matt Gibson,** *Director of MGA+D*

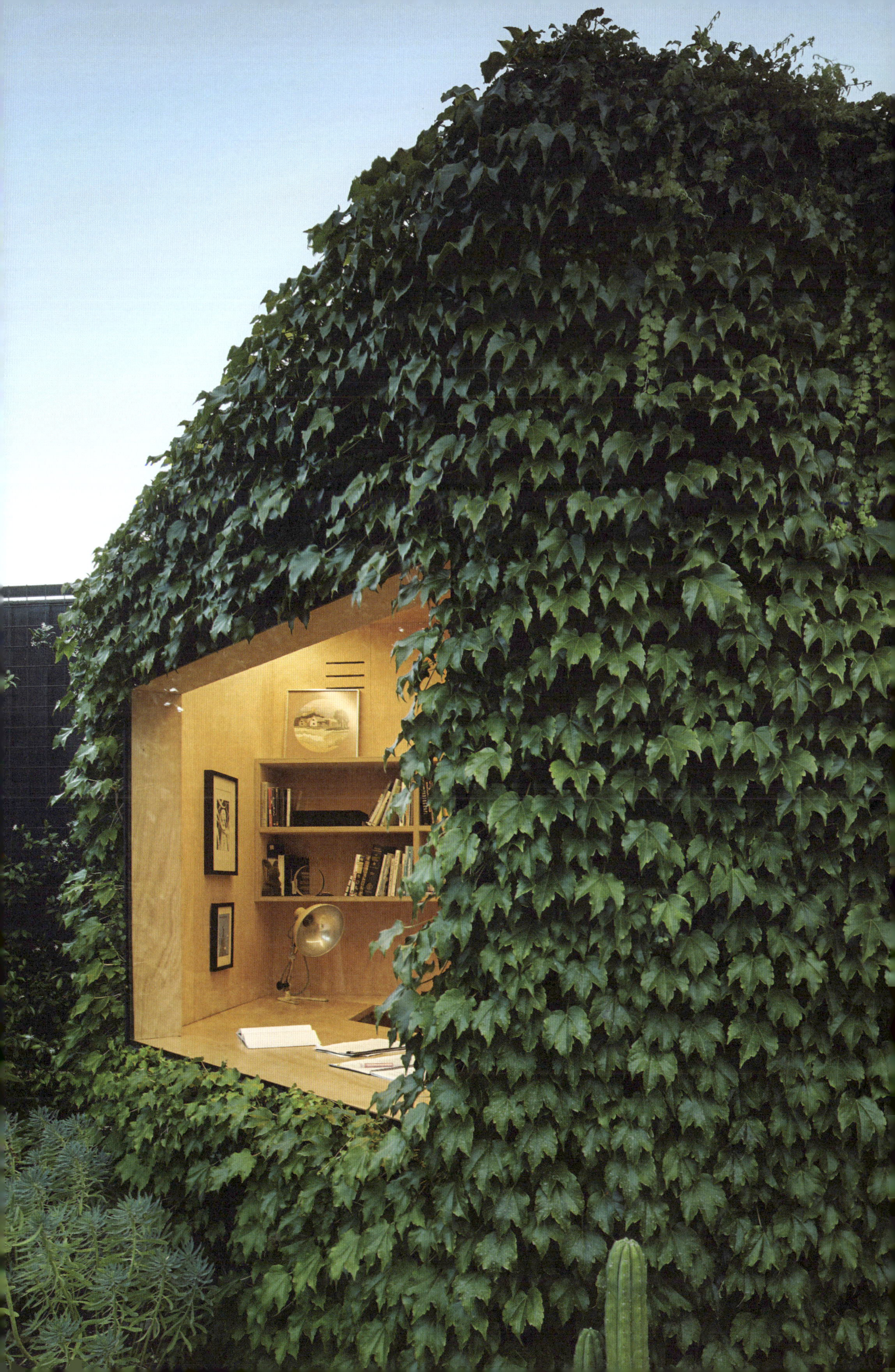

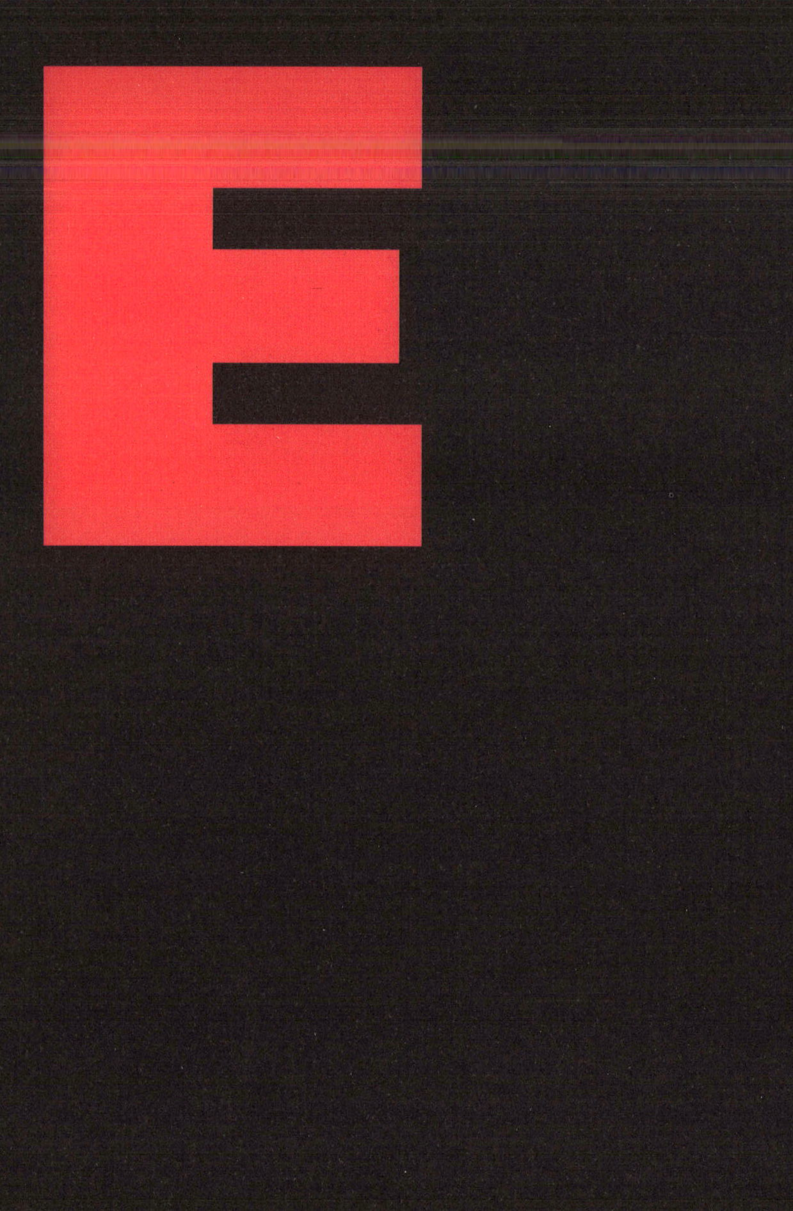

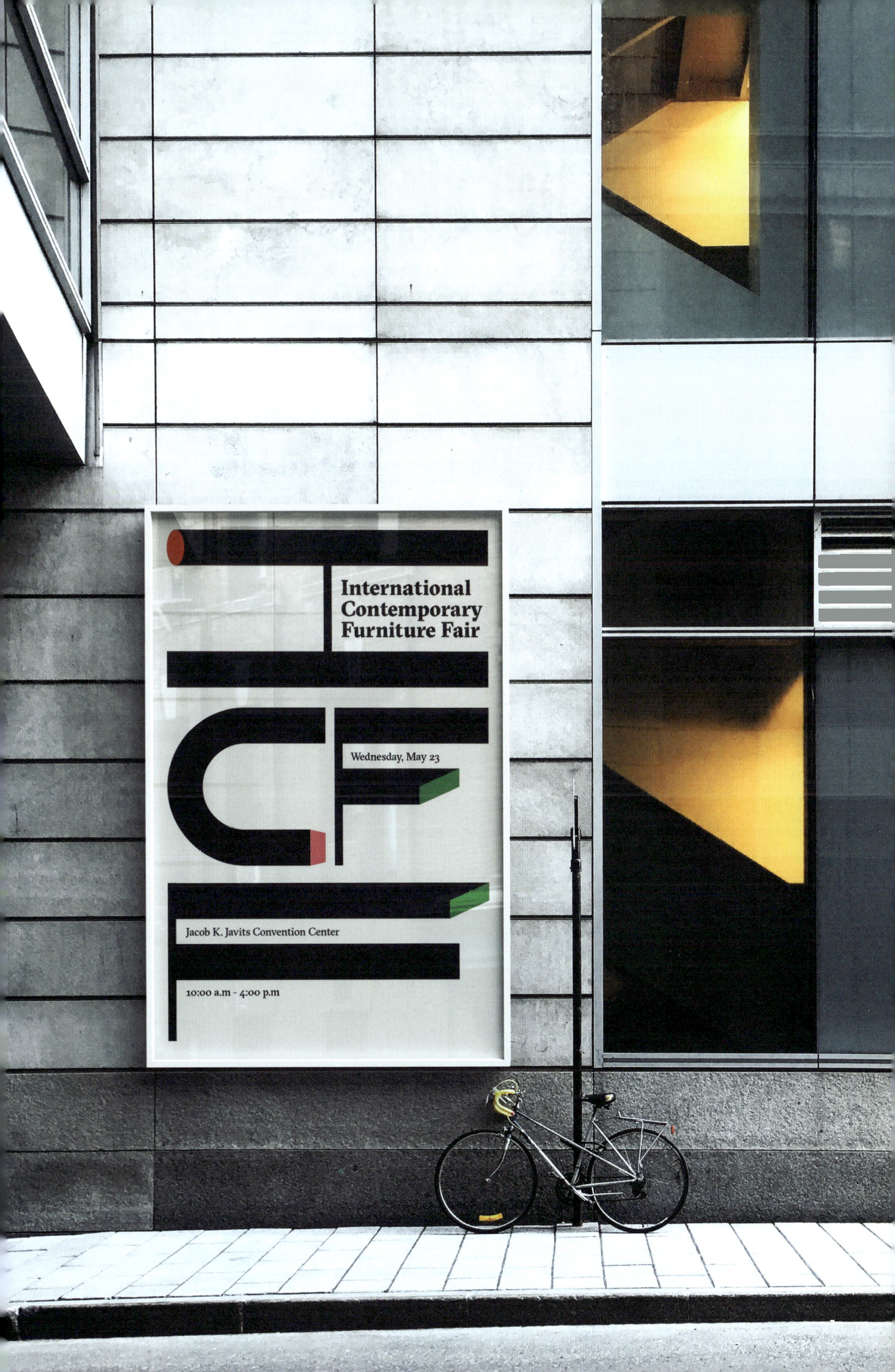

International
Contemporary
Furniture Fair
Wednesday, May 23
Jacob K. Javits Convention Center
10:00 a.m - 4:00 p.m

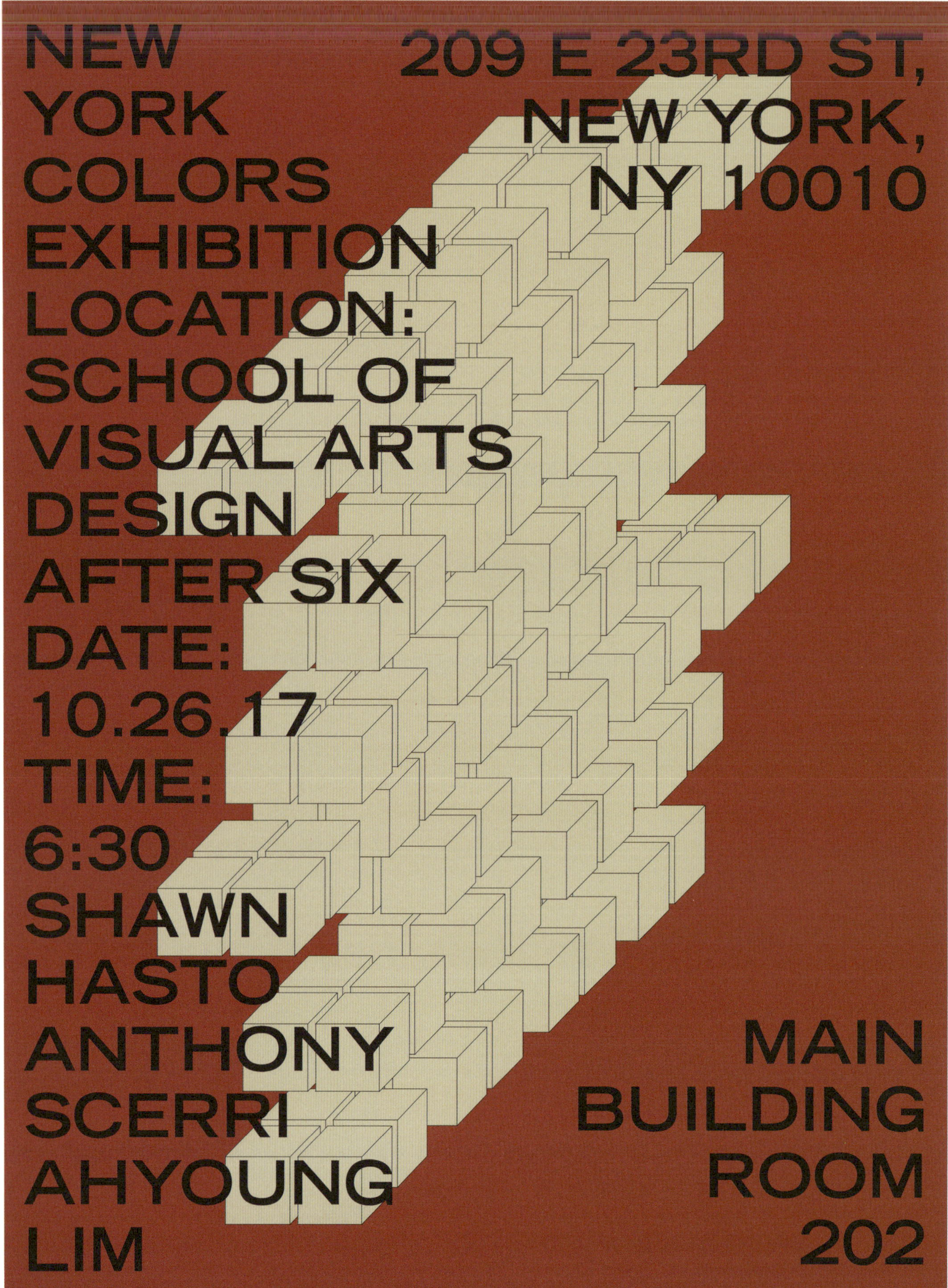


Instructor: Shawn Hasto | Student: Ahyoung Lim

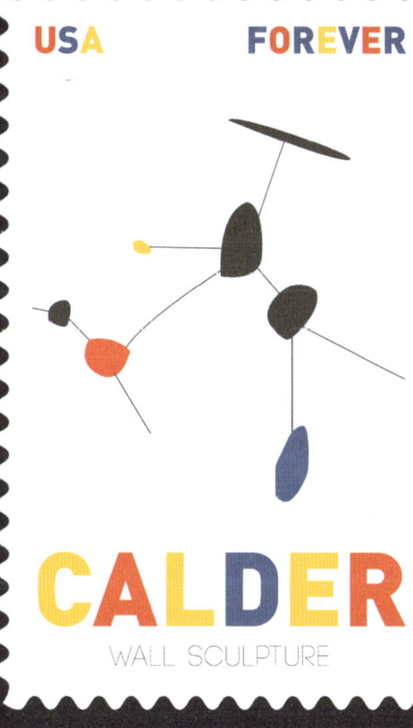


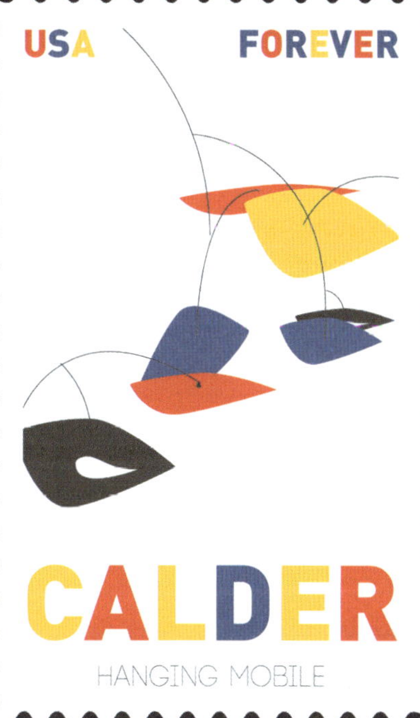


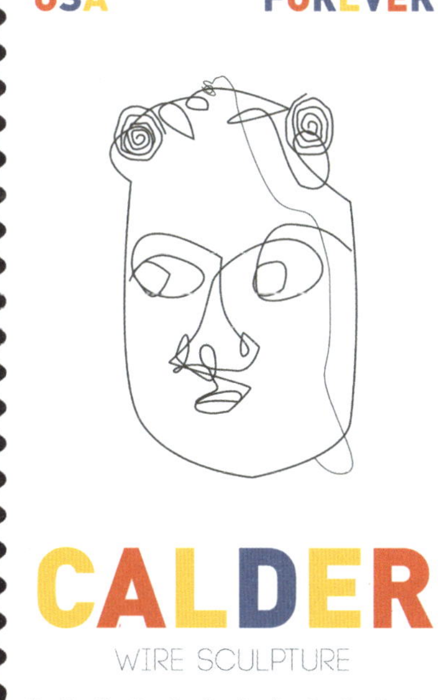


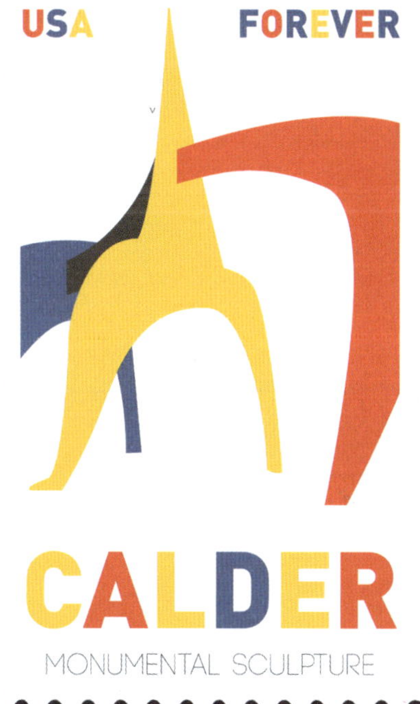


Instructor: **Renée Stevens** | Student: **Yingying Yue**

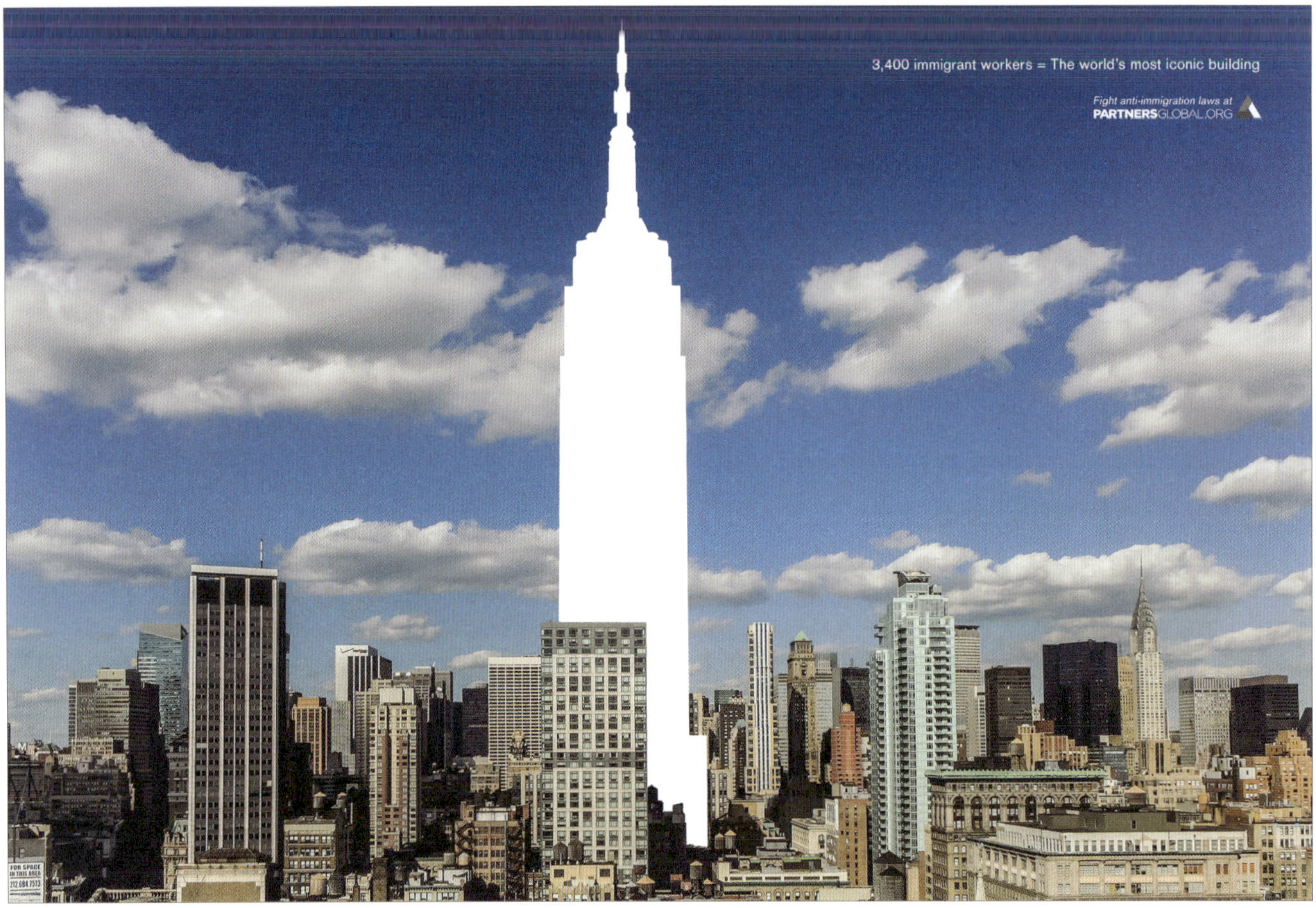

Instructor: **Frank Anselmo** | Students: **Josi Liang Matson, Seona Kim**

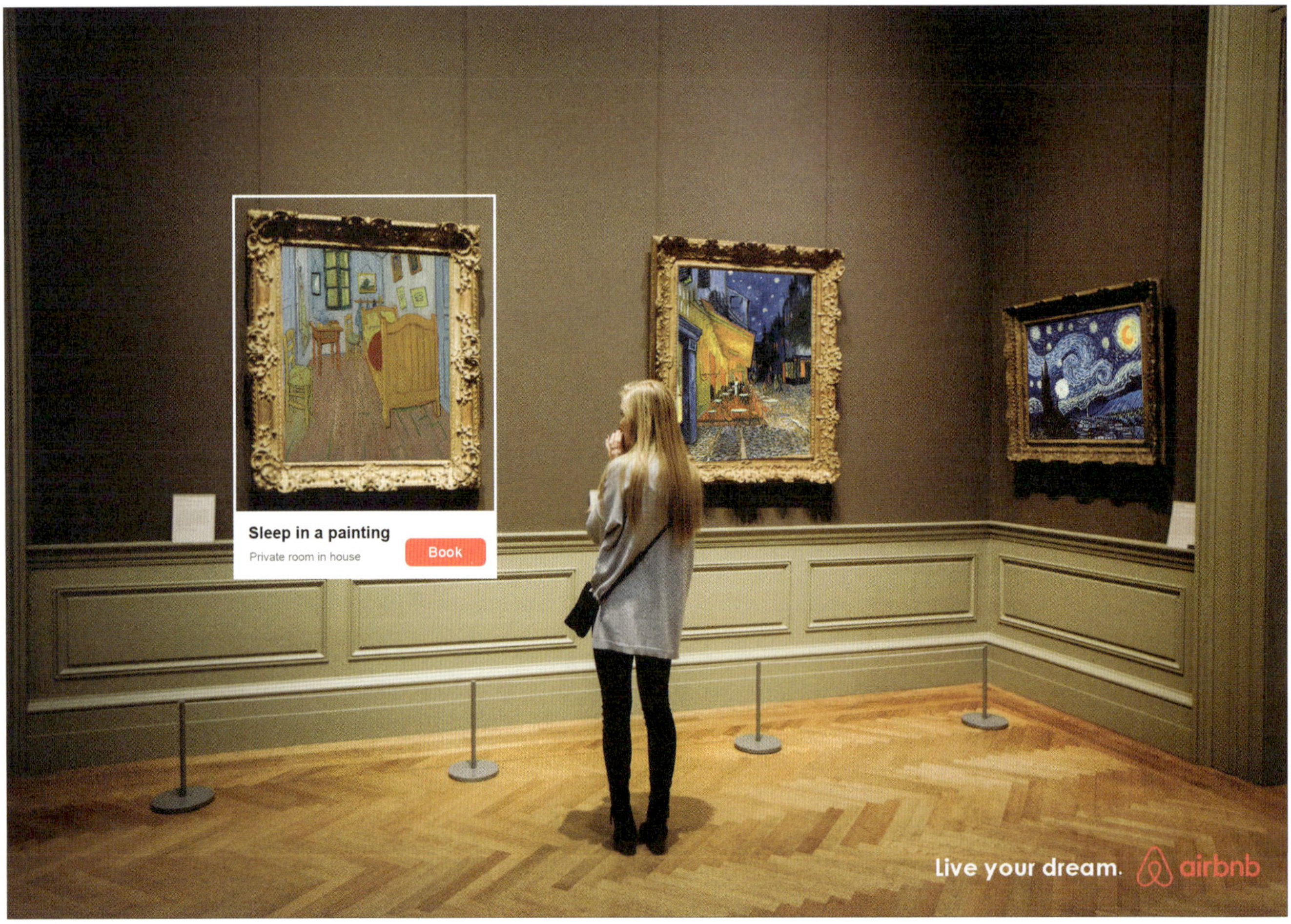

Instructors: **Mel White, Kevin O'Neill** | Student: **Ning Zeng**

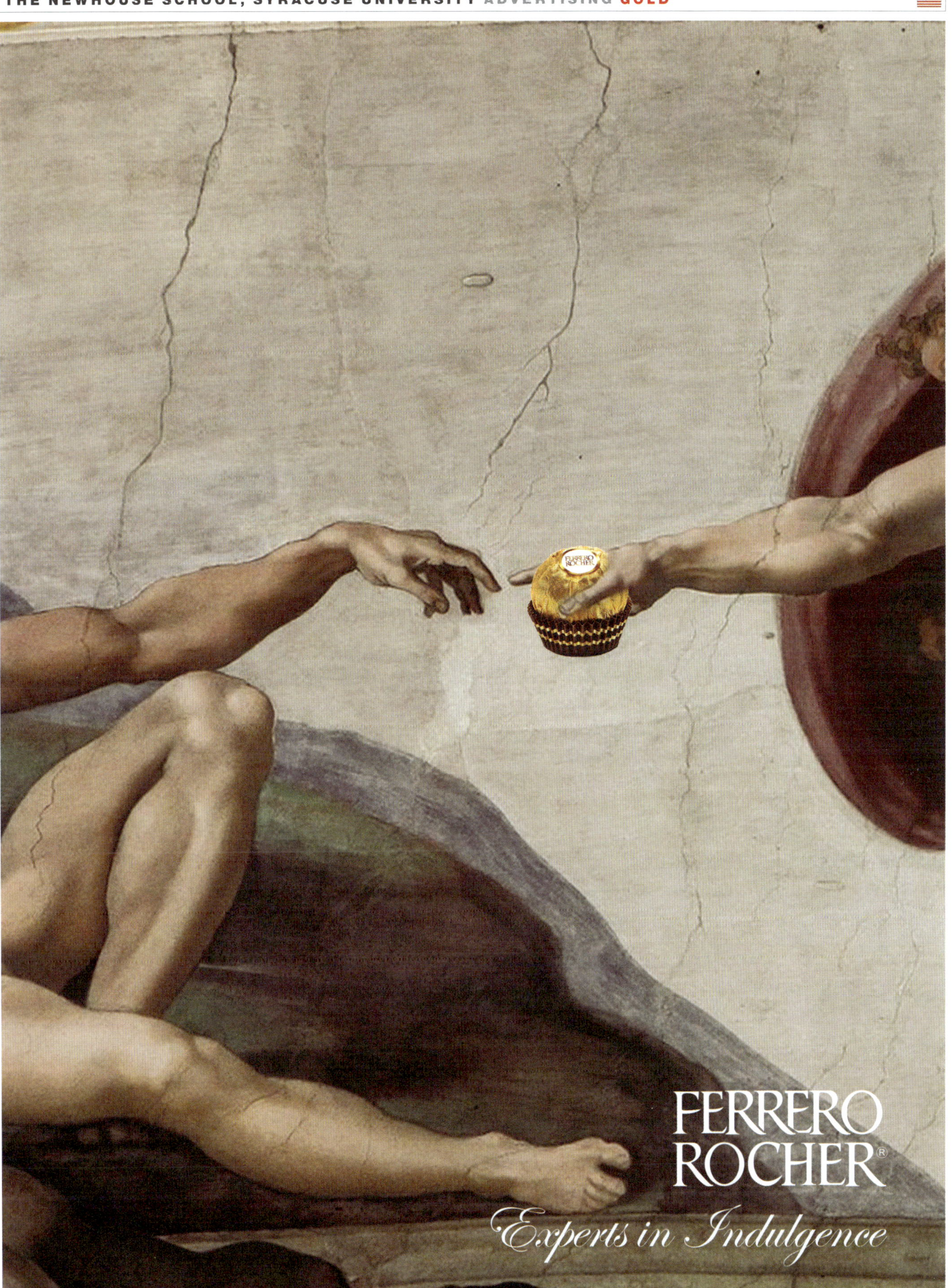


Instructors: **Mel White, Kevin O'Neill** | Student: **Emma Bhayani**

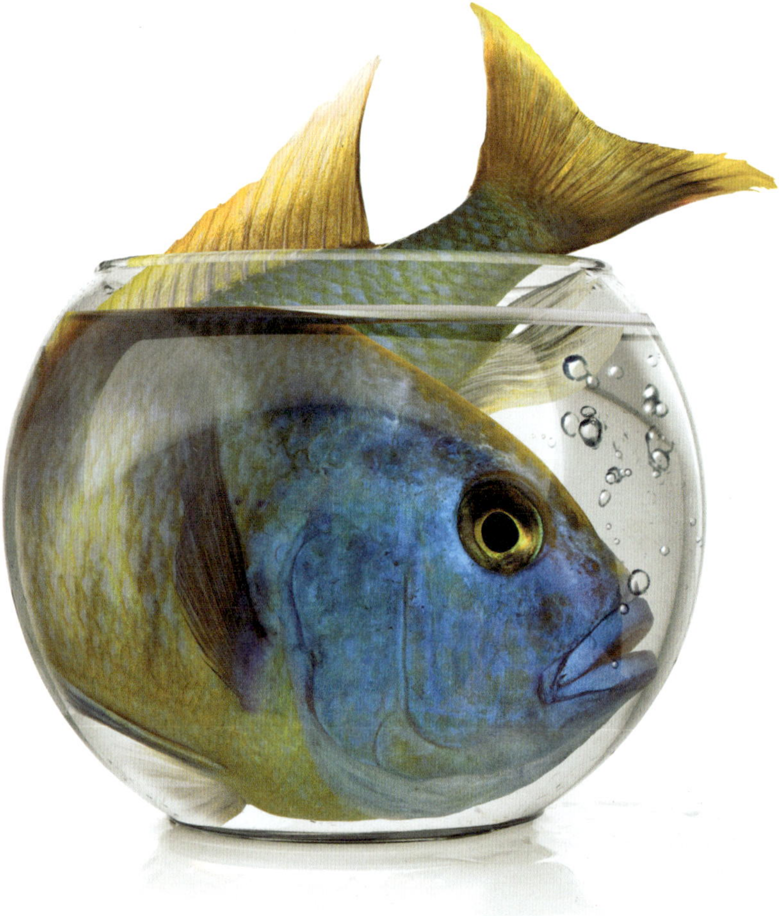

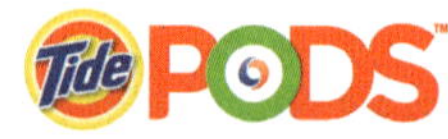

Sometimes smaller is better.

Detergent, brightener, & stain remover. All in one small pod.

Tide PODS

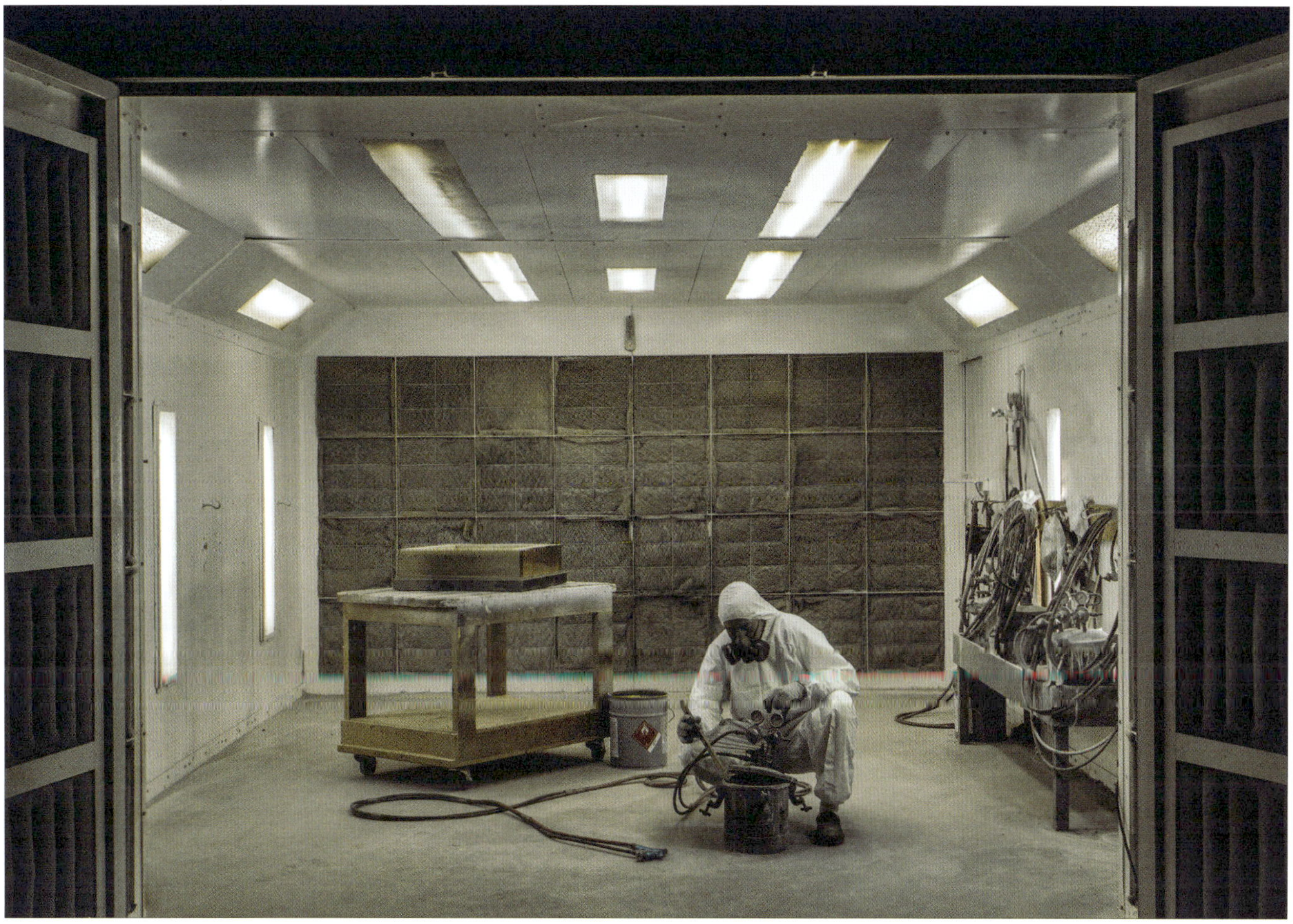

Instructor: **Lynda Green** | Student: **Tyler King**

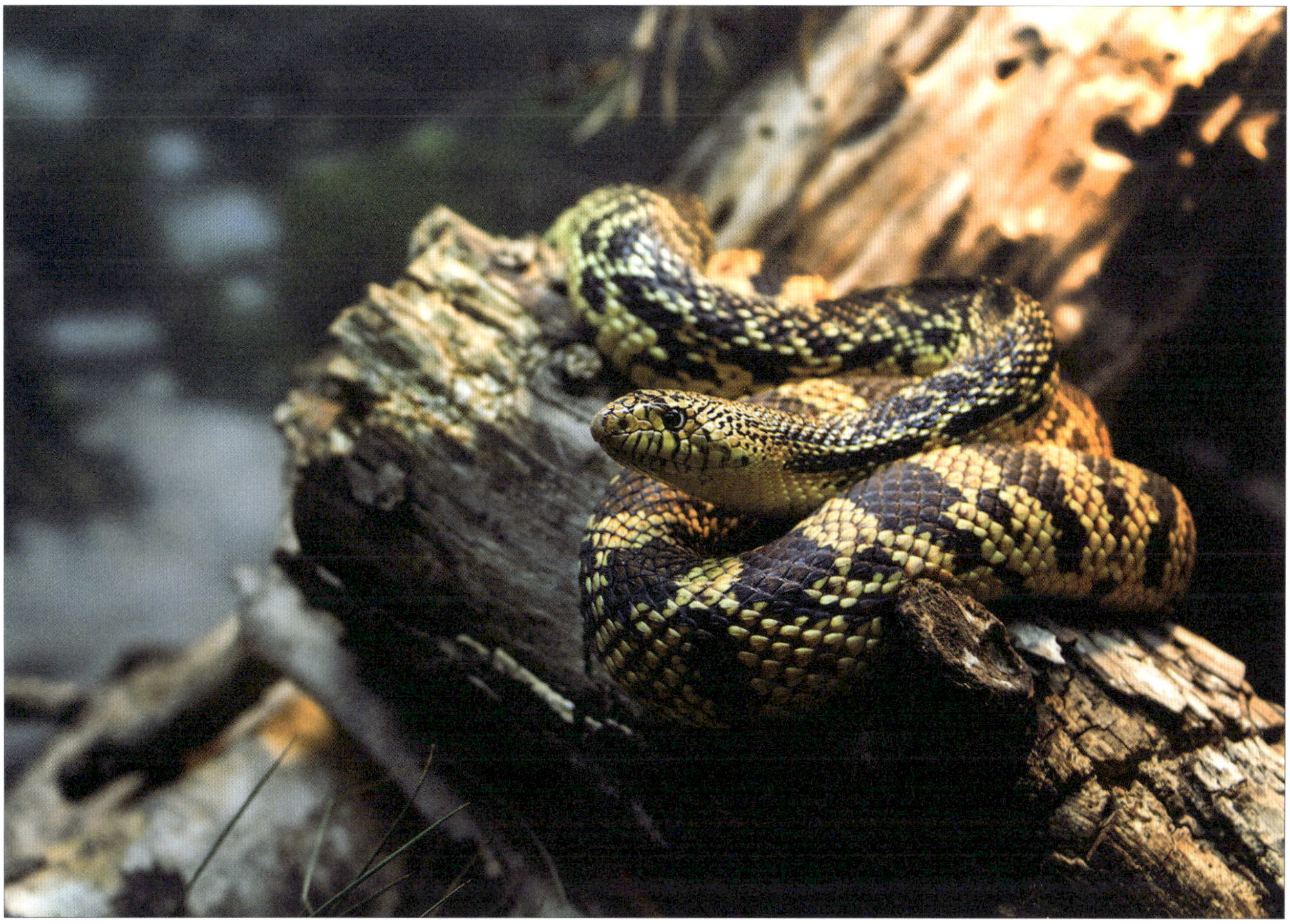

Instructor: **Dusty Crocker** | Student: **Mackenzie Malpass**

## Design Annual 2020

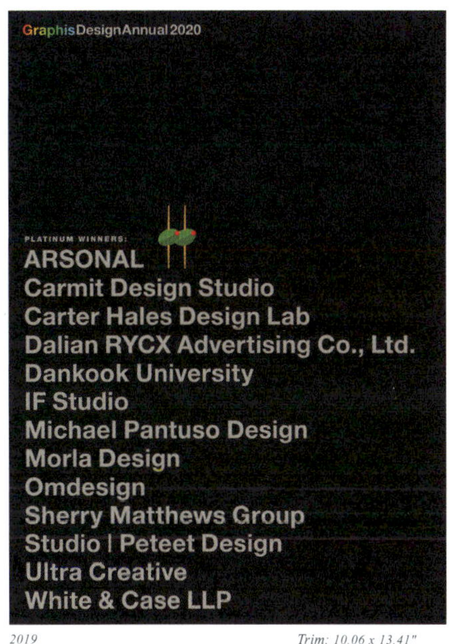

2019
Hardcover: 272 pages
200-plus color illustrations
Trim: 10.06 x 13.41"
ISBN: 978-1-931241-82-3
US $90

**Awards:** 12 Platinum, 163 Gold, and 268 Silver Awards, totaling more than 700 winners, along with 273 Honorable Mentions. **Platinum Winners:** ARSONAL, Carmit Design Studio, Carter Hales Design Lab, Dalian RYCX Advertising Co., Ltd., Dankook University, IF Studio, Michael Pantuso Design, Morla Design, Omdesign, Sherry Matthews Group / Studio | Peteet Design, Ultra Creative, and White & Case LLP.
**Judges:** Fa-Hsiang Hu, Toshiaki & Hisa Ide, Jennifer Morla, Shadia Ohanessian, Michael Pantuso, and Rene V. Steiner.
**Content:** The best of design with 716 winners, as well as Platinum and Gold-winning work by each of this year's Judges. Our Design Museum Directory and annual In Memoriam are also presented.

## Nudes 5

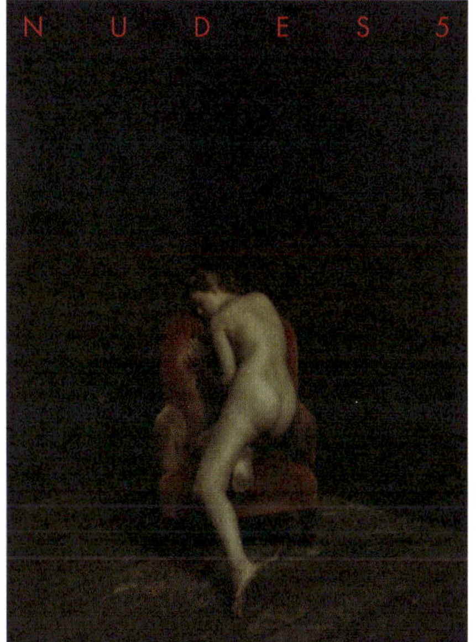

2019
Hardcover: 256 pages
200-plus color illustrations
Trim: 10.06 x 13.41"
ISBN: 978-1-931241-84-7
US $90

The fifth volume in this series, Nudes 5 continues to present some of the most refined and creative nudes photography. Just as this genre helped elevate photography into a realm of fine art, one will find that many of the images on these pages deserve to be presented in museums. Award-winning Photographers include Erik Almas, Rosanne Olson, Klaus Kampert, Howard Schatz, Phil Marco, Joel-Peter Witkin, Chris Budgeon, among others.

## Poster Annual 2020

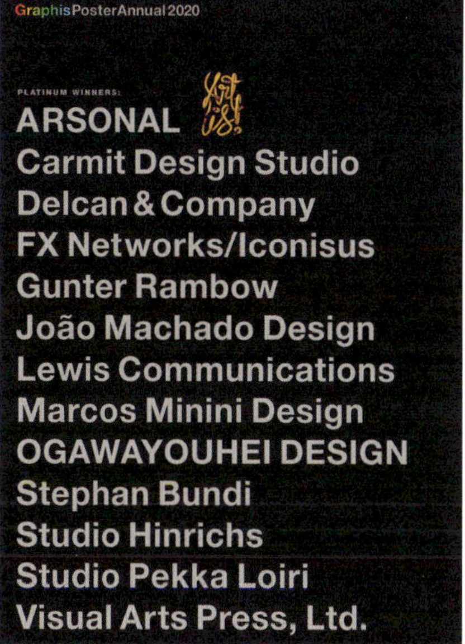

2019
Hardcover: 240 pages
200-plus color illustrations
Trim: 8.5 x 11.75"
ISBN: 978-1-931241-81-6
US $90

**Awards:** 12 Platinum, 107 Gold, and 230 Silver Awards, along with 149 Honorable Mentions. **Platinum Winners:** ARSONAL, Carmit Design Studio, Delcan & Company/Visual Arts Press, Ltd, FX Networks/Iconisus, Gunter Rambow, João Machado Design, Lewis Communications, Marcos Minini Design, OGAWAYOUHEI DESIGN, Stephan Bundi, Studio Hinrichs, and Studio Pekka Loiri.
**Judges:** Entries were judged by highly accomplished Poster Designers: Takashi Akiyama, Rikke Hansen, Dermot Mac Cormack, Patricia McElroy, Gunter Rambow, and Hajime Tsushima. **Editorial:** Designs by Graphis Masters and previous Platinum Winners, who continue to win awards today: Stephan Bundi, Melchior Imboden, Taku Satoh, and Shin Matsunaga. Their Platinum-winning designs from the Poster Annual 2010 competition are shown in full-page images.

## New Talent Annual 2019

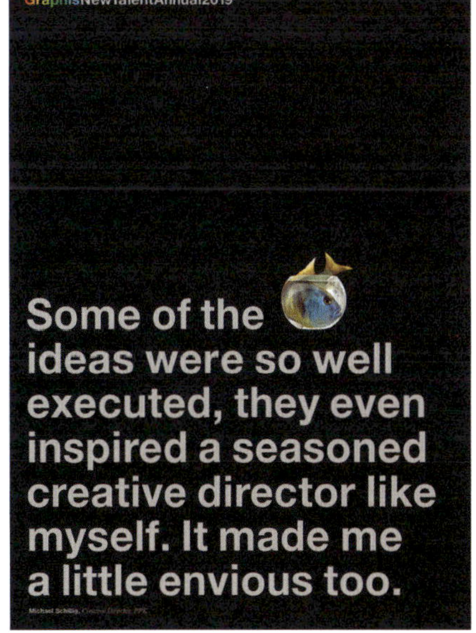


2019
Hardcover: 256 pages
200-plus color illustrations
Trim: 8.5 x 11.75"
ISBN: 978-1-931241-77-9
US $90

This Annual presents work from award-winning Instructors and students. **Platinum:** Advertising: Frank Anselmo, Josh Ege, Larry Gordon, Seung-Min Han, Patrick Hartmann, Kevin O'Neill, Dong-Joo Park, Hank Richardson, Eileen Hedy Schultz, and Mel White. Design: Brad Bartlett, Devan Carter, Eszter Clark, Carin Goldberg, Seung-Min Han, Marvin Mattelson, Kevin O'Callaghan, Dong-Joo Park, Adrian Pulfer, Ryan Russell, and Kristin Sommese. **Gold:** Advertising: 88; Design: 85; Photography: 5; Film: 36. **Silver:** Advertising: 95; Design: 185; Photography: 9; Film: 40. We award up to 500 **Honorable Mentions**, encouraging new talent to submit. All winners are equally presented and archived on our website. This book is a tool for teachers to raise their students' standards and gauge how their school stacks up.

## Advertising Annual 2019

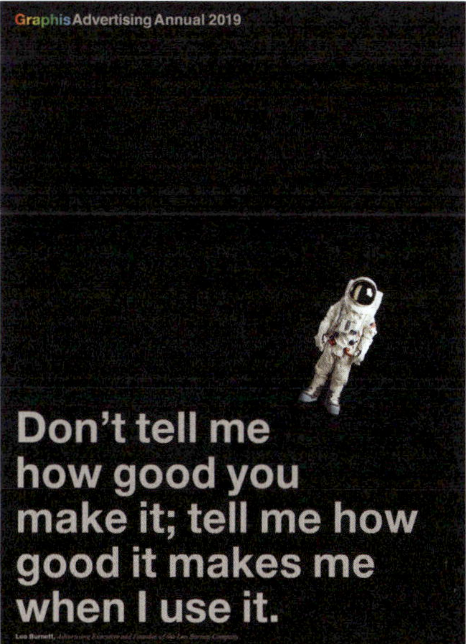


2018
Hardcover: 240 pages
200-plus color illustrations
Trim: 8.5 x 11.75"
ISBN: 978-1-931241-74-8
US $90

**Awards:** 16 Platinum, 122 Gold, and 310 Silver Awards, totaling more than 600 Winners, along with 197 Honorable Mentions.
**Platinum Winners:** 21X Design, Earnshaw's Magazine, Entro, Fred Woodward, hufax arts, IF Studio & Magnus Gjoen, Ken-tsai Lee Design Lab/Taiwan Tech, Michael Pantuso Design, Morla Design, Shadia Design, Steiner Graphics, Stranger & Stranger, Studio 5 Designs Inc., Toppan Printing Co., Ltd., and Traction Factory.
**Judges:** Ronald Burrage of PepsiCo Design & Innovation, Randy Clark, John Ewles, William J. Gicker, Matthias Hofmann, John Krull, and Carin Stanford.
**Content:** Designs by the Judges and award-winning student work.

## Branding 7

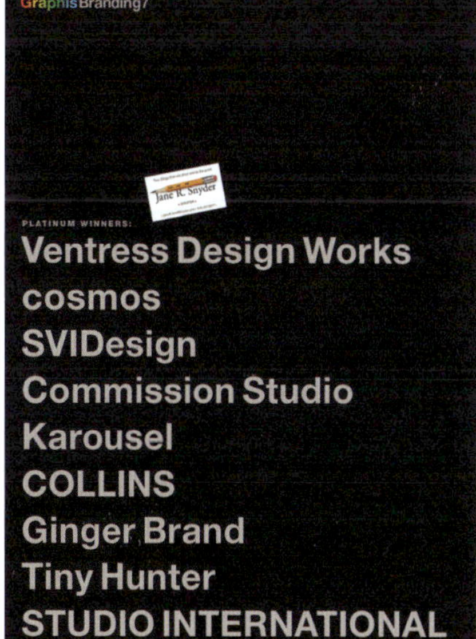

2018
Hardcover: 240 pages
200-plus color illustrations
Trim: 8.5 x 11.75"
ISBN: 978-1-931241-73-1
US $90

**Awards:** 10 Platinum, 73 Gold, and 194 Silver Awards, totaling nearly 500 winners, along with 124 Honorable Mentions.
**Platinum Winners:** Tiny Hunter, COLLINS, cosmos, Ventress Design Works, Karousel, SVIDesign, Ginger Brand, Commission Studio, and STUDIO INTERNATIONAL.
**Judges:** All entries were judged by a panel of highly accomplished, award-winning Branding Designers: Adam Brodsley of Volume Inc., Cristian "Kit" Paul of Brandient, and Sasha Vidakovic of SVIDesign.
**Content:** Branding designs from New Talent Annual 2018, award-winning designs by the Judges, and Q&As with this year's Platinum Winners, along with some of their additional work.

**Books are available at www.graphis.com/store**

# At $90 each, these books showcase award-winning talent. Become a Professional Member and receive 50% off.

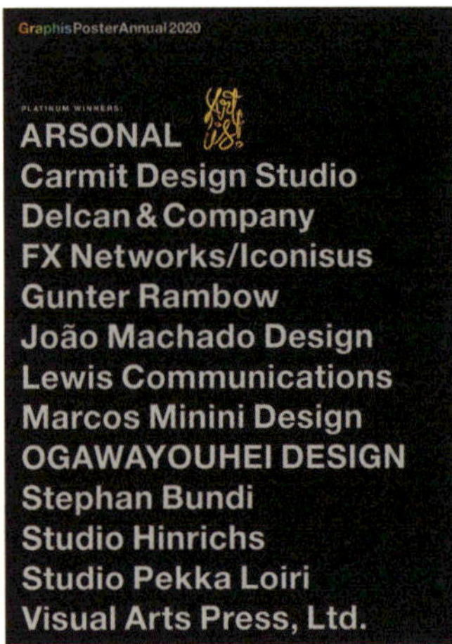


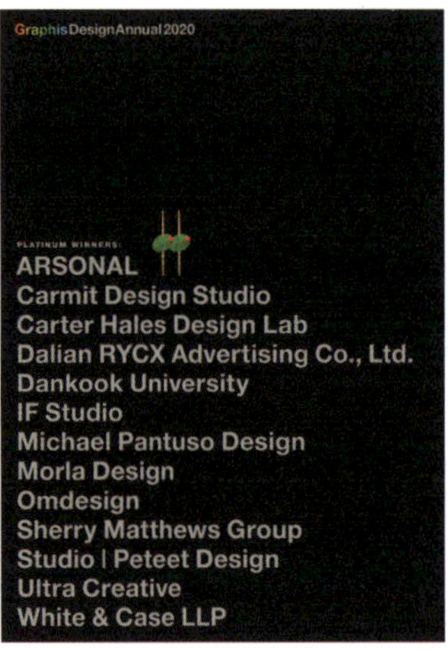


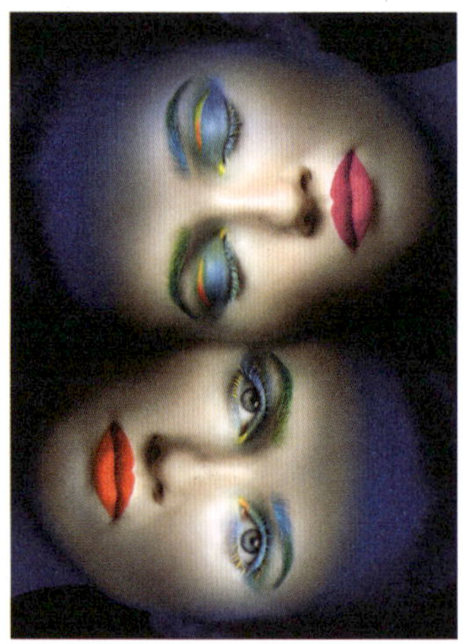

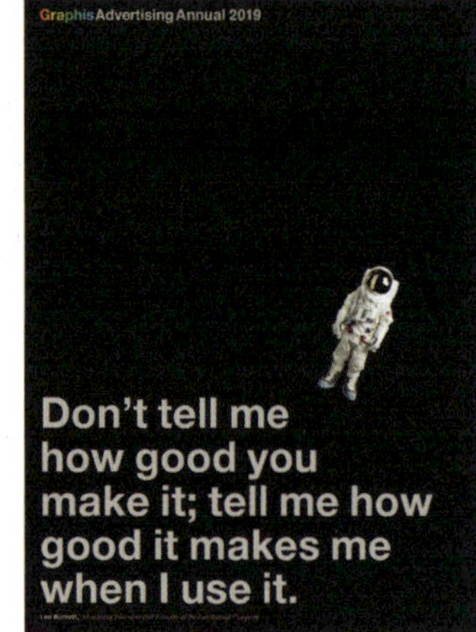


**POSTER ANNUAL 2020 PLATINUM WINNERS:**

ARSONAL
Carmit Design Studio
Delcan & Company
FX Networks/Iconisus
Gunter Rambow
João Machado Design
Lewis Communications
Marcos Minini Design
OGAWAYOUHEI DESIGN
Stephan Bundi
Studio Hinrichs
Studio Pekka Loiri
Visual Arts Press, Ltd.

**DESIGN ANNUAL 2020 PLATINUM WINNERS:**

ARSONAL
Carmit Design Studio
Carter Hales Design Lab
Dalian RYCX Advertising
  Co., LTD
Dankook University
IF Studio
Michael Pantuso Design
Morla Design
Omdesign
Sherry Matthews Group
Studio | Peteet Design
Ultra Creative
White & Case LLP

**PHOTOGRAPHY ANNUAL 2019 PLATINUM WINNERS:**

Athena Azevedo
Dan Humphreys
Jonathan Knowles
Joseph Saraceno
Juan Cruz Durán
Michael Schoenfeld
Parish Kohanim
Stan Musilek
Staudinger+Franke

**ADVERTISING ANNUAL 2019 PLATINUM WINNERS:**

Angry Dog
ARSONAL
BRAND DIRECTORS
BVK
Darkhorse Design
designory.
Fältman & Malmén
FCB Lisbon
Lewis Communications
PPK, USA
Splash Worldwide
Traction Factory
xose teiga, studio.
Zulu Alpha Kilo

# HOW CAN I CREATE A COMPELLING VISUAL NARRATIVE IN WHICH THE SOLUTION DOESN'T TURN INTO A STYLISTIC CONCEIT?

**Jennifer Morla,** *President and Creative Director of Morla Design*

# DON'T LOOK TO THE INDUSTRY FOR INSPIRATION. DON'T TRY TO FIGURE OUT THE SYSTEM. HACK THE SYSTEM. BE INTERESTED AND INTERESTING

**Carolyn Hadlock,** *ECD | Principal, Young & Laramore*

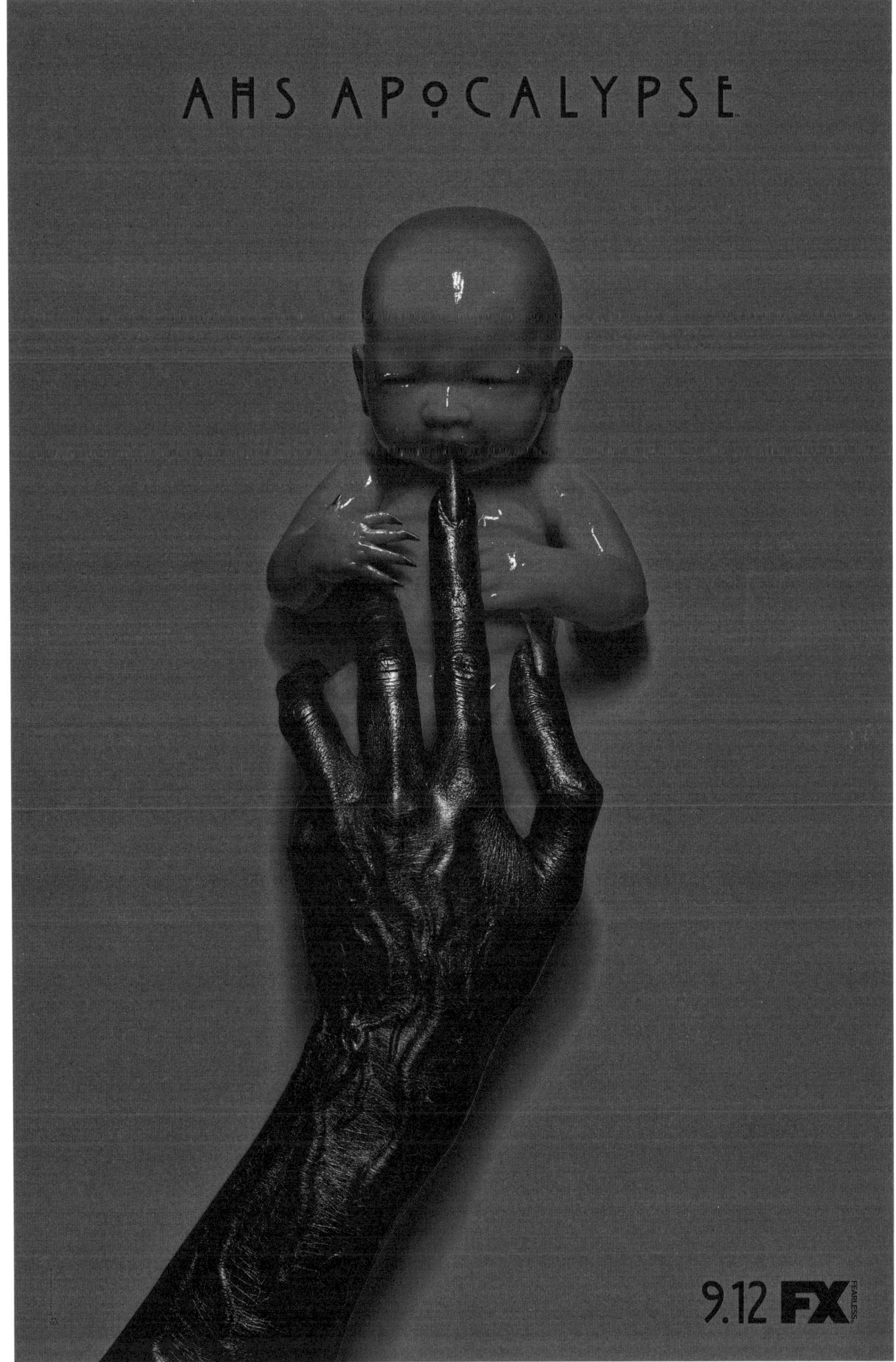


Design Firm: **ARSONAL** | Client: **FX Networks**

Designer: **Michael Pantuso** | Client: **Private Art Collector**



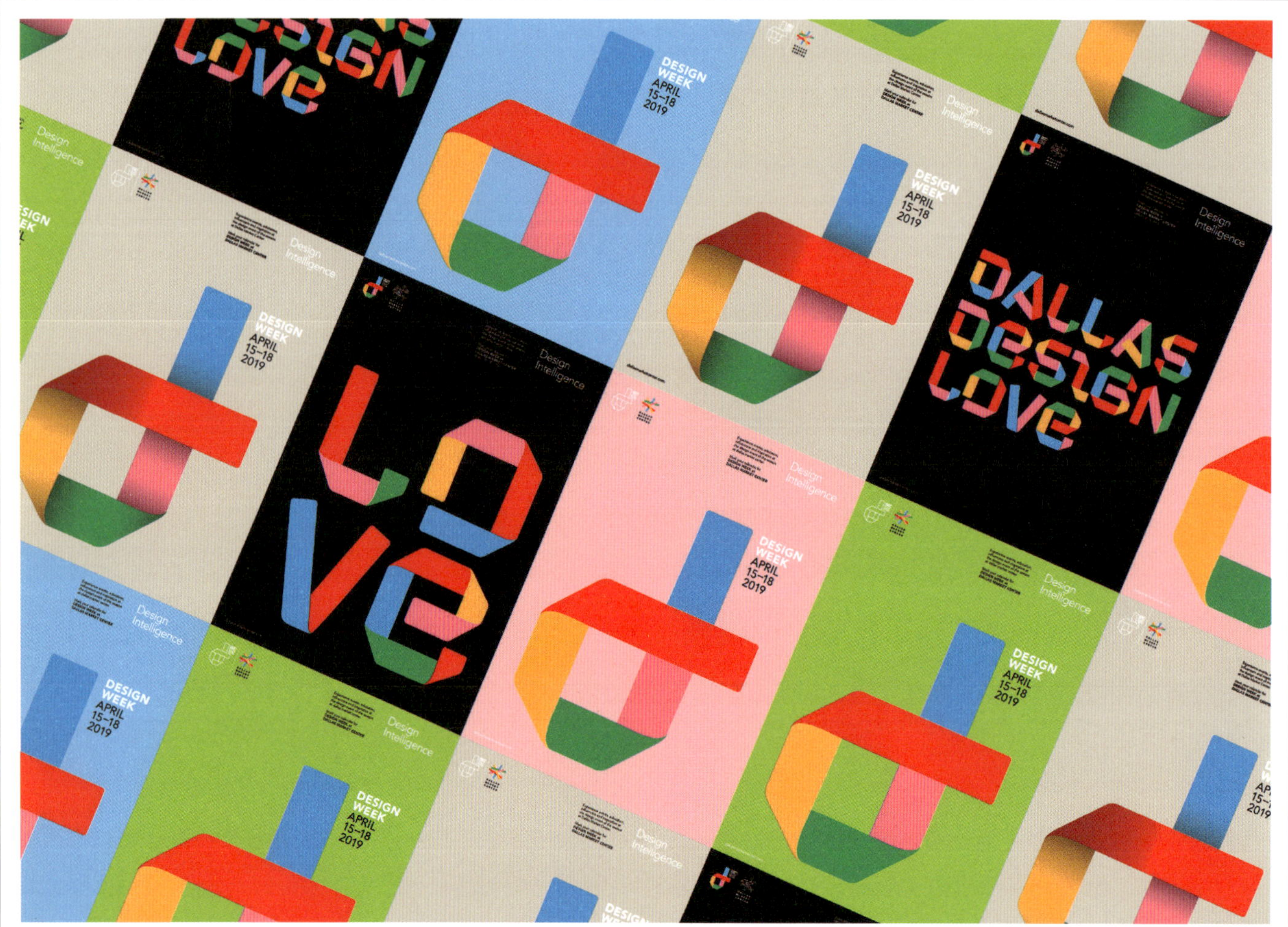


Design Firm: **studio'farrell** | Client: **Dallas Market Center, guillermo tragant**

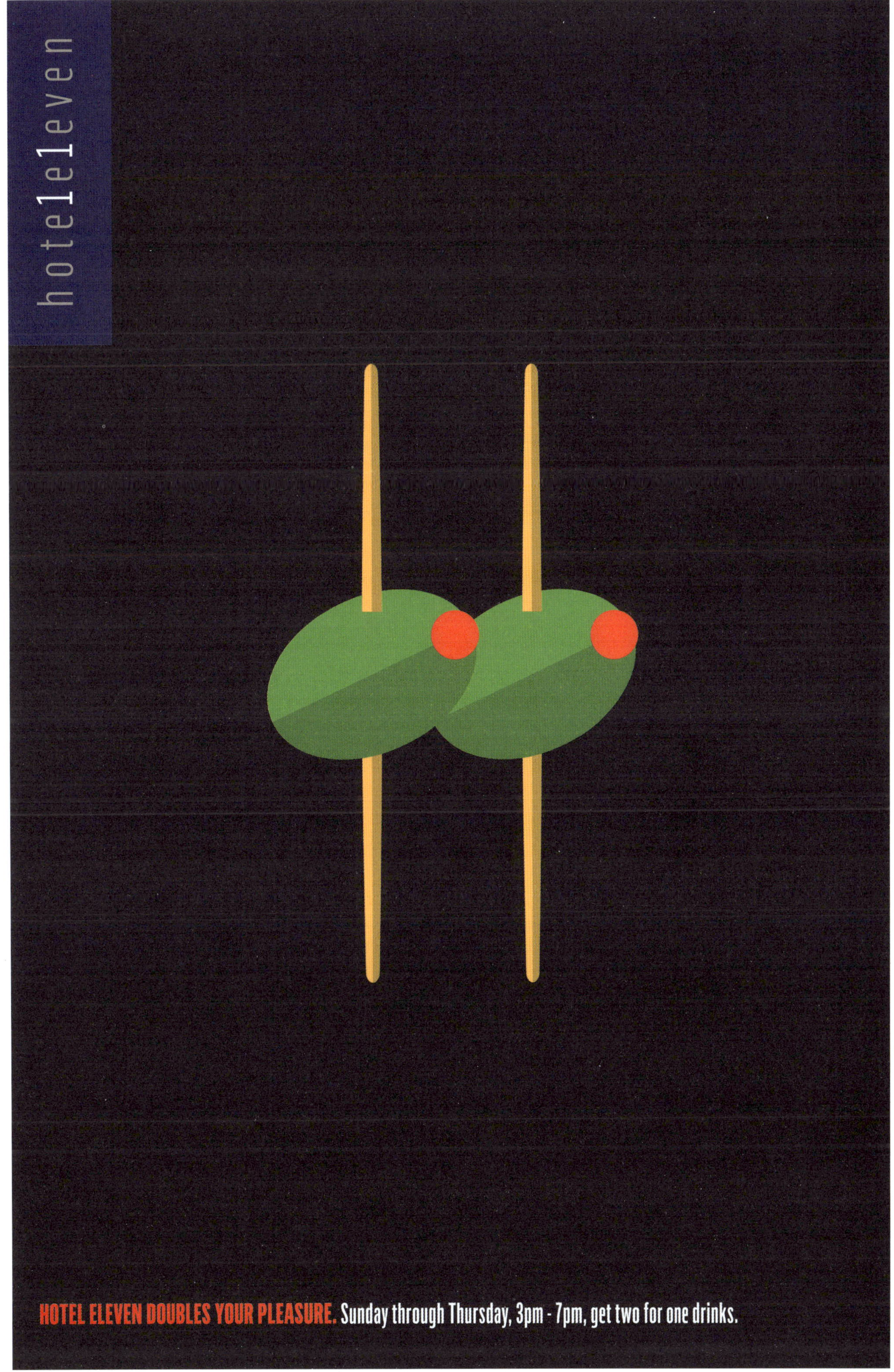


Design Firm: Peteet Design | Client: Hotel Eleven

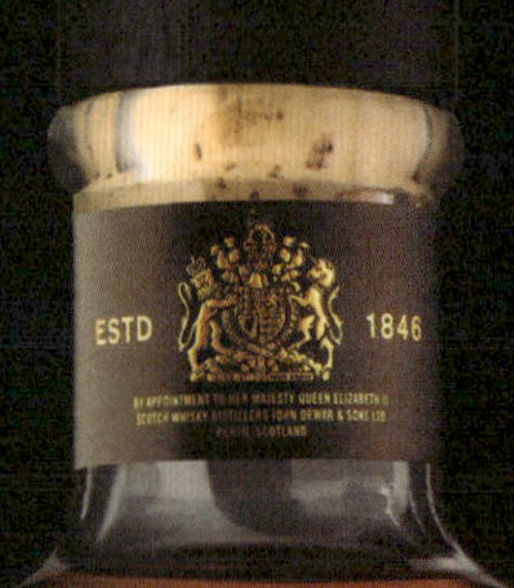

ESTD 1846
BY APPOINTMENT TO HER MAJESTY QUEEN ELIZABETH II
SCOTCH WHISKY DISTILLERS JOHN DEWAR & SONS CO
PERTH, SCOTLAND


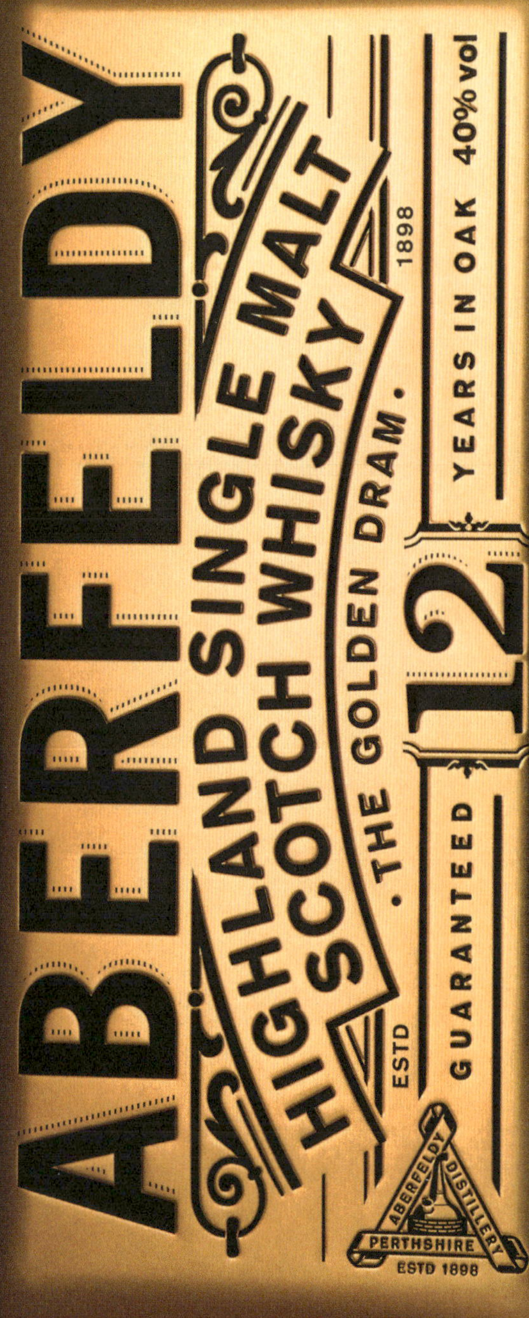

ABERFELDY
HIGHLAND SINGLE MALT
SCOTCH WHISKY
GUARANTEED 12 YEARS IN OAK
MELLOWED FOR TWELVE YEARS IN HANDMADE OAK
CASKS, THIS SMOOTH, SWEET DRAM OFFERS RICH
REWARDS FOR THOSE WHO LIKE TO DIG DEEPER
LIMITED BOTTLING BATCH NO. 2905
WE LOSE OUR FAIR SHARE TO THE ANGELS
ABERFELDY
HIGHLAND SINGLE MALT SCOTCH WHISKY
THE GOLDEN DRAM.
1898
12 YEARS IN OAK 40% vol
ESTD GUARANTEED
ABERFELDY DISTILLERY
PERTHSHIRE
ESTD 1898

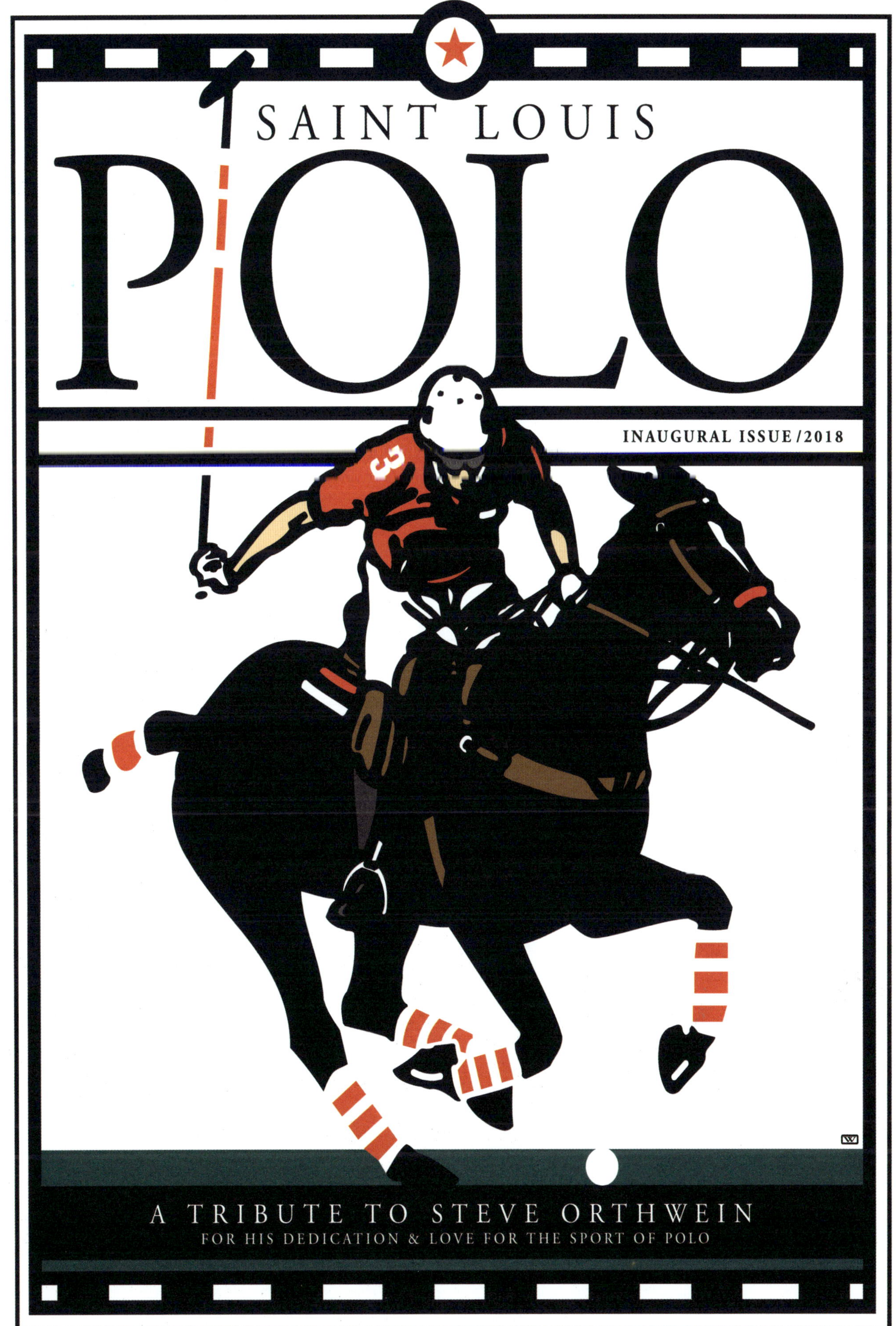


Designer: **Ted Wright** | Client: **St. Louis Polo Club**

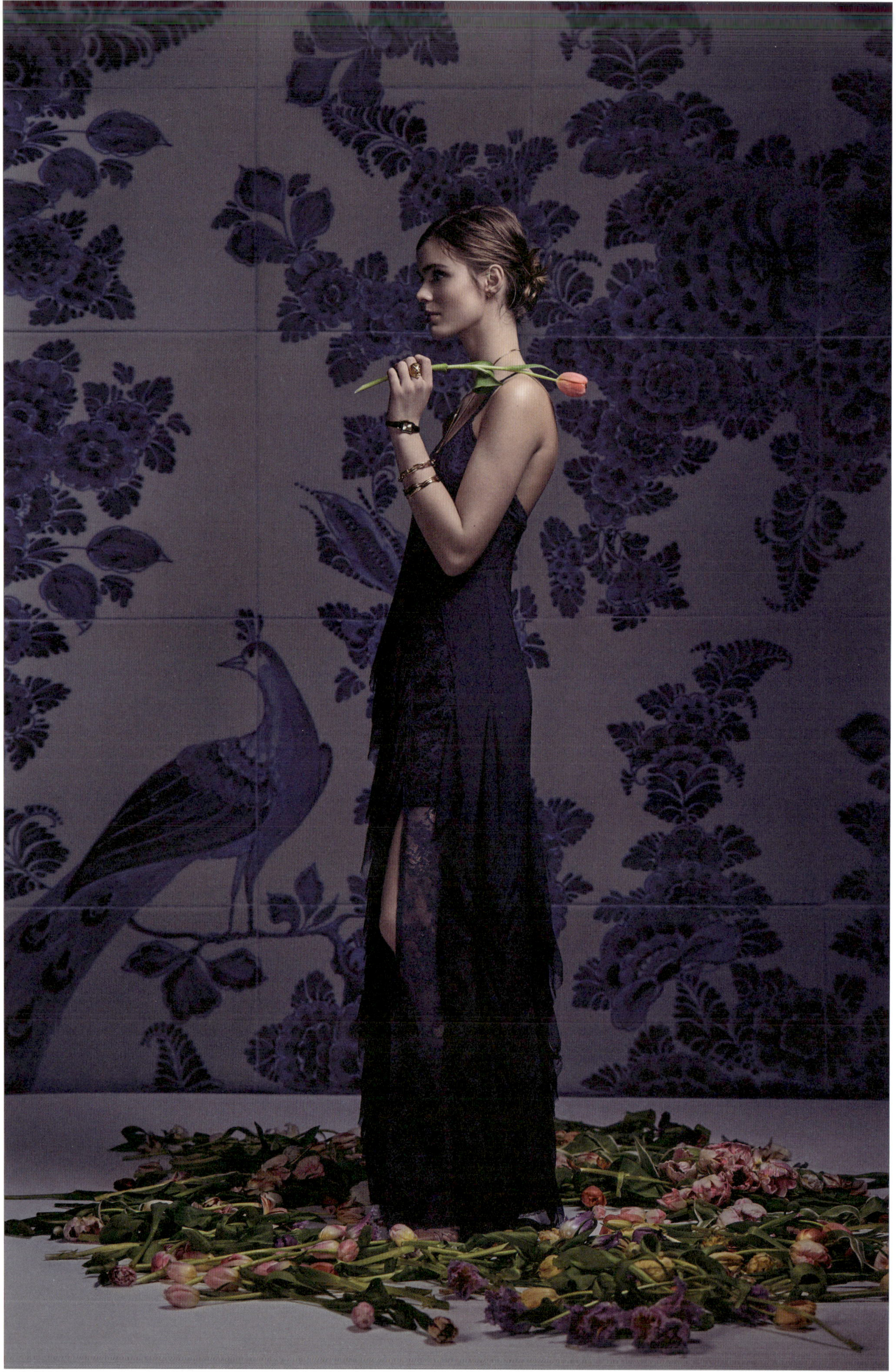

Photographer: **Athena Azevedo** | Client: **Carmel Partners**

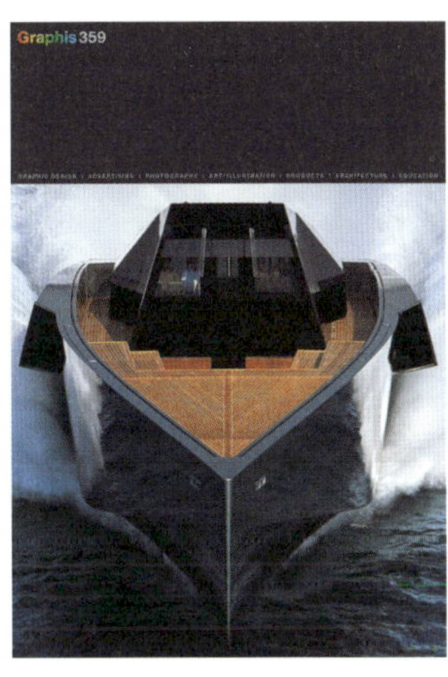
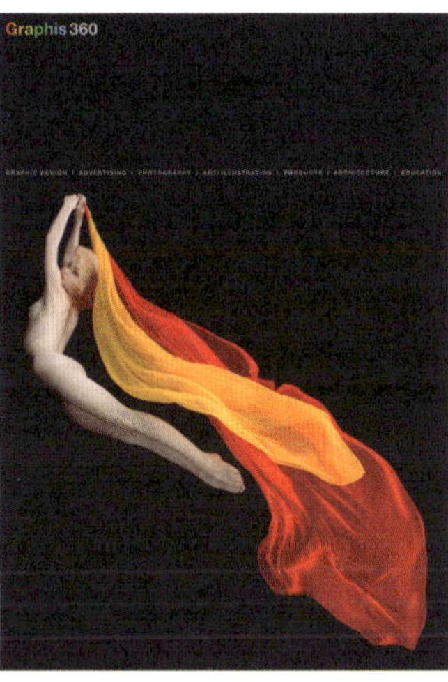
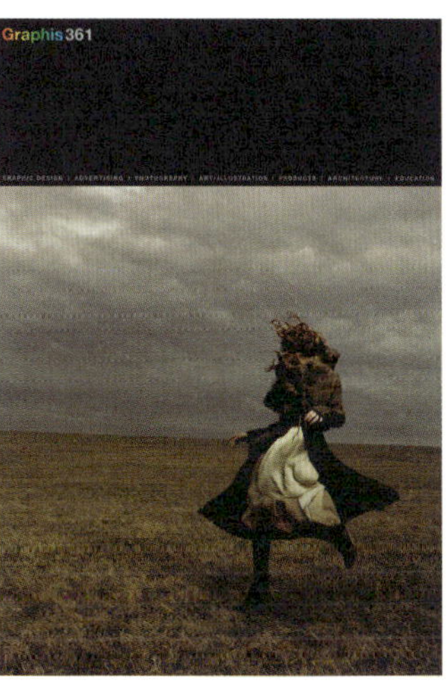
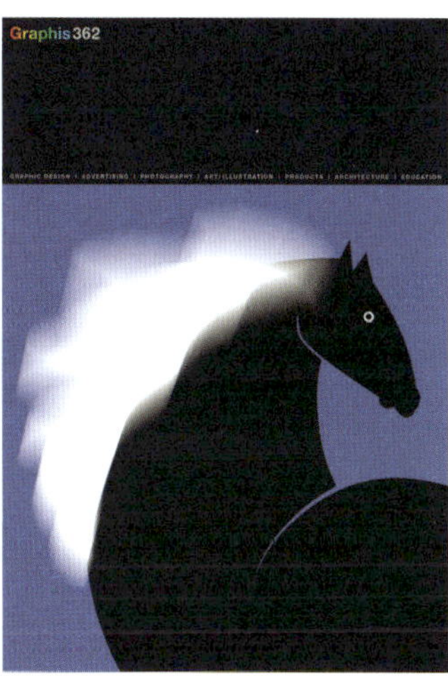



Subscribe to our quarterly journals and experience Platinum and Gold award-winning work for $140

Or become a Professional Member and pay only $70

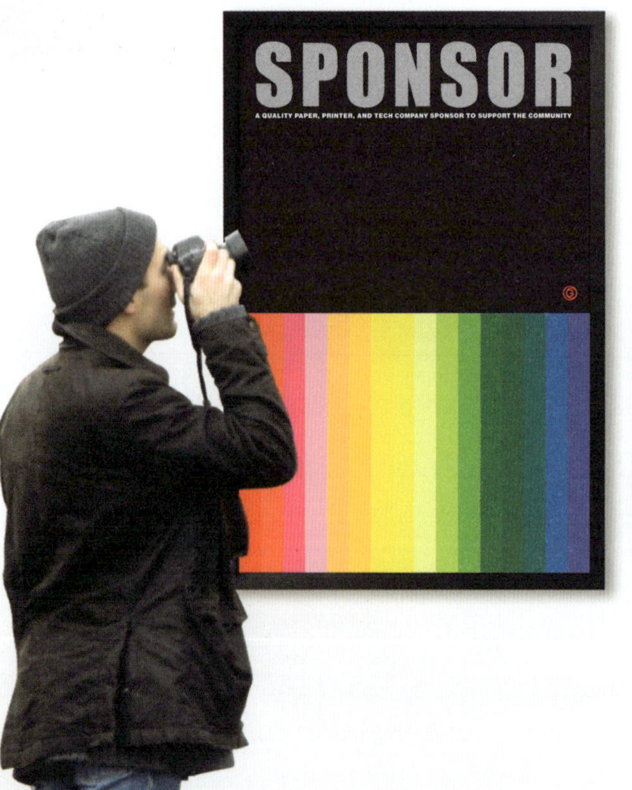

Graphis Exhibitions
GOLD AWARD-WINNING WORK
SPONSOR
A QUALITY PAPER, PRINTER, AND TECH COMPANY SPONSOR TO SUPPORT THE COMMUNITY
DESIGN ANNUAL 2020

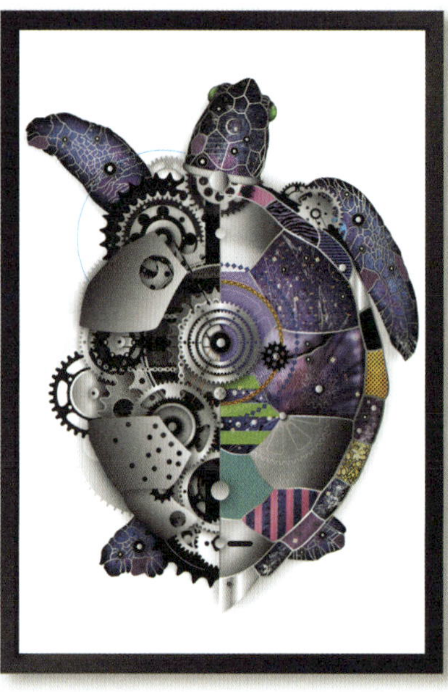
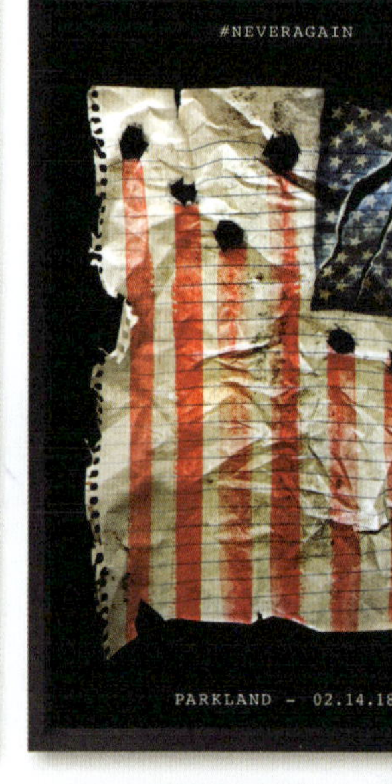

#NEVERAGAIN
PARKLAND — 02.14.18
DESIGN ANNUAL 202

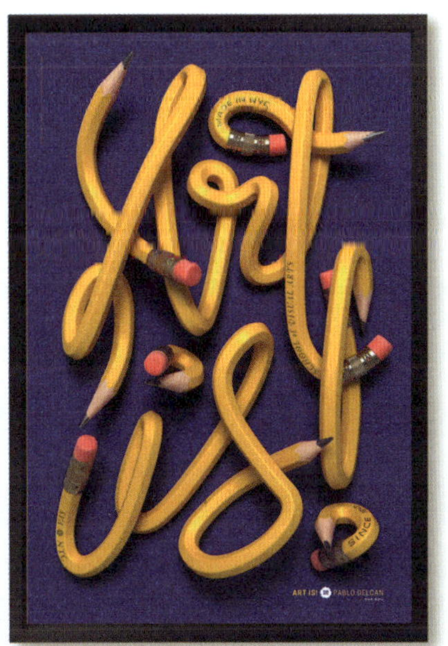


POSTER ANNUAL 2020

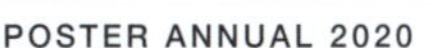

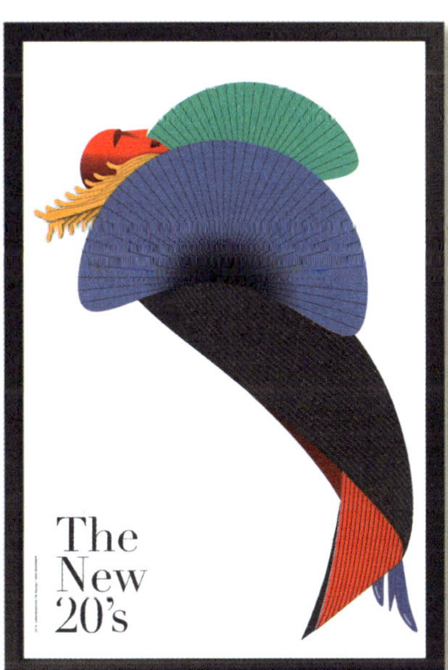


POSTER ANNUAL 2020

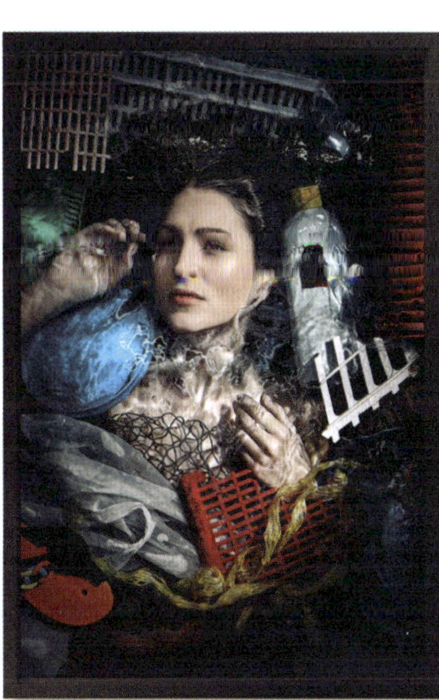

PHOTOGRAPHY ANNUAL 2019

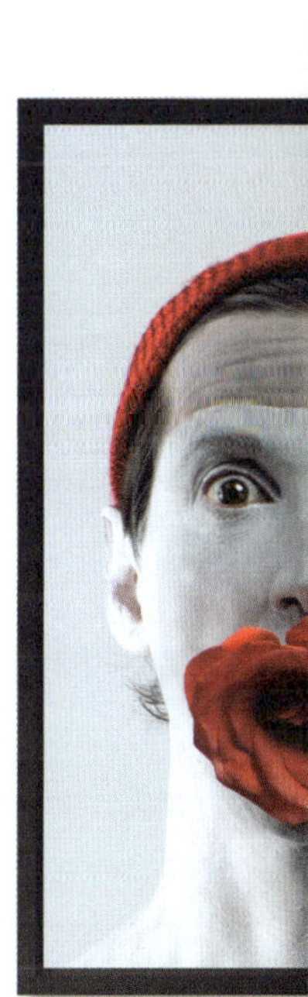

PHOTOGRAPH

www.**Graphis**.com